# THE MANY LIVES OF
# CATWOMAN
## THE FELONIOUS HISTORY OF A FELINE FATALE

## TIM HANLEY

CHICAGO REVIEW PRESS

An A Cappella Book

Published by Chicago Review Press Incorporated
814 North Franklin Street
Chicago, IL 60610
ISBN 978-1-61373-845-0


Library of Congress Cataloging-in-Publication Data
Names: Hanley, Tim, author.
Title: The many lives of Catwoman : the felonious history of a feline fatale
    / Tim Hanley.
Description: Chicago, IL : Chicago Review Press, 2017. | Includes
    bibliographical references and index.
Identifiers: LCCN 2017006163| ISBN 9781613738450 (paperback) | ISBN
    9781613738481 (epub edition) | ISBN 9781613738474 (kindle edition)
Subjects: LCSH: Catwoman (Fictitious character) | Women heroes in literature.
    | Women heroes in motion pictures. | Women heroes in mass media. | Comic
    books, strips, etc.—United States. | Women in popular culture—United
    States. | BISAC: SOCIAL SCIENCE / Popular Culture. | LITERARY CRITICISM /
    Comics & Graphic Novels. | SOCIAL SCIENCE / Feminism & Feminist Theory.
Classification: LCC PN6728.C39 H36 2017 | DDC 741.5/973—dc23 LC record
    available at https://lccn.loc.gov/2017006163


*Unless otherwise indicated, all images are from the author's collection*
Front cover design: Tim Hanley
Cover layout and interior design: Jonathan Hahn

Printed in the United States of America
5  4  3  2  1

*To my sister;*
*me, I say*
*that she's okay.*

# Contents

# Introduction

"It's too bad she has to be a crook!"

So lamented Batman after one of Catwoman's earliest comic book appearances in the autumn of 1940. She'd just gone on a robbery spree throughout Gotham City and roped Batman into freeing her from the clutches of her shady underworld associates. Catwoman then escaped Batman's attempt to arrest her for the third straight issue; this time she stunned him with a kiss before shoving him out of her way and taking off in a stolen car, leaving her free to commit another series of dazzling crimes just a few issues later.

Catwoman completely enraptured Batman. She was cunning, fierce, and beautiful, a femme fatale and master thief rolled into one. She was also one of the few villains in the Golden Age of superhero comics who was able to escape Batman and his resolute war on crime. While many of Batman's other foes ended up dead or behind bars, Catwoman constantly outsmarted him. He adored her nonetheless, but he knew that his affection was futile. She was a crook, after all.

For more than seventy-five years, Catwoman has been a mercurial character, with her many incarnations ranging from criminal to hero. In the black-and-white world of superheroes, she exists in shades of gray, yet she is ultimately defined by her villainy. When she's not outright engaged in criminal activity, she's a mistrusted ally cautiously held at arm's length. Because of her felonious history, Catwoman is a perpetual outsider, and her existence on the periphery of society led her to avoid both the tropes and triumphs typically associated with the evolution of female characters.

Female superheroes are generally held to the prevailing cultural standards of what a woman should be. When the Cold War culture of the 1950s emphasized the importance of wives and mothers, female superheroes wanted to settle down and become homemakers. When women's lib became mainstream in the 1970s, female superheroes began to embrace the tenets of feminism. The history of female heroes in the superhero industry is a familiar narrative that mirrors the conventional history of American women as a whole.

Catwoman is not beholden to these standards, and thus her history exists outside this typical framework. She has forged her own path, with its own twists and turns. No female villain has had as long or as varied a career as Catwoman, and her journey is wholly unique in the world of superheroes.

At times, Catwoman's depiction was an intentional counter to the dominant portrayal of women in comics. As a villain, she was meant to represent the opposite of what a good woman should be, but her supposedly negative traits came off looking like far more fun. When many women in superhero comics were damsels in distress pining for their hero, Catwoman was independent and carefree, reveling in corruption and using her sexual wiles to her advantage. However, being a villain had its drawbacks. Over the decades, Catwoman was considered expendable and prone to lengthy absences. Furthermore, the primarily male creators behind the character sometimes depicted Catwoman in objectified and degrading ways that they couldn't show heroines.

For good and ill, Catwoman's criminal role allowed her to escape the familiar evolution of female characters throughout her history. The standards for a female villain were different, and for nearly eight decades her adventures have charted a varied journey of empowerment and exploitation. Catwoman has been a popular character across a variety of media at every stage of her career, an iconic embodiment of both villainy and a unique independence, and her history showcases a compelling alternate viewpoint in the world of superheroes.

# 1

# *Perjured Origins*

otham City's feline fatale is a familiar sight for superhero fans. From comics to television to movies, Selina Kyle has burgled her way through the city in her sleek costume and cat-eared cowl as the fiendish Catwoman for decades. However, her original incarnation would be almost unrecognizable to those familiar with her more recent exploits. When she first debuted in the spring of 1940, she wasn't even called Catwoman. She was simply the Cat for her first appearance, and then became the Cat-Woman; the hyphen eventually disappeared in the mid-1940s. She wasn't Selina Kyle, either. Instead of one regular alter ego, she adopted a string of different aliases to aid in her felonious schemes. Whatever name she gave was inevitably a ruse.

Her costume was different as well, in that she didn't actually have one. She relied on disguises, using false identities to get near the items she wanted to steal rather than the sly breaking-and-entering tactics that became her modus operandi years later. Catwoman also adapted her clothes and hair to the circumstances at hand so that she could blend in, whether she was pretending to be an old woman vacationing on a cruise ship or a society gal throwing legendary soirees. She donned a mask in her third appearance, but it was nothing like her modern, form-fitting cowls. Instead, it was a realistic cat's head, which was large enough to fit over her own and came complete with brown fur and whiskers. This mask stuck around for a few issues.

Catwoman eventually settled into a regular costume and adopted a consistent alter ego, leaving behind her enigmatic origins and cumbersome mask for more typical comic book villain fare. Despite her lack of resemblance to her modern incarnations, the original Catwoman was familiar at her core. She was a clever thief, almost impossible to pin down, and a constant headache for the Caped Crusader. Catwoman was a crafty, independent cat burglar from her very first appearance, firmly establishing the heart, if not the look, of the character for the myriad versions that followed.

## The Men Behind Catwoman

The creation of Catwoman is usually credited to Bob Kane, the man also credited with Batman, Robin, and a host of Gotham City's other iconic characters. All the live-action adaptations of Catwoman, from the *Batman* television show in 1966 to *Batman Returns* in 1992 to *Catwoman* in 2004, have prominently featured a credit in their opening sequence that declares, "Based on characters created by Bob Kane." Creating Batman and his universe was Kane's entire identity, an accomplishment he traded on for decades until his death in 1998. Kane's tombstone even reads, "GOD bestowed a dream upon Bob Kane. Blessed with divine inspiration and a rich imagination, Bob created a legacy known as BATMAN."* Understanding the creation of Catwoman requires a closer look at Kane and the development of the Batman mythos as a whole.

The standard Bob Kane legend begins in 1939, with DC Comics editor Vin Sullivan searching for another hit superhero after the surprise success of Superman a year earlier. Comic books were still a young medium in America and the Man of Steel was the industry's

---

* Kane's tombstone also reads, "Bob Kane. Bruce Wayne. Batman—they are one and the same. Bob infused his dual identity character with his own attributes: goodness, kindness, compassion, sensitivity, generosity, intelligence, integrity, courage, purity of spirit, a love of all mankind." One would be hard pressed to find anyone who knew Kane and agrees with this list.

first unique success, so every editor was keen to find the next caped hero. Kane, a young cartoonist with a few credits in other DC titles, accepted the challenge. After speaking with Sullivan on a Friday, Kane came back to the office Monday morning with the Bat-Man, millionaire playboy Bruce Wayne by day and masked vigilante by night. Sullivan loved the character and made him the cover story for *Detective Comics* #27 in May 1939. He was an instant hit, quickly spinning off into other titles like *Batman* and *World's Finest.*\* For the next twenty-five years every Batman story featured the byline "By Bob Kane," and Kane created all of the Dark Knight's most infamous friends and foes in this span, including Catwoman.

Like most legends, this is an inaccurate and incomplete tale, but it's the story that everyone believed for decades. Then, in the letter column of *Detective Comics* #327 in May 1964, editor Julius Schwartz offhandedly mentioned Bill Finger for the first time, calling him the man "who has written most of the classic *Batman* adventures of the past two decades." A year later, Finger appeared at New York Comicon and confirmed that he'd written the bulk of Kane's Batman stories. Soon after, an article by Jerry Bails in the comic book fan magazine *CAPA-alpha* claimed that Finger was responsible for the bulk of Batman's design and his many supporting characters.

Kane was furious. He sent a lengthy response to *Batmania*, another fan magazine, in which he unequivocally claimed that he was "the sole creator" of Batman. Kane threatened to sue Bails for "misrepresentation and distortion of the truth" and blasted, "Your article is completely misleading, loaded with untruths fed to you by Finger's hallucinations of grandeur." While Kane admitted that Finger "literally typed" many scripts, he contended that Finger was working off Kane's own ideas and that Finger had little to do with the vast majority of the Batman mythos. As proof, Kane cited the fact that "it remains obvious that my name appears on the strip alone," and thus he must be the true creator. Kane also claimed that he drew all the Golden Age Batman comics himself, and that he continued to draw 90 percent of the Batman stories being published at the time.

---

\* Much like Catwoman, Batman quickly lost his hyphen.

These statements, along with most of the rest of Kane's missive, were all lies.

The real story behind Batman began like the legend, with Vin Sullivan looking for a follow-up to Superman and Kane taking a shot at the gig. But instead of going home, hunkering down, and creating Batman, Kane called up Bill Finger. The two had met at a cocktail party a few years before and discovered that they shared an interest in science fiction and adventure pulp books.* Kane was an artist who couldn't write and Finger was a shoe salesman with literary aspirations, so Kane began to pay Finger for scripts that he then drew and submitted to comic book publishers as his own work. Kane had been working for Eisner & Iger, a sort of comic book story factory with many writers and artists churning out material for several emerging comics publishers. With Finger writing him stories, Kane was able to strike out on his own and get better pay directly from DC Comics, where he sold some humor and adventure stories.

When Finger showed up at Kane's apartment, Kane had already sketched out an idea for his new superhero: the Bird-Man. He had red tights, blond hair, a black domino mask, and large black wings. Finger was unimpressed and recommended something more along the lines of the pulp hero the Shadow, a dark and mysterious vigilante. The Bird-Man quickly became the Bat-Man. Finger suggested adding a cowl and gloves, changing the wings to a scalloped cape, and trading the bright costume for a gray-and-black color scheme. He then set about writing the first six-page script for the new hero, "The Case of the Chemical Syndicate." The story established the Bat-Man's detective skills, featured his socialite alter ego Bruce Wayne, and also introduced police commissioner James Gordon.

Meanwhile, Kane took the new design in to Vin Sullivan, who bought the feature straightaway. Kane's father had asked around for some legal advice before the meeting, and when Kane came in, he knew he didn't want to just sell the story. He wanted a regular job

---

* They also grew up in the same neighborhood, though they didn't know each other, and shared a Jewish heritage. Both of their names are anglicized, to allow them to better fit in and afford them more work opportunities; their given names were Milton Finger and Robert Kahn.

with his name attached, and Sullivan agreed, giving him a decent page rate, a guarantee of work, and a degree of control over the character. The contract was between DC Comics and Bob Kane alone; at this point, Sullivan didn't even know that Bill Finger existed.

Finger's early scripts established several iconic elements of the Batman universe. Along with his dual identity, Finger gave Gotham City its name, introduced the Batmobile and the Batcave, and created Batman's sidekick, Robin.* When Batman launched an eponymous solo series in 1940, it was Finger who wrote the stories that introduced iconic villains like the Joker and Catwoman in *Batman* #1. Ultimately, Bill Finger was the man behind almost every significant part of the Batman mythos. Bob Kane just drew the pictures.

Except that Kane didn't actually draw much of anything. Recent research has found that a fair amount of Kane's artwork was swiped, meaning that he copied the basic forms and figures of other artists' work, altered them somewhat, and passed them off as his own. For example, Batman's iconic first appearance on the cover of *Detective Comics* #27 was a blatant copy of a panel drawn by Alex Raymond in a 1937 *Flash Gordon* Sunday comic strip. The body position and the angle of the head were almost exactly the same; the only changes were that one arm was posed differently and that Kane put the figure in the Batman costume. Many examples of other swipes have been found in Kane's interior art as well, including a litany of images copied from *Gang Busters in Action*, a 1938 children's book illustrated by Henry Vallely.

What Kane didn't swipe he farmed out to other artists. Initially, Kane hired young artists to ink his penciled artwork and fill in backgrounds, a common practice at the time, but this quickly grew into artists drawing entire stories that Kane submitted to DC as his own work. One of his first ghost artists was Jerry Robinson, who is today regarded as a legend in the comic book world. Robinson did the majority of the art in the story that featured the Joker's first appearance, and many now credit him, instead of Kane, with the

---

* When Finger first brought up a sidekick, Kane suggested a hero inspired by and named for the mythological Mercury. Finger wisely went another direction with Robin the Boy Wonder, a.k.a. Dick Grayson, the orphaned son of murdered circus performers.

creation of the Joker. DC eventually hired Robinson away from Kane, and he worked for them directly for several years, but Kane simply found replacements. Some of his ghost artists, like Sheldon Moldoff and George Roussos, worked for DC while doing Kane's work on the sly.*

Despite his often complete reliance on ghost artists, Kane refused to give them any recognition whatsoever. After Kane's Batman contract made him a wealthy man, Jerry Robinson approached him and said, "Look, you're very successful now, and you can afford to give me credit for what I did." Kane simply replied, "I don't see it that way."

Kane's editors were aware of his reliance on ghost artists but generally let it go. When Kane turned in some work in the late 1940s that was very obviously not his own, his editor Jack Schiff told him to stop using ghost artists, but he didn't. Later on, Schiff's replacement, Julius Schwartz, knew that Moldoff was doing Kane's work at the time but recalled, "We continued with the charade of working with Bob as if he actually did the work." Kane's contract with DC guaranteed him a good enough page rate that he could pay someone else to do the work at a lower rate and still clear a decent amount of money for himself. So long as the art came in on time, it seems that DC Comics didn't particularly care who did it. Every story still said "By Bob Kane" regardless.

Kane was notoriously quiet about his contract with DC, but he definitely came out ahead when he renegotiated it in the mid-1940s. Some sources say that when Superman's creators Jerry Siegel and Joe Shuster sued DC for the rights to the Man of Steel in 1946, Kane came in and claimed that he was underage when he signed his contract for Batman. DC's moneyman Jack Liebowitz then granted him partial ownership of Batman, a higher page rate, and a percentage of subsidiary rights for his silence. Another version says that Kane's lawyer threatened legal action that would derail DC's plans for a

---

* Kane drew so little that he didn't even do his own sketches. At the height of the *Batman* television show's popularity in the mid-1960s, Kane had a regular gig drawing sketches on a children's television show. He hired one of his ghost artists, Joe Giella, to outline the sketches beforehand, light enough that the cameras wouldn't see them, and then he traced them during the show.

Batman serial film, and so DC granted him an annual stipend and a percentage of Batman's merchandising profits. Whatever the case, Kane lived quite comfortably and made an absolute killing when the *Batman* television show started a Batman craze in 1966. Legendary comics creator Will Eisner, Kane's former boss and colleague, said of Kane's ability to make so much money through such minimal work and talent, "Bob was the luckiest man in the world you ever knew. He's an example of how to succeed out of pure luck."

While Kane was making a fortune and getting all the credit, Finger languished in obscurity. DC eventually found out about his arrangement with Kane and hired him directly, and he continued to write Batman comics for many years, as well as Green Lantern and Superman stories. Robinson said of Finger: "He was a very good visual writer; he knew what could translate visually. Bill wasn't a cartoonist himself, but he knew the limitations and the potential of the art form." However, Finger was slow and often late with his assignments. He was a perfectionist, and he wouldn't submit a script until it was just right.

Finger never made any money off Batman's success other than his page rate for new stories. He certainly had a claim to more, but he didn't pursue any legal action. The most common term Finger's associates used to describe him was "agreeable," though his son put it far more bluntly when he said, "My father had a very weak spine." Finger's pay wasn't great, and he moved to smaller and smaller apartments as the years went on and money became increasingly tight. He was fired briefly in the 1960s for asking his boss at DC about a health care program, though he returned a few years later. Finger was drinking heavily at that point, and he passed away in 1974 at the age of fifty-nine. He wrote Batman comics for decades but never saw his name in the credits.*

Meanwhile, Kane became a millionaire because of Batman, and he tirelessly defended the legend that he was the sole creator of the Batman universe for his entire life. He took all the credit in

---

* Finger does receive official credit on Batman properties today, though only since late 2015. From comics to television to movies, Batman's adventures now include the line "Created by Bob Kane with Bill Finger."

early comic book features about him, including a profile in *Batman* #1 that ironically declared, "Bob Kane is certainly not a copyist; his work shows a definite originality and freshness." In a two-page article decades later in *Detective Comics* in 1964, he didn't mention Finger or any of his ghost artists at all. Instead, he suggested that young aspiring artists should work hard and rely on "good old elbow grease" because "I've never found a short cut." Kane also claimed grandiose inspirations for Batman as he grew older, including Leonardo da Vinci's flying machine; his autobiography even included "early sketches" of a da Vinci–inspired design that most scholars believe to be backdated forgeries. Kane eventually did say, "I must admit that Bill never received the fame and recognition he deserved," but only long after Finger was dead.

In short, Bob Kane was a liar and a fraud, and his discussion of the creation of Catwoman should be viewed with a very critical eye. In his 1989 autobiography, *Batman & Me*, Kane claimed a specific inspiration for Catwoman: 1930s sex symbol Jean Harlow. Kane recalled, "She burned up the screen with her sensuous face and torrid figure," and added, "At my impressionable age she seemed to personify feminine pulchritude at its most sensuous." How much of Catwoman's first appearances Kane actually drew is debatable, but regardless of the true artist, she didn't look a thing like Harlow. Harlow was known as the "platinum blonde" and the "blonde bombshell," while the original Cat was a brunette. Her face structure wasn't at all similar and she lacked any of Harlow's signature facial elements, like her dimpled chin and her mole.*

This wasn't the only time that Kane cited an iconic actress as his inspiration for a character. He not only claimed that Marilyn Monroe inspired the look of Gotham City reporter Vicki Vale, who first appeared in 1948, but also spun yarns about meeting the actress

---

* While Harlow was the only actor associated with Catwoman in his autobiography, Kane later claimed that Hedy Lamarr and her "feline beauty" inspired Catwoman. This has been the generally accepted inspiration since, probably because the early Catwoman artwork does resemble Lamarr; the two are now so closely associated that Anne Hathaway studied Lamarr before portraying Catwoman in *The Dark Knight Rises*. But this so-called inspiration seems to be a later invention of Kane's, a visual coincidence that he decided to claim as intentional far after the fact.

twice while visiting Hollywood during the filming of the Batman serials. Supposedly, they first met at a Hollywood party in 1943 when she was still just Norma Jean, and the pair danced all night long. Then Kane ran into her again five years later and they spent a lovely day at the beach, where Kane drew sketches of her in her bathing suit that he later used as reference while creating Vicki Vale. Unsurprisingly, these all seem to be lies. The details ring false; Monroe was an entirely unknown munitions factory employee in 1943, and the timing of their 1948 encounter was all wrong.* Plus, Lew Schwartz drew the bulk of the story in which Vicki Vale first appeared anyway.

While Kane citing Harlow's influence on Catwoman was a far less elaborate whopper, it was in keeping with his fondness for manufacturing grandiose inspiration long after the fact. From da Vinci for Batman to Monroe for Vicki Vale to Harlow and Lamarr for Catwoman, Kane often made up stories to appear more cultured and impressive when the actual origins of his supposed creations either had nothing to do with him or were entirely mundane.†

Beyond the Harlow chicanery, Kane's autobiography did shed some light on Catwoman's creation. Kane actually mentioned Finger's involvement in her development, which adds some legitimacy to his words. He wrote:

> We knew we needed a female nemesis to give the strip sex appeal. So Bill and I decided to create a somewhat friendly foe who committed crimes but was also a romantic interest in Batman's rather sterile life. She was a kind of female Batman, except that she was a villainess and Batman was a hero. We figured that there would be this cat and mouse, cat and bat byplay between them—he would try to reform her and bring her over

---

* Kane claimed that Monroe had just been dropped from her Columbia contract when they met up in 1948, but that actually occurred in 1949.
† The true inspiration for Catwoman may have lacked any Hollywood glitz. In a recent interview, Bob Kane's cousin Ruth Steel revealed that Kane based the look of Catwoman on her. She also said, "Bob Kane always loved me and said if I wasn't his cousin he would've married me, although I never would've married him."

to the side of law and order. But she was never a murderer or entirely evil like the Joker.

The idea was to have a female character that girls and women reading the comics could relate to while also making her sexy because "male readers would appreciate a sensual woman to look at." Kane wrote that they decided to associate their new character with a cat because a cat embodied the aloof, untamable nature they wanted to imbue in her, saying, "Cats are cool, detached, and unreliable . . . cats are hard to understand, they are erratic, as women are." *

Finger's perspective on the creation of Catwoman is largely unknown. He never wrote an autobiography, and he did very few interviews before his untimely passing. His peers credited him with coming up with the character; Jerry Robinson said that Catwoman was wholly Finger's creation, as were other villains like the Riddler and the Penguin. Thomas Andrae, the cowriter of Bob Kane's autobiography, agrees with Robinson's assessment, and after the book was published he admitted disappointment that Kane took so much credit for Catwoman and other characters that he had very little to do with.

In a 1970 interview with artist Jim Steranko for his *Steranko History of Comics*, Finger gave a handful of specifics about his inspirations for Catwoman, but they weren't particularly illuminating. He mentioned that "*National Geographic* had a great issue on cats" that he found helpful, and that he used "Bartlett's book of quotations and the dictionary to invent puns about cats. Very methodical." That was it. Finger's few interviews focused more on Batman, and Catwoman was mentioned only in passing.

Even though the behind-the-scenes details are sparse, the bulk of the credit for Catwoman, and for the majority of the Batman mythos in general, should go to Finger. There's a reasonable chance that Kane didn't actually draw most, if any, of Catwoman's early appearances, and his input on the creation of the character was

---

* Kane then used this discussion of cats as a springboard to talk about women generally. He opined, "You always need to keep women at arm's length. We don't want anyone to take over our souls, and women have a habit of doing that. So there is a love-resentment thing with women. [...] With women, when the romance is over, somehow they never remain my friends." How odd, Bob.

probably minimal. Finger laid the foundation of Catwoman, creating a cunning, captivating thief, while Kane likely farmed out or swiped the art. It's telling that while Catwoman's characterization has remained the same from her earliest appearances, her look has changed dramatically since then.

## The Cat Debuts

The Cat first appeared in *Batman* #1 in the spring of 1940, and the book began with Robin going undercover as a steward at a high society yacht party. The wealthy Mrs. Travers brought along her famed necklace, valued at half a million dollars, and Batman suspected that someone might try to steal it. Robin was unable to prevent the necklace's inevitable theft, but he did find a note that showed that Mrs. Travers's nephew, Denny, was working with the mysterious burglar, the Cat. Batman and Robin tried to decipher which of the other passengers could be the elusive thief, and, playing on a hunch, Batman set off the boat's fire alarm. Denny's elderly friend, Miss Peggs, took off running for the lifeboats, and Batman noted, "Nice legs for an old woman!"

After the Dynamic Duo gave chase and caught her, Batman removed Miss Peggs's white wig and wax makeup to reveal the Cat. She yelled, "Let go of me!" but Batman retorted, "Quiet or papa spank!" As everyone looked on in shock, the Cat snarked, "Well, what's the matter? Haven't you ever seen a pretty girl **before**?" Batman then explained her cunning plan: she came aboard as Miss Peggs, feigning an ankle injury, and then snuck into Mrs. Travers's cabin, stole the necklace, and hid it in her ankle bandages.

Once captured, the Cat tried to sell Batman on teaming up. She explained that she had been planning to split the half-million dollars with Denny, but now she'd gladly partner with him instead, proclaiming, "You and I—King and Queen of Crime! We'd make a great team!" Batman admitted that he was tempted, but he refused her offer. Then, as Batman and Robin transported the Cat back to land where the police were waiting, she leaped off the speedboat. When Robin moved to go after her, the narration read, "Batman clumsily 'bumps' into him!" Robin was incensed and accused Batman of bumping into him on purpose and intentionally letting the Cat escape. Batman casually brushed away his concerns before remarking, "Hmm, nice night, isn't it?" He then spent the story's final panel musing about the Cat's loveliness and how he hoped to run into her again.

This was an unusual story in a variety of ways. First, it was a Batman comic that featured a female character in a speaking role. This was extremely rare in the early years of the Golden Age. In the four years following Batman's first appearance in *Detective Comics* #27, women appeared in just 7 percent of the panels in the series' Batman stories. Moreover, they spoke in just 4 percent of the books' panels. Men, on the other hand, appeared in 96 percent of the panels and spoke in 80 percent of them. Of the forty-eight issues published in this four-year span, sixteen didn't feature a single woman anywhere in the story, and twenty-one didn't have a woman speaking any dialogue. Women in early Batman stories were few and far between.

The women who did appear were given very little to do. They were often damsels in distress for Batman to save, briefly introduced before one of the Caped Crusader's fiendish foes nabbed them, and once freed they were rarely seen again. They were lucky to even get a name. Even Batman's mother was anonymous. Batman's origin story in *Detective Comics* #33 depicted a young Bruce Wayne witnessing the murder of his parents during a stickup. His father's name was mentioned twice: the family was described as "Thomas Wayne, his wife, and son," and Bruce's mother called out "Thomas! You've killed him!" after the crook shot him, but her name wasn't revealed.*

Aside from Catwoman, the only regularly appearing female characters were Bruce's girlfriends. Bruce had a fiancée named Julie Madison during his first few *Detective Comics* appearances, and her main function was to be captured or become involved in a dangerous situation so that Batman could rescue her. She had a comedic purpose as well, regularly wishing that her foppish, playboy beau could be

---

* She didn't get a name until nearly a decade later, when a retelling of Batman's origin in June 1948 called her Martha Wayne for the first time. She was shot and killed in the first origin story, but in this later version "Martha Wayne's weak heart stopped from the sudden shock!" after Thomas was killed.

more like Batman. Bruce never seemed terribly interested in Julie; his true love was stopping evildoers. When Julie broke off their engagement in *Detective Comics* #49, Bruce responded, "I understand! It's all right," and moved on instantaneously.

After Julie, Bruce dated Linda Page but was similarly flippant about their relationship. When he noticed a clue for a big case while out on a romantic walk with Linda, he abruptly declared, "Well, Linda . . . gotta go now," and left. Linda assumed he was heading off to a night club, and Bruce didn't bother to correct her. On a later date at a carnival, he saw the Bat-Signal while he and Linda were trapped high in the air on a broken ride, so he undid his safety belt and pretended to fall and miraculously survive, then drove off to answer the call.

For Batman, women were just pawns he could use to portray Bruce Wayne as a carefree socialite and protect his alter ego. Being Batman was his only priority and romance didn't interest him in the slightest. Until Catwoman, that is. When the Cat first appeared, Batman fell for her immediately. Bruce was still engaged to Julie at the time, and as he rhapsodized about the Cat's beauty in the story's final panel, he suddenly declared, "Say—mustn't forget I've got a girl named Julie!" He then continued to fixate on the Cat anyway, and said, "Oh well—she still had lovely eyes!"

Piquing Batman's romantic interest for the first time was a considerable achievement, but even more impressive was the Cat's ability to make Batman forget his commitment to fighting crime. Batman's many male villains didn't escape. They were captured or, in some of the early stories before Batman had a stricter moral code, killed. Either way, justice was served to every criminal Batman encountered, except for the Cat.

She returned as the Cat-Woman in *Batman* #2 and the Dynamic Duo quickly nabbed her, but Batman let her go when she traded information on the Joker's whereabouts. Later, the Joker interrupted her plans to steal a cask of jewels from a castle, and Batman showed up to make it a three-way fight. At the end of the battle, Batman left an unconscious Joker behind in the now-fiery castle and escaped on a rope ladder to the Bat-Plane with Cat-Woman in tow. Once they were away from the castle's flames, Cat-Woman leaped into the ocean, again evading capture. Batman had gotten the jewels back, at least, but she remained free.

The Cat-Woman was back in the following issue, performing a series of crimes that culminated in her disguising herself as a model and pulling off a daring theft in the middle of a diamond show. Wanting a bigger cut, her allies betrayed her, but Batman came to her rescue. When he told her that he had to take her to the police, she replied, "It doesn't matter! You saved my life! I'd like to thank you for that!" She then kissed Batman and, using the kiss as an excuse to get close to him, shoved him away and escaped out the door. Robin was about to give chase, but Batman called him off as he mused, "What a night! A night for romance, eh, Robin?"

After a short break, Cat-Woman deployed her most ambitious plan yet in *Batman* #10. She pretended to be Marguerite Tone, a wealthy society woman, and hosted a scavenger hunt for Gotham City's richest citizens. Then, while everyone was out on the hunt, her goons looted all the empty mansions. Her men later posed as butlers and cooks in wealthy homes across Gotham and were about to pull another heist when Batman intervened. Cat-Woman kissed him again, leaving him momentarily stunned, and when Robin finally ran in to snap him out of it, she was gone. The police were perplexed over why Batman failed to capture her, but he brushed them off with a vague explanation. Robin later alleged, "I've a feeling you **let** the **Cat-Woman** escape!" but Bruce feigned outrage before praising her cleverness and beauty.

A clear pattern ran through all of Catwoman's earliest appearances, one that was strikingly at odds with Batman's usual methods. Catwoman outsmarted him repeatedly, and he was complicit in her doing so. When she tried to talk him into joining with her to rule the criminal underworld together he always refused, but she didn't need to turn him completely to achieve her ends. She got enough of what she needed from him, and he happily gave it. Catwoman had corrupted the incorruptible.

## Feline Fatale

As Catwoman established a presence in the early Batman comics, a similar type of character became a mainstay in American cinemas. The femme fatale was a classic archetype in literature going back millennia, a mysterious woman who seduced a good man into danger and vice, controlling him with her sexual wiles. These temptresses became key players in film noir pictures of the 1940s, where the criminal underworld provided the perfect trap in which to lure private investigators and other stalwart citizens. From murdered spouses to mob machinations to blackmail, femmes fatales were a busy bunch in many of the decade's most popular films.

However, there was often a tragic element to their tales. The hero usually found his way out of the femme fatale's web, foiling her scheme and leaving her imprisoned or, in many cases, dead. Few femmes fatales got out unscathed. It was the 1940s, after all, and wanton sexuality and manipulation couldn't go unpunished. A femme fatale was everything that women at the time were not supposed to be, and thus the balance had to be restored by bringing them down, often harshly.

Those who study cinematic femmes fatales sometimes look behind their many tragic demises to appreciate the power they represented. Scholar Janey Place says of this era, "It does give us one of the few periods of film in which women are active, not static symbols, are intelligent and powerful, if destructively so, and derive power, not weakness, from their sexuality." Showcasing these rarely seen attributes in female characters was significant, regardless of the outcome, and expanded the scope of what women in film could be and do.

At the same time, these films were written, directed, and produced by men, for men. As Mary Ann Doane writes, the femme fatale "is not a subject of feminism, but a symptom of male fears about feminism." While the films showed men as weak and easy to manipulate, they still flocked to them in droves because they knew how things would end. The male audience enjoyed watching the sexy actress with the knowledge that no matter how much trouble she got the male lead into, he was going to escape and she was going to be punished. The genre played on male fears of impotence and power-ful women but ultimately restored their confidence by highlighting women's inability to topple men and undo the patriarchal system. The femme fatale didn't challenge male beliefs; she reinforced them.

Her punishment was key to this process. The woman who acted outside the bounds of her prescribed gender role always paid the price, and a story in *Batman* #5 illustrates such a tale. A femme fatale named Queenie was part of a criminal gang that teamed up with the Joker to rob a gambling ship, a plan that involved her getting playboys drunk so that they'd be easier to steal from. One of those playboys was Bruce Wayne, and Queenie committed the cardinal comic book sin of piecing together that he was Batman by noticing a shaving nick on Bruce's chin that matched Batman's. In the story's final confrontation, she realized that she was in love with Bruce and stopped her associate from shooting Batman; one final act of goodness after a life of crime was a common send-off for femmes fatales. Her associate then shot her, and Queenie died in Batman's arms. Her last words were, "I'm going . . . please, kiss me . . . kiss me before it's too late." Queenie's death was immediately forgotten as Batman ran off to chase down the Joker, and she was mentioned again only at the story's end when Bruce briefly recalled "that girl who died back there."

Catwoman met all the femme fatale criteria. She was a beautiful woman committed to a life of crime who used her feminine wiles to corrupt Batman and make him do what she wanted. She got herself into dangerous situations knowing full well that Batman would show up to save her if things got too bad, and then easily escaped his grasp with just a kiss. But while Queenie shared the fate of most femmes fatales, Catwoman was able to escape the usual cycle.

Because of the nature of superhero comics, Catwoman avoided punishment repeatedly in the early years of the Golden Age. Unlike a film or a pulp novel, comic book narratives didn't end. There had to be new stories every month, and coming up with different, excit-ing villains was a taxing job. By the time Catwoman debuted, many superhero comics were in the practice of bringing back popular vil-lains and giving their stories an open-ended conclusion so that they could return again. Queenie died because she wasn't a primary villain; she was a secondary character in a Joker story and thus expendable. The Joker, however, escaped that story when he was thrown off a lighthouse to his "death" in the ocean below; of course, no body was found and he was back at it a few issues later. Catwoman regularly escaped Batman as well, albeit through more conniving means. Because of her higher profile, she too was untouchable.

By eluding punishment and death, Catwoman broke the tragic cycle of the femme fatale, embodying all the unique and progressive elements of these characters without the sharp lesson that wiped them away to restore male superiority. She was the femme fatale at peak power, the male lead wrapped around her little finger as she bounced from crime to crime, walking away scot-free from each of them.

# 2

# A Conspicuous Pause

When the superhero boom began in the late 1930s, the critical reaction was swift and wide ranging. Many parent and teacher groups took issue with the entire medium, and were outraged that kids were reading comics instead of "real" books. They saw comics as the junk food of the written word, a treat kids loved that offered nothing beneficial to them and ultimately would rot their brains. Some critics even got up in arms about the poor production of comics, fearing that the badly printed books might give children eye strain.

Other critiques were of a moral nature. Parents and educators were joined by religious groups in condemning the crimes and violence portrayed in superhero comics. Many early superhero books featured realistic villains like thieves, mobsters, and murderers, and their crimes were depicted in detail. Heroes often killed their foes, taking justice into their own hands. Batman wasn't particularly lethal in his early years, at least not intentionally; a lot of his villains did end up dead when Batman's defensive maneuvers "inadvertently" flipped them off a roof or snapped their necks. The initial years of the superhero genre were a dark mix of tragic origins and regular violence.

In response to these criticisms, DC Comics put together an editorial advisory board composed of education professionals and children's psychologists. When the panel was introduced in all DC books in late 1941, the publishers wrote, "A deep respect for our obligation to the young people of America and their parents and our responsibility as parents ourselves combine to set our standards of wholesome entertainment." The editorial advisory board was made up of consultants with limited power, and profit usually trumped their concerns. In one notable instance, Josette Frank had her name removed from the regular advisory board listing in *Wonder Woman* because she was upset at the book's bondage imagery; despite her concerns, DC had sided with the book's creator, William Moulton Marston, because the series was a bestseller. Nonetheless, the editorial advisory boards looked good, and criticism of superhero books quieted down for a time.

The introduction of advisory boards coincided with America's entry into World War II, and the two combined to create a significant shift in tone across DC's superhero titles. Characters like Superman and Batman were born out of a 1930s Depression-era mindset that distrusted authority, and the heroes often battled against the powerful forces in society that kept the common people down. With America at war, the country banded together and that mindset disappeared from the comics. Everything about the American way of life became unassailable. Authority figures were now friends, the justice system was key, and superheroes became model citizens. Violence lessened, real crime was reduced, and the good guys always won.

For Catwoman, this meant that the free ride was over. Her years of manipulating Batman and escaping him came to an end as the Caped Crusader became even more of a paragon of moral virtue. Catwoman had been his one vice, but now her power over him was gone.

## Capturing Catwoman

In February 1943, Catwoman returned in *Batman* #15 with a new scheme. She posed as a beautician named Elva Barr and used a mud-pack treatment on a society reporter's face as a mold to make a mask that she then wore to infiltrate a wealthy heiress's lavish wedding. When Batman caught her, she told him that she was in love with Bruce Wayne and that she'd give up her life of crime if she could be with him. Batman let her go and then began to date Elva as Bruce, and soon they were engaged. However, their relationship was a scheme by Batman to reform Catwoman, and when she learned that Bruce didn't really love her she returned to her old ways and set off on a massive crime spree. Batman and Robin ultimately captured her, and Batman declared, "I'm afraid you're hopeless, **Catwoman!** There's only one place where I'm sure you'll go straight! In prison!" For the first time ever, Catwoman was behind bars.

This issue was the end of Catwoman's early femme fatale era. Whatever desire Batman felt for her had disappeared. Catwoman, on the other hand, was now awash in romantic desire. There had been hints of this before; Catwoman wasn't a cruel, hardened criminal, and she didn't hate the Dynamic Duo like some of their other foes did. In *Batman* #3, Catwoman drove off at the end of the story after she escaped from Batman and said, "I sort of wish the **Batman** were driving this car [. . .] and we were just another boy and girl out for a ride on a moonlight [*sic*] night. That would be sort of . . . of . . . **nice!!**" Then in *Batman* #10, Catwoman observed Batman and mused, "How brave and strong he is!" though that thought quickly turned into a plan for them to become an unstoppable criminal duo.

The Elva Barr episode marked a major shift for the character, in which romance trumped her criminal nature. She legitimately gave up crime when she got engaged to Bruce Wayne, firing her goons and going straight. His subsequent betrayal soured her on Bruce, but Catwoman's affection for Batman became a regular part of her appearances in the comics that followed. After hitting Batman in the head allowed her to momentarily flee in one issue, Catwoman worried "**Batman** wasn't hurt was he? I only meant to scare him." In a Christmas story, she tried to make time with Batman under the mistletoe, then stopped a goon from killing him, prompting the goon to ask, "What's de idea? You soft for dis guy?" In a later issue, Catwoman posed as a fashion magazine editor and took advantage of her disguise to plant a big kiss on the Caped Crusader.

Catwoman's romantic inclinations were part of a larger change in the Bat-books' approach to gender roles. By falling in love with Batman, Catwoman slipped into a more typical role, trading some of her unusually independent nature for a traditional desire to settle down. Batman followed suit; while he couldn't settle down because he was wholly devoted to justice, Bruce's cavalier approach to dating lessened. He showed genuine concern for his girlfriend Linda Page's feelings when he pretended to date Elva, letting her in on his plan to ease her concerns. As Batman, he went beyond crime fighting in a variety of stories in which he and Robin helped couples that were in difficult situations, solving their problems so that they could get married. DC's commitment to "wholesome entertainment" led to an increased focus on love and marriage across the board.

This shift in gender roles also came with a degree of domestication for Catwoman. Batman viewed her as a troublesome pet that needed to be sorted out, not a fierce feline on the prowl. After he foiled another of her elaborate plans, he crowed, "Well, kitten, I've just hung a bell on **you**!" Along with the taming implications of a collar and bell, the "kitten" moniker also made her appear childish. This was reinforced in a later issue when Batman's butler, Alfred, nabbed Catwoman and decided to mete out justice himself, saying, "A little spanking will do the trick. And, believe me, it will hurt you more than it will me!" The continued juvenilization of Catwoman was a stark contrast with her earlier commanding depiction.*

Despite her new romantic role and the petulant-kitten angle, Catwoman nonetheless possessed all the accoutrements of a proper supervillain. As DC Comics moved away from real crime scenarios, costumed supervillains with elaborate traps and themed gadgets became the norm. Catwoman shifted from thief to supervillain, completing the transformation with a new costume in 1946. The earliest incarnation of the outfit debuted in *Batman* #35; Catwoman traded her large, realistic cat mask for a more streamlined, purple cat-eared

---

* The comic didn't actually show the spanking, and instead cut away as the narration read, "Let us be discreet and withdraw as Alfred pays his private debt to the Catwoman." With *Wonder Woman*'s constant bondage imagery, including spankings, an ongoing concern, perhaps the editors of the Bat-books wanted to avoid anything that might be misconstrued.

cowl. She paired the new mask with a knee-length, short-sleeved purple dress, long purple gloves, and a short green cape. The now-iconic version of the costume premiered a few months later in April 1947's *Detective Comics* #122 with the same color scheme but a different design: the dress was now a long gown with green trim and a high slit up the leg, and the full-length sleeves led into clawed gloves.

Catwoman also possessed a variety of supervillain accessories. She had a loyal cat named Hecate, after a Greek goddess of the moon, to whom she could outline her fiendish plans. The belt of Catwoman's costume was also a cat-o'-nine-tails that she could whip off and use to repel Batman and Robin. While the Dynamic Duo had the Batmobile, Catwoman drove around in her Kitty Car, a sleek open-topped vehicle with a cat face on the front grille and an upraised, curled tail on the back. The purple car was fast and, like a cat, had the ability to leap a fair distance. After successful outings in the Kitty Car, Catwoman drove back to the Catacombs, her lavishly appointed secret hideout where she, Hecate, and a rotating cast of goons resided.

The first issue with Catwoman in her new costume was absolute supervillain spectacle. The story began with Catwoman blackmailing three of Gotham's wealthiest citizens, sending them letters promising a black cat would cross their paths and give them bad luck unless they each paid her $50,000.* When the first man refused, Catwoman and her goons dragged a blimp into the path of his landing plane full of expensive furs, blowing up both vehicles when they collided. After the second man refused, she unleashed a black panther in the middle of his crowded circus show. When the third refused, Catwoman hijacked his freighter, but Batman and Robin intervened. This led to a dramatic chase up the Statue of Liberty and a daring helicopter escape, culminating in the Kitty Car leaping off a drawbridge and into the river.

The conclusion of this issue was one of the rare instances where Catwoman didn't end up in jail, though she did prove herself to

---

* Adjusted for inflation, in today's money Catwoman was gunning for more than half a million dollars from each man.

be resourceful in her many other prison stints. In *Batman* #35, she hypnotized her jailer and broke out. In *Batman* #42, she arranged for her gang to send her a specially treated book, folded the pages correctly to activate the chemicals hidden in them and turn the book into a bomb, and blew apart her cell door in a dramatic escape. In *Batman* #45, she just made a run for it and dove from the prison's tall walls into the sea below. Getting arrested may have become the new normal for Catwoman, but no jail could hold her.

Once released, Catwoman was a criminal mastermind with malevolent motivations. Her amplified romantic feelings didn't soften her nefarious leanings at all. In one issue, her goons no longer trusted her because Batman had caught her so many times, so she orchestrated a series of elaborate hoaxes to convince them that she had nine lives and ultimately won them back. After she was left out of a book about famous lady rogues a few issues later, spite compelled her to break out of prison in order to "**prove** that the **Catwoman** is the greatest woman criminal of **all time**."* In another story, she came up with clever, literary crimes just for the fun of it, including one where she chained up Batman and Robin behind a brick wall; her bricklaying was reminiscent of Edgar Allan Poe's "The Cask of Amontillado," and Catwoman laid the bricks in a manner that made her vanish until just her head and then only her smile remained, a direct reference to the Cheshire Cat in Lewis Carroll's *Alice in Wonderland*.

Catwoman was clever, often gleefully malicious, with all of the trappings that went along with her position. She was a consummate supervillain, until one day she wasn't.

## Pet Shop Gal

December 1950's *Batman* #62 began in fairly typical fashion. A new, mysterious criminal named Mister X was making waves in Gotham City, but he needed a partner to help him pull off higher-profile heists. He decided to bring in "the most cleverest, most

---

* After Batman stopped Catwoman and returned her to prison, the author of the book visited her to explain why he'd left her out of the book: "**Your** exploits are so terrific that I was writing a book about **you alone!**"

dangerous—and most beautiful lady of crime in the country—**the Catwoman!**" and broke her out of jail. Mister X was impressed by her ability to commit big crimes without killing, thus avoiding an onerous murder rap, and he offered her a partnership in which they would split the loot evenly.

Catwoman accepted, and when she went out to commit her first robbery she ran into Batman and Robin. As she unleashed one of her cats on them and made her escape, she noticed that the wall of a condemned building was about to fall on Batman. Unable to stand by while the man she loved died, she leaped back and saved Batman but was knocked unconscious by falling bricks.

Batman and Robin took her back to the Batcave, where the dazed Catwoman murmured, "Fasten your safety belts! If we remain calm the pilot will get us down safely!" When she woke up, she didn't remember Batman and Robin at all, had no recollection of her time as Catwoman, and was shocked to learn that it was 1950. She told them that her name was Selina Kyle, and that she was a stewardess for Speed Airlines. Years earlier, she had fallen out of a plane during a crash, and the last thing she remembered was hitting her head. Batman deduced that she'd had amnesia during her time as Catwoman, and that the blow to her head from the wall's collapse restored her memory.

Commissioner Gordon suggested that to atone for her crimes, Selina could go undercover as Catwoman and help them capture Mister X. She reluctantly agreed and returned to the gang, feeding information back to Batman and the police. After her cover was blown, Selina was nearly killed before Batman intervened just in the nick of time. With Mister X captured, she handed her costume over to Batman and declared, "That's that! From now on I'm plain Selina Kyle! The **Catwoman** has **retired!**"

The transition stuck. When Selina returned six months later, she was running a pet shop. Bruce Wayne and Dick Grayson stopped in one day and recognized underworld czar Whale Morton visiting the shop, but Selina gave the criminal an earful and told him to leave, explaining to Bruce, "He came here to remind me of another life . . . a life I'd rather forget!" But when a series of cat-themed crimes were committed soon after, Batman and Robin became suspicious. Even Selina was concerned, fearing that her amnesia had returned and she was committing the crimes without knowing it. Later in the issue, Batman was disappointed to see Selina in her Catwoman costume alongside Whale Morton, and then dismayed when she ensnared him and Robin in an elaborate trap, but it was all a clever trick. Selina figured out that Morton was framing her, so she pretended to work with him while drawing in the Dynamic Duo to help her capture him. When he realized her plan, Batman said, "He knew you'd believe yourself guilty and, for a bit, I'll admit I did, too!"

Batman's doubts continued in *Batman* #69, despite Selina already proving herself twice over. When a new villain, the King of Cats, started to commit crimes in Gotham, Batman stopped by Selina's pet shop to ask her about it. She was reluctant to talk about him, and Batman became even more suspicious when she received flowers from a secret admirer with a note signed "K." As the story went on, Batman assumed that Selina was falling in love with the King of Cats, and worried that she would return to a life of crime even though she swore that she wouldn't. In a final confrontation at the zoo, Selina saved the lives of both Batman and the King of Cats, and out of gratitude the King of Cats promised to give up his life of crime. Selina then exclaimed, "Oh Karl! Now I really am proud to be your sister!" A flummoxed Batman had missed what was actually going on: the King of Cats was Selina's brother, and she had been cagey about his behavior because she didn't want him to get in trouble.

In January 1954, a couple of Catwoman's old underworld associates visited the pet shop to poke fun at Selina, laughing, "She's been reformed since **Batman** nipped her claws!" Batman stopped by to shut them up, but warned her, "Unless you forget your former life as **Catwoman**, there's no future for you, ever!" Later that night, Selina finally had enough of civilian life. She donned her Catwoman suit and said, "No one laughed at me when I wore **this**! And I'll wear it again! I'll stun Gotham City with such cat-crimes that they'll never ridicule **Catwoman** again!"

After a dazzlingly impressive job in which she stole valuable chemicals from a transport helicopter in midair, all the goons in

Gotham wanted to work with her again. Once her team was assembled, one of the gang observed, "This new **Catacomb** is even splashier than your old one," and Catwoman added, "Yes, and my new **Kitty Car** is even more powerful!" Catwoman and her team stole the box office receipts from a popular circus known for its lion show and then nabbed cat's-eye jewels from a yacht. She was back a few months later in *Batman* #84, infiltrating a beauty contest as part of a diamond-smuggling scheme. Her law-abiding days were over.

In the early 1950s, superhero comics weren't written with an overarching plan. Stories were churned out each month at a breakneck pace by an assortment of different writers and artists—especially Batman stories, because he starred in a variety of series. Bill Finger was still a writer on the Bat-books, but Edmond Hamilton, David Vern, and William Woolfolk were all part of the regular rotation. The art was drawn by Sheldon Moldoff, Win Mortimer, Dick Sprang, and whomever Bob Kane was paying to ghost his issues; in this era, it was usually Lew Schwartz. Most of these men also worked on other characters at DC at the same time, and their workload was considerable. There was no master plan for the Bat-books and there were no larger character arcs, just a mad dash to get the books out on time, followed immediately by everyone scrambling to figure out what to put in the books the next month.

Nevertheless, Catwoman's reformation and recidivism make for an intriguing arc when read as a single tale decades later. The supervillain left behind the underworld for the sort of conventional life a woman of the early 1950s was supposed to have, but Batman, the man who had most wanted Catwoman to reform, never fully trusted Selina. No matter how many times she proved herself, she remained forever tainted by her criminal past. With Batman constantly doubting her, and her powerless life wearing on her, she returned to crime with renewed vigor. The story line can be read as a commentary on the role of women in this era, from Selina's unhappiness with her new conventional lifestyle to the lingering stigmas of the damaged woman. No one at DC intended such commentary, but voracious young fans who faithfully picked up each issue may have been able to piece together a harsh critique of their patriarchal society.

In September 1954 Catwoman appeared in *Detective Comics* #211 in typical supervillain fashion. She stole a case of diamonds, used the steel claws on her Cat-Plane to rip off the wings of the Bat-Plane, trapped Batman and Robin on a jungle island, and then dressed them in skimpy cat skins and set them free so she and her gang could hunt them for sport. Batman stopped her in the end, but she ultimately escaped on her Cat-Plane and flew off into the dawn sky.

Catwoman then disappeared for twelve years.

## Into Thin Air

Dr. Fredric Wertham was, for the most part, a very progressive fellow. Born in Germany and educated in London and Munich, he moved to America in the early 1920s to work at a psychiatric clinic in Johns Hopkins Hospital and moved to New York a decade later to help run the Bellevue Mental Hygiene Clinic. Wertham also opened a low-cost mental health clinic in Harlem to treat the underserved black youth community of New York City.

He wasn't afraid to take controversial stances. In 1950 Julius and Ethel Rosenberg were arrested under suspicion of being Soviet spies. At the height of the Red Scare, Wertham testified about the harmful effects of solitary confinement and argued that it was cruel to imprison Ethel in such a manner. A few years later, his research on the damaging psychological ramifications of school segregation was used in the landmark Brown v. Board of Education case that ultimately led to the integration of American schools. Wertham did a great deal of important work that was significant to American history and progress.

However, most of that is now forgotten. Instead, Wertham is remembered as the man who almost destroyed the comic book industry with his 1954 book *Seduction of the Innocent*. Today, Wertham is often dismissed as a crackpot who blamed all of society's ills on comic books and wanted to ban them from the newsstands, but the truth is more complicated. His extensive psychiatric work with children led him to believe that comic books were a contributing factor to juvenile delinquency and, more important, a factor that could be easily remedied. Wertham wanted comic books to be rated so that children couldn't read books that weren't appropriate for their impressionable young minds.

The comics that dominated the newsstands in the early 1950s showed that Wertham had a fair point. After the end of World War II the popularity of superheroes quickly faded, and within a few years DC was the only superhero publisher left, with just Batman, Superman, and Wonder Woman headlining series. With superheroes all but gone, the industry was dominated by crime and horror comics that were often shocking and gruesome.

EC Comics was at the forefront of this new wave. With its sharp writers and now-legendary artists, EC's crime and horror books told compelling stories, usually with a clever moral lesson. EC titles were much more than just outrageous schlock, but this wasn't the case for their slew of imitators. Newsstands and spinner racks were full of gory, frightening tales of violence and murder from other publishers that copied the broad strokes of EC's line without any of the panache.

For Wertham, all of these books, including EC Comics' well-constructed tales, were problematic. He argued that even if the villains were defeated and a moral lesson was taught, children were more apt to focus on the many initial pages of horror imagery or crimes being committed rather than the single final page of resolution and right winning the day. Young readers didn't have the ability to understand the nuance. For example, in a story about racism and lynchings, the bulk of the story with racist rhetoric and crimes against African Americans would weigh far heavier on their minds than the final page where the racists got their comeuppance. As such, Wertham believed that children shouldn't be allowed access to these books.

At its core, it was a reasonable argument. A lot of the imagery in these books was shocking, and many crime comics were essentially how-to manuals for all manner of felonies. Suggesting that kids shouldn't read them was a fair point. But Wertham went further than that, tearing into the industry as a whole with vitriolic rhetoric and a critical eye that even landed on America's favorite nocturnal superhero.

*Innocent* debuted. The timing suggests that this was because she was one of the only other characters mentioned by name in Wertham's Batman section.

And unkindly so. Square in the middle of Wertham's homoerotic discussion, he stated, "In these stories there are practically no decent, attractive, successful women." As an example, he suggested, "A typical female character is the Catwoman, who is vicious and uses a whip." These are uncharitable descriptions of Catwoman but not enough to damn her to obscurity. More damaging was Wertham's association of Catwoman's role with the comics' gay undertones when he continued, "The atmosphere is homosexual and anti-feminine. If the girl is good-looking she is undoubtedly the villainess. If she is after Bruce Wayne, she will have no chance against Dick."

A twelve-year banishment for Catwoman was an excessive reaction, but not at all unusual relative to DC Comics' wider reaction to *Seduction of the Innocent* and the Senate hearings. Wertham called out other DC characters as well, labeling Superman a Nazi and Wonder Woman a lesbian. With the comic book industry reeling from so much negative publicity, DC executives helped lead the charge to save the industry's image and move past Wertham's many harmful allegations.

DC and several other publishers banded together to create the Comics Code Authority, an independent body that would regulate comic books based on a strict set of guidelines designed to make comics as inoffensive and unobjectionable as possible. Crime and horror books were essentially banned, and everything from language to violence to sexuality was closely monitored. The Comics Code Authority was officially formed in September 1954, and its iconic seal of approval began to appear on many comics early in 1955. Nearly every publisher who didn't submit to the code and change its line accordingly was out of business within the year. *

Public scrutiny began to fade, but DC Comics wasn't nearly finished. Internally, the Bat-books underwent big changes to appear

---

* Those who did submit to the CCA made out quite well. DC brought back their superheroes (because there was little else left to do under the strict code) to great success, launching what is now known as the Silver Age of superhero comic books.

wholly innocuous and avoid any potential hint of homoeroticism. Jack Schiff had been editing Batman comics since the early 1940s; when several of DC's editors were drafted into military service, Schiff moved from editing pulp novels to comics and did such a good job that DC kept him on after everyone returned from the war. He was well respected by the writers and artists who worked for him, known as an editor who was tough in his demands for good, solid plots but extremely fair when it came to wages. Schiff preferred action-packed supervillain stories, but now DC executives wanted to go in a different direction to make the books more unobjectionable.

Instead of fighting supervillains who were actual people, however ridiculously depicted, DC wanted Batman to go up against weird creatures, monsters, and other light, silly fare. That way, the violence that Wertham so decried would be lessened and goofier. When Schiff resisted, Mort Weisinger strong-armed him into it. Weisinger was the editor of the Superman titles, a bully who was generally reviled by most of the creators who worked for him. He'd been doing so-called monster stories in Superman for years, with decent success, and forced Schiff to have the Batman titles fully embrace this trend. Supervillains became much less of a factor.

To combat Wertham's more damning allegations, Schiff brought in some female characters to romance both Bruce Wayne and Batman. Catwoman would have been ideal for this role, but she was tainted by her mention in *Seduction of the Innocent* and also had unpleasant criminal associations. Instead, Schiff brought back Vicki Vale, a photojournalist at the *Gotham Gazette* who was basically a redheaded Lois Lane. She was first introduced in 1948 and appeared occasionally in the years that followed, then became a fixture of the Bat-books after 1954. Vicki dated Bruce Wayne and tried to prove time and again that he was Batman, but her efforts always proved fruitless.

To date Batman, Schiff introduced Batwoman in 1956. She was Kathy Kane, a wealthy heiress and former trapeze artist who used her money and skills to fight crime. In her first appearance in *Detective Comics* #233, she tracked criminals through a space exhibit with Batman and knelt to help him when he was knocked unconscious. Robin ran in, and seeing them together he exclaimed, "**BATMAN!** I—oh! Maybe I'm intruding!" Ultimately, Batwoman helped the Dynamic Duo stop the criminals, and even though Batman tried to talk her out of being a crime fighter because it was a dangerous business, she didn't heed his warnings and appeared frequently in the years that followed.

Batman's heterosexuality was often at the forefront of their meetings. Several stories involved romantic encounters or imagined the two married. Robin got a potential girlfriend as well with the introduction of Kathy's niece Betty as Bat-Girl in 1961. A pinup in *Batman Annual* #2 read "Greetings from the Batman Family" and showed them all as one big happy family. Batman and Batwoman were the parents, Robin and Bat-Girl were the precocious children, and Alfred and Commissioner Gordon appeared as kindly uncles.*

All the while, Catwoman remained conspicuously absent, not even mentioned except for one issue in January 1963 when *Detective Comics* #311 introduced a new villain, Cat-Man. He was Tom Blake, a wealthy socialite who captured big cats to sell to zoos and circuses, but even those adventures were beginning to bore him. When Blake returned home and saw his tame panther, he remarked, "Seeing you reminds me of the **Cat-Woman**—a criminal who was one of **Batman's** greatest foes until she reformed! But she was a mere woman! Imagine what I, a **man**, could do!" And so he decided to put his skills to ill use and become a criminal.

Blake donned a yellow outfit with an orange cape and cowl and committed a series of cat-themed crimes over three issues, all of which were ripped from the pages of previous Catwoman stories without any mention of their origin. Cat-Man battled Batman atop a giant "Cat and the Fiddle" statue, just as Catwoman did in *Batman* #42. He re-created all her literary crimes, including her mash-up of Poe's "The Cask of Amontillado" and the Cheshire Cat. He proved

---

* Also included were Bat-Mite, an imp from a different dimension who showed up to annoy Batman and who embodied the typical zaniness of the Bat-books' post-Wertham status quo, and Ace the Bat Hound, a German shepherd Batman and Robin got in the mid-1950s to be a tough, manly, not-at-all-gay pet and emphasize their familial father-son relationship.

he had nine lives, like Catwoman did years earlier in *Batman* #35. All the while, he drove a Kitty Car that could leap across chasms and rivers. In one issue, Kathy Kane even donned a new feline costume and went undercover as Cat-Woman to spy on Cat-Man, and the story didn't once mention that she wasn't the first woman to use that name.

Catwoman's absence was so glaring in this era that it had to be intentional, and her connection to *Seduction of the Innocent* is the only obvious explanation. While supervillains had less of a presence after the events of 1954, few of them disappeared entirely. The Joker still appeared regularly in the years that followed, and the Penguin and the Riddler eventually came back after brief hiatuses. New female villains were introduced, including Poison Ivy, but Catwoman remained a pariah. Her only appearances in the decade following *Seduction of the Innocent* were in reprints of older stories in a couple of oversized specials. DC bent over backward to distance itself from Wertham's allegations, and Catwoman paid the price.

Jack Schiff left the Bat-books in 1964 and was replaced by Julius Schwartz, an editor known for his forward-thinking ideas. He was one of the key architects of DC's resurrection of its superhero line after 1954, and he wanted to make big changes to modernize Batman comics. However, one of his first acts looked backward: Schwartz killed off Batman's butler, Alfred, and brought in Aunt Harriet to take his place. He later recalled that he did so because of lingering concerns about Wertham, even a decade after *Seduction of the Innocent* was released. Alfred had been the only other secondary Bat-character mentioned by name in Wertham's book, referenced as a key component of the Dynamic Duo's sumptuous, homoerotic home life. In a world where DC was willing to murder Alfred a decade after the fact, benching Catwoman for twelve years was about par for the course.

# 3

## Same Cat Time, Same Cat Channel

*W*hen Catwoman returned after her twelve-year hiatus, it wasn't in a comic book. It was on television, at 7:30 PM on a Wednesday night, March 16, 1966. She was the "Special Guest Villainess" on *Batman*, ABC's new hit show that had premiered two months earlier. Iconic comic book villains like the Joker, the Penguin, and the Riddler appeared in the program's early episodes to great acclaim and excitement, as well as massive ratings, so Catwoman was freed from her Wertham-induced purgatory to join her fellow villains on the small screen.

Very few people inside ABC believed that *Batman* was going to be a hit. They had been looking for a new, hip show to appeal to young audiences and thought that something from the comic book world could do the trick. Batman wasn't their first choice; they wanted Superman, but the rights were tied up in the short-lived Broadway musical, *It's a Bird . . . It's a Plane . . . It's Superman*. ABC settled for Batman and brought in William Dozier to develop the series.

Dozier was a television veteran who'd produced several shows, though few of them lasted for long. Nonetheless, he was given wide creative control over *Batman*. He read up on old Batman comics when he was first offered the program, and was intrigued by what he saw. Dozier had a different vision for the show than ABC; while the network wanted something trendy, he wanted to play everything as square as possible and turn the program into something of a pop art piece. The show would be pure camp, with over-the-top plots, ridiculous death traps, and outlandish villains, but the comedy would come less from the zaniness than from all the actors playing the zaniness dead straight.

For Batman, Dozier found Adam West, an actor who'd starred in small roles in television shows and B-movies. West embraced Dozier's vision of the show and played Batman with a righteous seriousness. He spoke slowly and emphatically, as if each ridiculous word was of the utmost importance.* For Robin, Dozier brought in newcomer Burt Ward, who impressed the producer with his enthusiasm and martial arts training, as well as his chemistry with West.

The show was shot cheaply and quickly, often in a rush. ABC didn't greenlight *Batman* until November 1965, and they wanted it ready to go in January 1966. The actors rarely had more than two takes to do a scene, and then they were off to the next shot. Footage was often reused to save time and money; the classic shot of Batman and Robin sliding down the Batpoles and running to the Batmobile was only shot once, but it appeared in almost every episode. They even cut corners on stunts, to Burt Ward's dismay. Unlike Batman, it was harder to get decent coverage on Robin because his mask wasn't a full cowl, and thus it was obvious when his stunt double took his place if it wasn't shot carefully, a luxury rarely afforded to them. It was cheaper just to have Ward do the stunts, which resulted in many hospital visits for the banged-up and burned actor.

The hastily produced pilot went over poorly with ABC's test audiences, and the executives weren't enthused about it either, but they had nothing else to air in its place. *Batman* debuted in January to very low expectations, and it was a surprise hit. Kids loved the silliness and adults were amused by the camp, and millions of viewers

---

* West's costar Burt Ward believed that West's slow delivery was less about him embracing the camp aesthetic and more about West trying to get himself as much screen time as possible.

tuned in twice a week. The Wednesday episode set up the villain's crime and ended in a cliff-hanger with Batman and Robin ensnared in a convoluted death trap, and on Thursday night they escaped and ultimately defeated their foe. The formula proved popular, and Batmania quickly swept the nation. Batman's comic sales soared, Batman merchandise was everywhere, and Adam West even appeared on the cover of *Life* magazine in full Batman regalia. The show was an instant phenomenon that burned brightly, but briefly.

## Julie Newmar: Season 1

When William Dozier decided to add Catwoman to the rogues' gallery of *Batman*, he had Suzanne Pleshette lined up for the role, but negotiations with the actress fell through shortly before the episode was due to start filming. Dozier reached out to his second choice, Julie Newmar, who was initially put off by the short notice; Newmar lived in New York while Batman was shot in California, and they called her on the weekend, wanting her there and ready to shoot on Monday. Her younger brother was down from Harvard visiting her at the time, and when he heard that she had an offer to be on *Batman* he flipped out. He explained that *Batman* was a massive hit on campus, with students even skipping classes to watch the show, and he urged her to take the job. Convinced by his enthusiasm, she accepted.

Julie Newmar was born Julia Chalene Newmeyer in Los Angeles in 1933, the daughter of an engineer and a dancer. She began ballet lessons at a young age and studied several other varieties of dance throughout her childhood. Newmar was a bright student and graduated high school at the age of fifteen, then attended UCLA before she left to pursue dancing. She was on Broadway by the time she was nineteen, where she soon moved from dancing to acting, and she won the Tony Award for Best Featured Actress in a Play in 1959 for her role in *The Marriage-Go-Round*. Along with several film roles in the 1950s and 1960s, Newmar also costarred in the short-lived television sitcom *My Living Doll* in 1964.

Before Catwoman debuted on *Batman*, female characters had been rare throughout the show's first season. The only regular female cast member was Madge Blake as Aunt Harriet, Dick Grayson's flighty caretaker who didn't have the slightest idea that Bruce and her nephew were running around as Batman and Robin, despite their innumerable hasty exits from Wayne Manor.* The other women who appeared on the show were often molls, the attractive companions of the many male villains, or the targets of their crimes.

The only female villain to appear before Catwoman was Zelda the Great, an escape artist turned thief played by Anne Baxter. Once a year, $100,000 was stolen from one of Gotham City's banks and the culprit was Zelda, who used the money to pay the genius inventor who crafted daring escapes for her stage act. The story was based on an issue of *Detective Comics* that starred a male escape artist, and the producers changed the role after Dozier noticed the lack of women on the show and told his staff that they "should work in dames where possible." However, the episode regularly highlighted the oddity of a female villain. When Commissioner Gordon learned the thief's true identity, he exclaimed, "Good heavens, a woman?! What is the world coming to?" When Bruce found out that Zelda had kidnapped Aunt Harriet and had her suspended over a vat of flaming oil, he declared, "You devil! How could a woman stoop to such a trick?" Her gender was constantly commented upon by the bewildered crime fighters.

The story ultimately ended in a bundle of gendered clichés. Zelda wasn't a real criminal at heart; she was just put in a difficult position by her cruel and demanding inventor associate, the true villain of the piece. When his hired guns were about to take out Batman and Robin, Zelda couldn't stand the guilt of harming such noble heroes and called out to warn them. Instead of escaping in the ensuing chaos, she waited around and gave herself up to Batman as tears of genuine contrition rolled down her cheek. Romantic music swelled as Batman put the Bat-Cuffs on her, and she suggested that in another life perhaps they could have had something together. Zelda later gave Bruce Wayne a rose to deliver to Batman when Bruce visited her in

---

* While Aunt Harriet knew nothing about Bruce and Dick's vigilante secret, the only other resident of Wayne Manor, their butler, Alfred, was not only in on the secret, he appeared as Batman on several occasions when Bruce was indisposed.

prison. He was there to offer her a job as a magician at a children's hospital upon her release, and she enthusiastically replied, "Oh, how wonderful! What a joy to entertain small children!" In the end, Zelda was less of a villain and more of a romantic interest in disguise.

Newmar's Catwoman was a very different kind of character. Her first two-part show was written by Stanley Ralph Ross and Lee Orgel, and Ross would go on to write the majority of Newmar's appearances. He had a good handle on Catwoman and what Newmar brought to the role. The production of *Batman* was so slapdash that Newmar did most of her own makeup, and she had a fair amount of control over her costume as well. One key change she made was lowering the belt from her waist to her hips in order to emphasize her figure. It was a subtle difference that gave Newmar the sensuality she was looking for.

This sensuality continued in Newmar's physicality. Despite the limited time she had to prepare for the role, Newmar's dancing background allowed her to slip into the lithe movements of a cat with ease. She rarely just sat or stood; she sprawled, or curled up, or stretched out in a variety of feline poses that showcased her five-foot-eleven frame. Other actresses might have been intimidated by the close-fitting costume, but the former ballerina later recalled, "It seemed so natural to put on those slinky tight pants because it felt like a leotard, and then to do those sort of outrageous things."

Newmar also embraced the villainy of the character, relishing the opportunity to be evil. While there was a hesitancy to the crimes of Anne Baxter's Zelda, Newmar's Catwoman was wholeheartedly crooked. Newmar said of her time on *Batman*, "It was so wonderful being on that show, because you could be nasty and mean, and in the 1960s women could never be mean, bad, and nasty. It was so satisfying; I can't tell you how satisfying it was."

Catwoman's first episode began with a shadowed figure breaking into the Gotham City Museum. The claw of a gloved hand scratched a circle into the glass of a display, knocked out the glass, and stole a golden cat statue. Catwoman then boldly sent a kitten with a note to Commissioner Gordon, declaring her intention to steal the statue's matching counterpart; it was also a plot to get

Batman and Robin on her trail so that she could eliminate them. One of her goons, dressed in cat ears and a tiger-patterned coat, mentioned that others had tried to take out the Dynamic Duo and failed, but she responded, "The Catwoman is not like the others! I'll show you how to clip Batman and Robin's wings! I will prevail!" She easily stole the second cat despite the fact that Batman and Robin were lying in wait for her, knocking out Robin and then sending her goons after Batman in a brawl with the usual BONK!, OOOOFF!, and THWACK! effects.

Batman had planted a tracker on the second statue, but Catwoman was prepared. When the Dynamic Duo showed up at her hideout, located in the abandoned Gato & Chat Fur Company warehouse, they were immediately trapped in a locked room. Catwoman gleefully toyed with them in a cruel cat-and-mouse game. Spiked walls closed in on them, but the spikes were rubber. She tossed in a bomb, but all it did was pop up a flag that said, "Meow!" When she snatched Robin away in a suction tube, a frustrated Batman exclaimed, "You feline devil!" to which Catwoman replied, "Tsk, tsk, and another tsk, Batman! Why don't you just admit I'm smarter than you are and let it go at that?" At the end of her cruel games, she unleashed a ferocious tiger, leading to a standoff between man and beast for the episode's cliff-hanger. Catwoman even took over the show's iconic narration when the announcer encouraged viewers to tune in to the finale the next night at the "same cat time, same cat channel!"

When the story resumed the following evening, Batman escaped as he always did and freed Robin as well, but Catwoman was on to the next part of her plan. While the cat statues she'd stolen were valuable, she was much more interested in the secrets they contained. When positioned back to back, the patterns on the cats revealed a map to a long-lost pirate treasure. The map led her to a chest full of gold and jewels hidden in a cave, and she knocked out her remaining goon so that she wouldn't have to share her prize. When Batman arrived to capture her, Catwoman attempted to escape by leaping across a bottomless cavern and didn't quite make the jump. Batman threw her a Bat-Rope as she hung from a ledge, but to grab the rope she would've had to let go of her treasure. She refused to give up her stolen goods, and instead plummeted into the abyss.

There was no redemptive arc to Newmar's Catwoman whatsoever, just clever machinations, multiple attempts to take out the Dynamic Duo, and an unwavering dedication to bringing her evil plans to fruition. This two-parter was Catwoman's only appearance in *Batman*'s first season, and it set the precedent for the character moving forward, even with different actresses in the mix.

## Lee Meriwether: *Batman: The Movie*

Following *Batman*'s massively successful debut season, production immediately began on a motion picture. ABC had originally planned to shoot the movie first and then launch the series from there, but the ratings for its 1965 fall television lineup were so poor that they rushed the development of the show to have something different to put on the air as soon as possible. When it turned out to be a hit, everyone involved thought that a movie would be a good way to make some money and help sell the program to overseas markets. Plus, the bigger movie budget would allow them to build some new sets and Bat-vehicles that they could then use in *Batman*'s second season.

To make the movie a real spectacle, Dozier brought together four of the series' most popular villains: the Joker, the Penguin, the Riddler, and Catwoman. Cesar Romero, Burgess Meredith, and Frank Gorshin all reprised their roles, but Julie Newmar was unavailable for the film. Decades later, no one is particularly sure why she couldn't do it. While some say that she was busy with another project and others that she had a back injury at the time, no one is confident of their recollections. Whatever the case, Newmar was out and Lee Meriwether was in.

Meriwether was born in Los Angeles in 1935 and spent most of her childhood in San Francisco. While attending college, friends nominated her for Miss San Francisco and she won the pageant. She then won Miss California in 1954, and ultimately became Miss America in 1955. After her year's reign, she got an on-air job with the

*Today Show* and later transitioned into acting, appearing on a variety of television programs throughout the 1960s including *Dr. Kildare*, *Perry Mason*, and *The Man from U.N.C.L.E.*

As a young girl, whenever Meriwether got a dime for pulling weeds or some other chore she'd go to the store and buy Batman comic books. She was excited when the part of Catwoman came up, but after she found herself waiting to audition for the coveted role in a room full of beautiful women, she knew she'd have to do something to stand out. When she was called into the audition room, Meriwether decided to simply act like a cat. She recalls, "I curled myself up in the chair, and I licked my hand like a paw and did a little preening and purring and things like that. Luckily, I had a lot of cats." The producers were impressed and gave her the part.

Shooting of the film was already underway when Meriwether auditioned. Much like the show, the movie's production was a mad rush and Newmar's unavailability caught the producers by surprise. There were several villain group scenes in the film where Catwoman should have logically appeared but she wasn't there, simply because she hadn't been cast yet.* Once Meriwether got the role, she was heartily welcomed by everyone involved and remembers the filming as "one of the nicest experiences of my life."

Meriwether wore the same style of costume as Newmar and looked the part, but she toned down the character's sensuality. Unlike Newmar, Meriwether found the costume unpleasant to wear and recalls, "I could not sit at all comfortably in that suit." The iconic mask she wore for most of the film also obscured her eyesight, narrowing it down to tunnel vision; Romero had to escort her around the sets so that she could hit her marks. As such, Meriwether's physicality was a little more subdued. She aimed for a softer take on Catwoman that she described as "Sexy, yes, but kittenish sexiness."

The film's set design tried to add some softness to Catwoman, and treated her differently than her male cohorts. The villains' submarine

---

* Catwoman wasn't part of the iconic scene where the villains, out in a submarine, had Batman and Robin trapped on a buoy and were about to blast them away with a torpedo when a valiant porpoise swam into the missile's path and sacrificed itself to save the Dynamic Duo.

had a cabin for each of them, with designs on the doors that were representative of each character. These designs were echoed on logos on the submarine's four-way periscope as well. The Riddler's door was adorned with green question marks to match his costume, and the Joker's door was purple, like his suit, with a jester to capture his clownish nature. Catwoman's door was a light pink, with a bouquet of pussy willows tied in a ribbon of a darker pink. The stereotypically girly coloring didn't match the character at all, and the decor proved to be the only part of the film where Catwoman was presented differently than the male villains. For the rest of the movie, she was as evil as they were.

The villains had come together to form the United Underworld, with the motto "Today Gotham City, tomorrow the world." Their plan was to break into the United World building, the movie's take on the United Nations, to kidnap the Security Council and demand a $1 billion ransom from each member's home country for their safe return. To do so, they had to first eliminate Batman and Robin, though that proved difficult as they escaped every death trap the villains laid for them.

Catwoman stayed busy keeping the bickering villains in line and focused on their task whenever one character's eccentricities riled the others into a fight. After an attempt to kill Batman failed and everyone was yelling at each other, Catwoman straightened them out and admonished, "United Underworld, feh! [. . .] What's the matter with you all?!" Chastened, her companions calmed down and set to work on a new plan. But Catwoman wasn't the group's babysitter; she was just the most sensible member. She gleefully joined in on the villainous fun throughout the rest of the movie as they hatched their many schemes. When the villains dehydrated the Security Council with a special gun, Catwoman cracked a joke as they gathered their dusty remains, playfully warning, "Boys, don't anybody sneeze."

Catwoman also had an important undercover role as Comrade Kitanya Irenya Tatanya Karenska Alisoff.* Better known as Miss

---

* A name that Meriwether had to memorize five minutes before she shot her introductory scene.

Kitka, she pretended to be a Russian reporter covering the Gotham City beat for the *Moscow Bugle*. This alias allowed Catwoman to traverse the city freely, get close to important people, and uncover information that she could report back to her associates. When the villains decided that they'd lure Batman into a trap by kidnapping Gotham's wealthiest citizen, Bruce Wayne, Miss Kitka was given the task of seducing the millionaire.

She did so with aplomb. Batman was already intrigued by Miss Kitka when he met her at a press conference, and Bruce was delighted when she stopped by Wayne Manor to ask him for his help with a mysterious letter. He was quickly smitten by the entrancing Russian, and invited her to dinner. The two danced to a French version of "Can't Help Falling in Love" and then shared a romantic hansom cab ride, where they had an innuendo-laden conversation about tearing down the iron curtain between them. An enraptured Bruce then closed his eyes and talked about a dream that "approaches a climax" as Catwoman nonchalantly communicated with the other villains via Morse code. After inviting himself up to her borrowed penthouse apartment, Bruce continued the flirtation by reciting verses from the Edgar Allan Poe poem "To One in Paradise."* Basically, he was head over heels. And just as he was about to kiss her, the Joker, the Penguin, and the Riddler showed up on rocket umbrellas and carried him away.

Bruce eventually escaped, but his infatuation with Miss Kitka became a key weapon in the villains' arsenal. He believed that they'd captured Miss Kitka as well, and his concern for her clouded his judgment. When Batman and Robin arrived to apprehend the criminals at the United World building, Batman ordered them to stop, but Catwoman replied, "I don't think you mean that, Batman. Miss Kitka dies if you take one more step!" Batman paused long enough for the villains to get the jump on him, and they escaped.

---

* "And all my days are trances, / And all my nightly dreams / Are where thy dark eye glances, / And where thy footstep gleams." Bruce altered the poem slightly to better reflect Miss Kitka; the original read "grey eye" instead of "dark eye." Meanwhile, she had to fight to stay in character and stop herself from clawing at Bruce when the rest of the villains showed up to nab him.

Catwoman maintained the ruse until the end of the film. She was the last villain to be captured, and she tripped while she fled from Batman, causing her mask to fall off. The truth was revealed as Robin exclaimed, "Holy heartbreak! It's Kitka!" Batman was devastated, and a reprise of the French "Can't Help Falling in Love" played as he looked on in disbelief. The villains may have been defeated, but Catwoman proved herself more than a formidable foe.

Meriwether didn't return as Catwoman, but she did appear in the second season of *Batman* as a woman that King Tut mistook for Cleopatra. She's gone on to an extensive film and television career since then, including arcs on *Mission: Impossible* and *The New Andy Griffith Show*, as well as a costarring role on eight seasons of *Barnaby Jones*, for which she was nominated for multiple Golden Globes and an Emmy.

## Julie Newmar: Season 2

The second season of *Batman* began in September 1966, with Julie Newmar back as Catwoman. Whatever had kept her out of the film was over, and Newmar returned with a vengeance. She appeared in eleven of the season's sixty episodes, more than any other villain. Her Catwoman was wildly popular after only one appearance in the first season, and producers brought her back whenever they could. Newmar starred in four two-part solo villain outings, teamed with the Sandman for another pair of episodes, and also cameoed in one episode set in the Gotham Penitentiary, still wearing her full Catwoman outfit despite being behind bars.

Catwoman's many crimes were varied but always big and bombastic. She targeted cat's-eye opals, priceless violins, and even the Gotham Mint, but she wasn't above old-fashioned ransom, either. She used a special device to steal the voices of the British folk duo Chad and Jeremy, who guest-starred on the show, and then demanded £8 million from the British government to give their voices back. Catwoman's technological prowess was impressive throughout the season; on top of the voice-stealing machine, she had a four-seat getaway rocket to escape a heist atop a skyscraper, and developed a drug that turned the gallant Boy Wonder into a villainous thug. Catwoman even had her own protégé, a young sidekick named Pussycat, played by pop singer Lesley Gore.*

Amid all her criminal fare, Catwoman got a new role with the addition of a romantic subplot that ran throughout the season. When Catwoman appeared in the season's third episode, she was up to her usual tricks, running a school for cat burglars and going on a crime spree. When Chief O'Hara heard that Catwoman was back, he fearfully gasped, "The princess of plunder! The saints preserve us!" She captured Batman and Robin at the end of the episode, and when Robin wondered what they were going to do to escape, she taunted, "What are you going to do? You're going to die. I'm not just pussyfooting around this time, Batman!"† Catwoman then greased the Dynamic Duo with margarine and left them tied outside to fry under a pair of giant magnifying glasses. Her villainy was on full display.

But before lashing Batman to her death trap, Catwoman admitted, "If we weren't on opposite sides of the law, Batman, I could go for you, in a small way. You're about the only man I've met lately who would be worthy of me." Robin replied, "Holy lovebirds, I think she's sweet on you, Batman!" At the end of the second episode, after Batman had escaped the trap and arrived to stop Catwoman's theft, he saved her life when she fell out of the window of a high rise. She was genuinely touched, and asked him, "Batman, are you spoken for?" Batman responded, "My crime fighting leaves me little time for social engagements," causing Catwoman to grin and say, "Boy, have I got a girl for you!" After Batman said that she'd still be beautiful even after serving her multiyear prison sentence, she gave him a kiss goodbye that caused him to blush tremendously.

Romance was a common theme throughout *Batman*'s second season, though it rarely affected the Caped Crusader. Marsha, Queen

---

* Gore was best known for the 1963 hit song "It's My Party," but her follow-up singles didn't perform as well. She was the niece of *Batman* producer Howie Horwitz, who got her on the show. Catwoman was trying to teach Pussycat to be a villain, but what she really wanted to do was sing. Gore performed her new single "California Nights" on the program, and it became her bestselling record in years.

† In response, Batman sputtered, "You can't frighten us with any of your threats, feline sorceress! Take heed; we shall overcome your satanic schemes!"

of Diamonds, played by Carolyn Jones, enraptured several prominent men in Gotham City with her love darts, including Chief O'Hara, Commissioner Gordon, and even Robin. They were so lovestruck by her potent formula that they consented to being kept in cages in her secret lair just so that they could be close to her. When she dosed Batman, he valiantly fought against the drug as it took effect. A frustrated Marsha demanded, "Worship me, I said! On your knees!" Batman continued to struggle and shudder, crumpling under the potion's power before rising to declare, "I prefer to stand, Marsha. Your drug didn't work." His willpower was just too great for him to succumb to her.

When the Dynamic Duo were faced with Ma Parker's curvaceous daughter, Legs, Batman was similarly unfazed. However, Robin was rather distracted by Legs, a woman so shapely that her prison number was 35-23-34.* Batman just chuckled at his young ward's stirrings and said, "You're growing up, Robin. Remember, in crime fighting always keep your sights raised."

But Batman was quite smitten with Catwoman, and she with him. In one episode, Batman broke into her headquarters and a surprised Catwoman exclaimed, "Batman!" before smiling and purring, "Batman . . ." In the brawl that ensued, she warned her goons, "Gentle with Batman, boys!" Catwoman drew a gun on Batman at the end of the episode, but she couldn't pull the trigger. She said, "Can't you see how I feel about you, Batman? How I want you by my side?" Once Batman secured the gun, she asked him if he would take her on a date when she got out of prison. After he stammered a response, she asked to kiss him but as the two leaned toward each other, Robin interrupted them. Batman requested a rain check on the kiss, Catwoman agreed, and the two walked off arm in arm as Robin turned to the camera and exclaimed, "Holy mush!"

More romance ensued. The couple shared a float with two straws at a diner in one episode, and in another Catwoman offered to surrender after a lengthy chase if Batman agreed to marry her. When

---

* A later episode revealed that Catwoman's prisoner number was 39-24-37. It was quite a sexist jail.

Catwoman fell off a tall building into the river below, presumably to her death, Batman had to pull out his Bat-kerchief to wipe away his tears. But Catwoman wasn't just in love with Batman; in fact, lust was her primary motivator. She created a trap that would render him essentially brain dead, musing, "Then you can be mine forever, Batman. True, I'd have to sacrifice your intellect . . . Oh well. With a build like yours, who cares?" Catwoman was perfectly happy to have a "handsome robot" to play with. She wasn't into Batman for his winning personality.

Catwoman also used Batman's romantic interest to her advantage. After the Dynamic Duo leveled Catwoman's goons and had her cornered, she began to cry and lamented, "Oh, nobody loves me!" She then asked if she could take out her Cat-kerchief to wipe her eyes and Batman, influenced by his feelings for her, agreed. It was all a trick, and Catwoman grabbed her knockout spray. When Batman and Robin came to, they were tied up in a giant coffee cup, with a giant kettle about to pour sulfuric acid on them. What's worse, the reason that Catwoman was out of prison in the first place was because of Batman's infatuation with her. As Bruce Wayne, he had sponsored her parole.

The conclusion of this coffee cup adventure was Newmar's last appearance as Catwoman, and the episode ended with her making a final play for romance. She was alone with Batman and about to be arrested, but she seemed to have other things on her mind as she cozied up to him. Batman admitted, "Your propinquity could make a man forget himself." Catwoman replied, "I don't know what that means, but it sure sounds nice." When she told Batman that she could make him happy, he earnestly inquired, "How do you propose to do that?" Catwoman gushed about how they would be partners and how it would be the two of them against the world, prompting Batman to ask what they would do about Robin. She instantly replied, "I'll have him killed . . . painlessly! Well, he is a bit of a bore with his 'Holy this!' and 'Holy that!'" Her response snapped Batman out of his distracted state, while Catwoman was flummoxed that he was even still standing; she'd put on a poison perfume before he entered and he should have been dead already. Unfortunately for her, Batman was wearing Bat-plugs in his nose just in case.

Catwoman was such an unrepentant villain that she couldn't even set aside her murderous ways long enough to properly distract Batman with her seduction. Killing Robin was the most logical course of action to her, so she blurted it right out, ending what had been a successful ploy thus far. At the same time, she did love Batman, even though she was trying to kill him. When she returned to prison, Bruce told her that he'd like to be her friend, to which she replied, "There's no room for another man in my life, Mr. Wayne. You're nice, but my heart belongs to Batman." Newmar's Catwoman was a complicated character, a love interest but in none of the traditional ways. She was just wired for villainy, and that was always the core of the character.

Newmar later revealed, "I wasn't so fond of that mushy stuff. [. . .] I felt that as the villain you made yourself too vulnerable." But she played it all wonderfully, so much so that she earned a role in *Mackenna's Gold*, a big-budget Western starring Gregory Peck and Omar Sharif, and was unable to return for the third season of *Batman*. The film went over poorly with viewers and critics, with the *New York Times* calling it "a Western of truly stunning absurdity," and Newmar's acting career consisted of guest roles on television and small film parts for some time. Nonetheless, her work as Catwoman made her a popular icon, and she found more successes elsewhere, including Broadway, modeling, and inventing.*

Fifty years after she debuted as Catwoman, Newmar reprised her role in *Batman: Return of the Caped Crusaders*, a 2016 animated film based on the *Batman* television show.† She, West, and Ward were the last surviving members of the principal cast, and they all lent their voices to the project. The film began with Catwoman, the Joker, the Penguin, and the Riddler reteaming for a high-profile heist, but when a chemical concoction turned Batman into a villain, Catwoman reluctantly partnered with Robin to end the Caped Crusader's reign of terror over Gotham City. Her turn for good was short-lived, however; after a cured Batman enthused, "She proves that even the most

---

* Newmar holds two patents, one for panty hose and one for a brassiere.
† While Newmar's Catwoman was the film's primary feline fatale, both Meriwether and Kitt's incarnations were included when Batman got hit on the head so hard that he saw three Catwomen, each corresponding with one of the three women who played her.

vile, depraved, and amoral villain is capable of redemption," Catwoman tried to run off with a bag of loot. The film ended with her leaping off a blimp, presumably to her doom, as a heartbroken Batman wiped away his tears with a Bat-kerchief yet again, but with a sequel already announced, the chances of Catwoman miraculously surviving the fall seem rather high.

## Eartha Kitt: Season 3

By the end of *Batman*'s second season, Batmania was fading fast. The program that millions of viewers initially found fresh and inventive now felt stale and formulaic, and its viewership declined sharply. As a result, ABC and William Dozier made some big changes for the show's third season. It was reduced to just once a week, doing away with the two-part death-trap cliff-hanger model, and the already low budget for the program was slashed significantly. To shake things up and add another crime fighter to the mix, they also brought in Yvonne Craig as Batgirl.

In the midst of all these changes came a new Catwoman, played by Eartha Kitt. Kitt was born in North, South Carolina, in 1927 and began touring the country as part of a performing company when she was just sixteen years old. Soon she was singing on Broadway and released several singles that charted well throughout the 1950s. She appeared in a few films later in the decade as well, but by the mid-1960s her career had stalled somewhat. The role of Catwoman came at just the right moment for Kitt; she later recalled, "I was in dire need of comfort at that time and as a starving cat I had to find a way to survive. And that was one of the most wonderful bones that was ever thrown to me."

Kitt was a natural for the part. Assistant producer Charles FitzSimons said of her, "We felt it was a very provocative idea, to hire Eartha Kitt. She was a cat woman before we even cast her as Catwoman. She had a cat-like style. Her eyes were cat-like and her singing was like a meow." Kitt said that playing Catwoman was her favorite role of her career: "I didn't have to think about her, I just did it."

Producers had replaced Julie Newmar with the physically similar Lee Meriwether when Newmar was unavailable for the *Batman* film, but Kitt was a whole new direction for the character. Whereas Newmar was five foot eleven before the heels, Kitt was only five foot four.* Newmar's Catwoman was flirty and devious, while Kitt's Catwoman was focused and ferocious. And, most significant for the time period, Kitt was black. Technically, she was part black, part Cherokee, and part German, but one aspect of her heritage outshone the others in 1967. The producers knew that it would be a bold choice to hire her, but they also knew that she was well suited for the role.

Aside from Kitt's performance, her three episodes as Catwoman were fairly run-of-the-mill. In the first, Catwoman interrupted a luncheon honoring Gotham City's ten best-dressed women. After Batgirl was given a special award, Catwoman burst in and declared, "Ridiculous! Nonsense! Foolish prattle! How can Batgirl be the best anything when Catwoman is around?" Later on, she tried to steal an assortment of expensive dresses and kidnapped Batgirl in the ensuing chaos. When Catwoman told Batman where Batgirl was trapped, he had to choose between saving Batgirl and stopping Catwoman from stealing a solid gold dress. Ultimately he sent Alfred to free Batgirl while he and Robin nabbed Catwoman and sent her off to prison.

Kitt's second story line was a rare two-part episode, as well as a team-up with the Joker. After the Joker earned an early release from jail for good behavior, Catwoman swung by in her green Kitty Car to pick him up as he left the facility. She had a scheme to locate a hidden cache of gunpowder and use it to blast into the Federal Depository to steal all the money inside. After several scrapes with the Dynamic Trio, Catwoman and the Joker were arrested at the beginning of the second episode, and the rest of the show was dedicated to their trial. It was a drawn-out affair in which Catwoman's lawyer, Lucky Pierre, refused to cross-examine witnesses or call any of his own because he'd replaced the jury with her goons. Batman figured out the plan, a brawl ensued, and Catwoman and the Joker returned to prison.

While the episodes were uneventful, Kitt's fierce performance was remarkable for the time. Not only was she a black woman playing a well-known character who had been white since her debut a quarter

---

* Yvonne Craig was glad for the change, saying, "I liked that she was my size. I could beat her up. I come up to Julie Newmar's bellybutton. Not good in a fight."

century before, she also made her stronger and more powerful than she'd ever been. Newmar's Catwoman was a tough villain, but her take on the character was also comfortable and languourous, like a powerful tiger in repose who occasionally lashed out with her full vigor. Kitt's Catwoman was a tiger on the prowl, aggressive and perpetually coiled to attack. She was always in control, even when she teamed up with the Joker. He was the show's most popular villain, appearing more than any other, but with Catwoman he was little more than a green-haired henchman. The plan was hers, the gadgets were hers, even the lawyer was hers, while the Joker just did what she said. Kitt's Catwoman was an indomitable force.

Moreover, the episode featured a black woman in charge of a man who was literally the whitest person on the program, owing to Cesar Romero's white greasepaint makeup. This stark contrast emphasized the racial and gender divide, showing that a black woman not only belonged in the show's hierarchy of villains but excelled among them. Similarly, Catwoman's involvement in the best-dressed women's luncheon was another assertion that black women belonged in traditionally white spaces. Almost all the luncheon's attendees were white, and after Catwoman declared that she deserved the prize instead of Batgirl, she deployed a hair bomb that blew up the women's straight hair into bushy masses. Historian Deborah Elizabeth Whaley sees this scene as an "an ironic, signifying statement on whiteness, Blackness, and beauty aesthetics." She writes, "Hair is a significant sign of race, and her transformation of the white socialites' hair to afros (which serves as contrast to Kitt's long and pin curled locks) via a 'hair bomb,' blurs and overturns hierarchies of beauty, hair, and their dependent relationship to race." The racial implications of these scenes, however subtle, emphasized Kitt's blackness in positive, progressive ways, a rarity for American television of the time.

However, Kitt's stint as Catwoman completely lacked the romantic tension with Batman that was a key component of Newmar's time in the role. There was no talk of marriage, or of killing Robin and running away together. There wasn't even any flirting. Both Catwoman and Batman were all business, and her three episodes were an entirely chaste affair. The only hint of Batman showing any emotion other than disdain for Catwoman's criminal leanings came when Robin sarcastically inquired, "How could a feline feloness like you also be a fashion model?" Batman quickly corrected him, "Credit where credit is due, Robin. She may be evil but she is attractive. You'll know more about that in a couple of years."

The episodes also appeared designed to keep Catwoman and Batman apart. Newmar's outings often involved a scene with just the two of them, usually talking about romance as Newmar draped herself over West. All Kitt's interactions with West were group events, and she spent far more time with Batgirl than Batman. On the few occasions when West and Kitt were in the same shot, they rarely stood next to each other. Instead, another character would act as a buffer between them. The show went out of its way to avoid any semblance of a connection between Catwoman and Batman.

This lack of romance was especially odd because Batman had been more susceptible to romantic advances throughout the third season, even unwanted ones. His former ability to call upon his willpower and resist artificially induced romantic impulses was gone. In the season's third episode, Bruce Wayne was entranced over the telephone by the call of the Siren, played by Joan Collins. He immediately left Wayne Manor to be by her side, and Batgirl and Robin had to team up to snap Bruce out of his infatuated state.

Continuing the flirty relationship between Catwoman and Batman would have made sense for a host of reasons, but the producers were obviously trying to stay away from any suggestion of interracial romance for fear of backlash. As cowardly as that may seem from a modern perspective, the fact was that television had yet to cross this line. The first unscripted interracial kiss on American television aired just three days before Eartha Kitt's debut as Catwoman in December 1967, when Sammy Davis Jr. and Nancy Sinatra pecked each other on the cheek after a musical performance on the special *Movin' with Nancy*. The first scripted interracial kiss came almost a year later in November 1968, when Captain Kirk and Lieutenant Uhura kissed on *Star Trek*.* Movies weren't much better; while there had been a

---

* It wasn't an actual romantic kiss, either. Kirk and Uhura were being mind controlled by aliens at the time.

handful of interracial romances in films before 1967, the landmark *Guess Who's Coming to Dinner* hit theaters after Kitt's time on *Batman* was wrapped.*

Furthermore, *Batman* was not a groundbreaking show. It aired in the earliest prime-time slot and had a substantial child audience, and so the network kept a tight clamp on its content. The executives were so concerned about offending viewers that in the first season they made Dozier add a scene in which Batman and Robin put on their seat belts after leaping into the Batmobile because the program's initial episodes hadn't explicitly shown them doing so. It was not the ideal platform for being culturally relevant, plus Batman was the ultimate square. When the show did address cultural changes, it was rarely positive and usually associated with criminals. During the second season Catwoman organized a sit-in, which Batman tried to break up, while the writers brought in women's lib in the third season when "woman power" advocate Nora Clavicle became Gotham City's new commissioner and used her post to run a crime empire. In such an environment, just having a black Catwoman was a fairly significant achievement.

It was also short lived. Catwoman made her final appearance on *Batman* in the second-to-last episode of the season, in which all of Gotham's greatest villains escaped from prison. The villains were played by stand-ins, filmed from behind or afar to disguise their faces. Catwoman was a tall brunette with white skin, an obvious analogue for Julie Newmar rather than Eartha Kitt. Whether it was an intentional reversion or a mistake due to the show's hasty schedule, the result was the same. Kitt's Catwoman was done.

After *Batman*, Kitt's strong stance against the Vietnam War temporarily hampered her career in America, but she toured Europe and Asia to much acclaim. She returned to Broadway in the late 1970s, earning a Tony nomination for her performance in *Timbuktu!*, had a new hit song in the 1980s, and starred in a variety of film, television, and voice-acting roles in the years that followed. Her distinctive

---

* Most of these rare interracial romances involved a white actor playing a light-skinned black role. Dorothy Dandridge was one of the few black actors to actually perform as part of interracial romances, doing so in a handful of films in the late 1950s.

voice was regularly in demand. Kitt passed away in 2008 at the age of eighty-one.

As for *Batman*, ABC canceled the show after its third season because the ratings continued to fall. There was a deal in place for NBC to pick up the program for a fourth season, but it fell through when the network learned that all the sets had already been destroyed. *Batman* has maintained a strong television presence throughout the decades in syndication, and recently enjoyed a renaissance during its fiftieth anniversary. There were scores of new merchandise, and DC Comics published a comic book series with new adventures of the Dynamic Duo set in the world of the program. The book featured both the Julie Newmar and Eartha Kitt incarnations of Catwoman, though it was perhaps too faithful to the show. Newmar's Catwoman appeared in several stories while Kitt's was only in a couple, both of which were Batgirl tales that kept Catwoman far apart from Batman yet again.

# 4

# A Streak of Heartbreaks

*C*atwoman finally returned to comics in November 1966 after her twelve-year hiatus, and her comeback was the direct result of her live-action popularity. The story's introductory narration read, "Holy cats! Who's this female fiend who's sic-ing her big-cat buddies on poor, invulnerable Clark Kent? Is it the **Catwoman?** Julie Newmar from the **Batman** TV show? Lee Meriwether from the **Batman** movie?" But the introduction came with a twist. After all of these questions, the narration revealed, "No . . . it's our **own** Lois!" Catwoman's return was in *Superman's Girl Friend Lois Lane* #70, the solo series of the *Daily Planet*'s ace reporter.

A book in the Superman line was an odd venue for Catwoman's revival. She had only appeared in Bat-books since her creation, and in 1966 she was one of the most popular characters on the *Batman* television show. This may have been a savvy move by editor Mort Weisinger, capitalizing on Catwoman's on-screen success by bringing her into the Superman line before his counterpart on the Batman line, Julius Schwartz, was able to do so. Such crafty undercutting of a peer would not have been out of character for the boorish Weisinger. A more likely explanation was that DC executives were still skittish about Catwoman's connection to Wertham's allegations of homoerotic subtext between Batman and Robin and wanted to bring her back away from the Dynamic Duo as a sort of test run.

The comic began at the *Daily Planet* offices, where Lois learned that a new bird sanctuary was opening in Metropolis just moments before news broke that the Penguin had escaped from prison. Lois sensed a connection, and thus a scoop, and went to the bird sanctuary to wait for the Penguin, only to be captured by Catwoman instead. The story offered no reason for Catwoman's lengthy absence, and she was introduced as if she were a familiar character, with Lois thinking, "The **Catwoman**. She's one of **Batman's** arch foes . . . She always uses cats as the inspiration for her crimes!" Catwoman's appearance was largely unchanged from a decade before, a purple outfit and cowl with a green cape. The only difference was that instead of a gown she wore pants.

Catwoman hypnotized Lois into thinking that *she* was Catwoman, and directed the reporter to defend the sanctuary from her foes. The plan was for the real Catwoman to take off with the loot while Lois stayed behind and took the fall for the crime, but Lois drew in Superman when his X-ray vision showed him that "Catwoman" was an entranced Lois. After Superman arrived, the real Catwoman saw a new opportunity. She broke Lois's hypnotic spell and put her in a cage, then prepared a trap for Superman while he was busy taking care of her menagerie of large cats.

When he was finished, Catwoman pretended to be a confused but still hypnotized Lois. She got a super-kiss from Superman, just for fun, and then lured him to her Catacombs hideout where she used the wand of the sorceress Circe, something she'd recently picked up in Italy, to transform him into a super-cat. With a superpowered cat at her disposal, Catwoman could become "the queen of crime." Lois had other plans, though. She escaped from the bird sanctuary and came after Catwoman, and the issue ended with the two women engaged in "the **cat**-fight of the century!" in a *Batman*-style cliff-hanger.

The next issue resolved everything quickly. Catwoman was arrested within three pages and Lois spent the rest of the story figuring out how to restore Superman from his cat state. It was more than a year before Catwoman returned to a Bat-book. She had a couple of cameos over the course of that year in the form of Bat-Mite in disguise and a mannequin on a parade float, but she didn't arrive in the flesh until *Batman* #197 in December 1967, more than thirteen years after her last appearance in the series.

## Trial and Error

Catwoman's return to *Batman* was motivated by the emergence of another female character in the Bat-books, Batgirl. When the producers of the *Batman* television show contemplated adding a woman crime fighter for the show's third season, they turned to Julius Schwartz and DC Comics, who quickly introduced Commissioner Gordon's daughter Barbara as Batgirl. She was an impressive character; she had a PhD, a photographic memory, and a brown belt in judo, and decided to use her skills to fight crime. Her day job as the head of Gotham City's library system allowed her to research information that helped her in her night job as Batgirl. Batman was initially resistant to her help because she was a woman, but she proved herself as a capable crime fighter and soon headlined her own solo feature in *Detective Comics*.

The new Batgirl was one of DC's earliest responses to the growing women's liberation movement, an educated, skilled woman who acted independently of any male hero. She had no romantic interest in Batman at all, wasn't a damsel to be rescued, and starred in her own stories. Her debut was a significant step forward for female characters in the DC Comics universe as the Silver Age of superhero comics gave way to the Bronze Age in the late 1960s.

Meanwhile, Catwoman's comeback was an intentional step backward. The story began with her Kitty Car prowling the streets of Gotham, but instead of going to commit a crime, Catwoman stopped them. She was jealous that Batgirl was spending so much time with Batman, and decided to best her as a crime fighter so that she could take Batgirl's place and ultimately win Batman's heart. After she nabbed a gang that the Dynamic Duo had been after for weeks, Catwoman told them, "It's a **purr**-fect demonstration that anything

**Batgirl** can do, I can do—**better!**" Eventually she bested Batgirl in a head-to-head showdown, and a demoralized Batgirl admitted defeat.

But Batman wasn't interested in Catwoman romantically, so she quickly returned to villainy. She captured Batman, Robin, and Batgirl in a dangerous trap, and told Batman that if he didn't marry her, she'd go back to her life of crime, demanding, "Now—give me your answer! Am I to be—**bride or burglar?**" Batman refused her proposal and escaped her trap, and Batgirl delivered the decisive blow that took out Catwoman.

While the story wasn't a great showcase for Catwoman, it marked a significant change in how creators and editors at DC Comics portrayed female characters. Strong and independent women used to be villains in their comics, and after years of limiting their heroines to passive, marriage-obsessed roles, now the dynamic was reversed. Batgirl's independence and romantic disinterest were presented as positive attributes that helped her be better at her chosen profession, while Catwoman's fixation on marrying Batman only gained her a trip to prison. It's a comic book villain's lot in life to embody the opposite of what the hero represents, so DC's turn toward stronger female heroes meant an unfortunate shift for Catwoman.

Societal change usually comes with a backlash, though, and such was the case with Catwoman's next major appearance a year later. After using her villainy to critique DC's old, narrow-minded approach to female characters in *Batman* #197, Catwoman's role in *Batman* #210 was instead a direct jab at women's lib. Written and drawn by a completely different creative team, the cover showed Catwoman with her whip wrapped around Batman as she declared, "It's all over, **Batman!** You just lost the **Battle of the Sexes!**" Catwoman was depicted as a radical feminist extremist, using the rhetoric of women's lib to turn her fellow women onto a criminal path.

Catwoman had her eye on a valuable pearl, and she decided that building her own gang of "feline furies" would help her nab it. To do so, she opened the Selina Slenderizing Salon and sent a free pass to eight women who were about to be paroled, along with a car to pick them up once they left prison. When they arrived Catwoman told them, "We all have a **common cause—**a **common enemy** . . .

men! It was **men** who led us astray—**men** who put us behind bars like caged tigers!" She proposed, "**You** help me outwit **Batman—I** help you revenge yourselves on the men who sent you to prison!" After nine days of exercising and training in the salon, she dressed all the women in costumes like hers and they went after the pearl. But Batman suspected that Catwoman would come after it and was waiting for her arrival. Despite having a team, Catwoman was quickly captured, along with her gang.

The story was a swift turnaround for Catwoman, and emblematic of a problem inherent in being out of commission for more than a decade: she had no established characterization. Nearly everyone who had worked on the character in the 1940s and 1950s was gone, and her stories were long forgotten. The result was a generic villain with a fondness for cat-related crimes, but no set character traits. They couldn't even settle on a costume. Catwoman donned her old look in *Superman's Girl Friend Lois Lane*, but in her first *Batman* appearance she wore a tight, scaled green suit with yellow gloves and boots as well as a yellow cat's-eye mask. In her "Battle of the Sexes" caper, she had another new costume consisting of a black halter top and gloves, white tights, red-lined boots, and a big red mask with yellow cat eyes, along with a new bob haircut.

With no definitive characterization, Catwoman became a vehicle for whatever the writer wanted to do, thus her contradictory appearances in *Batman*. Fans were split on her return, and wrote into the book's letter column to react to her comeback. Her first *Batman* issue received acclaim across the board, with fans just excited to have her back in a Batman series, but the second issue didn't go over as well. Steve Berry called the issue "in a nutshell, an unfortunate attempt," and lamented that Catwoman "has undergone her umpteenth change, and this time it's for the worse." Another fan wrote in to say that after her appearance was teased in the previous issue, he was angry that Catwoman wasn't on the cover before he realized that she actually was; her look had just changed yet again.

After these two appearances, Catwoman departed *Batman* for another five years. When Batmania trailed off midway through the television show's run, it fell hard, and editor Julius Schwartz quickly moved away from everything associated with the show. He'd tried to move the Bat-books in a new direction in the mid-1960s, trading Silver Age frivolity for more mature, slightly darker stories, but the success of the television show forced him to return to campy hijinks. After the program ended its run, Schwartz went back to his original plan and took things even darker. Robin was phased out, along with many of the villains who appeared on the show, and Batman became the ominous Dark Knight rather than the friendly Caped Crusader. Young creators dove into gothic horror and science run amok, with Denny O'Neil and Neal Adams's tenure in the early 1970s the most famous of this period. Their Batman was caught up in a complicated romance with Talia al Ghul, the daughter of Ra's al Ghul, a nigh-immortal leader of a global criminal empire, and Catwoman was again forgotten.

Catwoman didn't disappear entirely from the DC Comics land-scape during this period. She guest-starred in two issues of *Wonder Woman* in 1972 during the character's mod era. Wonder Woman had been revamped entirely in 1968, trading her superhero identity and her powers for a normal life as Diana Prince in an attempt to make the character more relatable to readers. Diana wore mod fashions and ran a boutique, but was soon caught up in a quest for vengeance that took her around the world as she searched for the villain who killed her boyfriend, Steve Trevor.

When Catwoman crossed her path, Diana was in Tibet search-ing for the Fist of Flame, a valuable ruby she was going to trade for the life of Jonny Double, the latest in her lengthy string of romances following the death of Steve. Catwoman was after the ruby as well, and the two fought before teaming up to defeat the warriors who guarded the gem. Diana saved Catwoman's life and they escaped into a cave that led them to Nehwon, a barbaric land in a different dimension. There they worked together to rescue Jonny and return home, with Catwoman setting aside her villainy in order to repay her debt to Diana.* Two issues later, Wonder Woman took back her

---

* It's an odd story, to be sure, but the first part was written by Denny O'Neil and the second by science fiction icon Samuel Delany. Both issues were drawn by comics legend Dick Giordano. It's got quite a pedigree.

superhero mantle and emerged as a feminist icon, while Catwoman remained on the bench for another few years.

When Catwoman returned to *Batman* in 1974, she infiltrated a circus to try to steal a pair of rare albino tigers and was ultimately captured by Batman. It was over a year before she was back again, and this time she donned her old costume from the 1950s and began a spree of jewel thefts that were again foiled by Batman. After a two-year gap, she reappeared in the same costume along with a widow's veil for a story in which the villains of Gotham City believed that Batman had been killed and met up to determine who had done the deed.* Her appearances were all one-offs, with no real connection or plan for the character, or any real impact on Batman's overarching story. Catwoman's personality varied; she was again an angry man-hater, then a criminal mastermind, then madly in love with Batman. It was all quite random.

DC's haphazard approach to Catwoman throughout the 1970s was indicative of the publisher's entire line. DC had emerged from the Wertham crisis of the 1950s as the nation's preeminent superhero publisher, but Marvel Comics debuted a slew of new heroes in the early 1960s and rapidly gained ground on DC with its serialized and more mature comics. By the late 1960s, Marvel was starting to pull ahead, so DC left behind its Silver Age silliness and aped Marvel's style. DC had some success, and launched many new titles in the early 1970s, but a series of economic factors threw the publisher for a loop.

The comic book market was shrinking, and DC was losing ground in an industry that was already on the decline. Newsstand distribution was slowly being replaced by the direct market of specialty shops that sold only comics books, and sales were down across the board. Combined with the inflation crisis of the 1970s, DC was making less money and comics were becoming more expensive to make. At the beginning of 1970, a regular-sized issue of *Batman* cost fifteen cents, not a huge change from when the series debuted three

---

* It was none of them. Batman faked his death repeatedly near each of them, leading the villains to gather together and each claim to be the victor. The whole scam was part of a plan to track down the Joker, who was wanted for an actual murder.

decades earlier and cost ten cents. By 1980 an issue of *Batman* cost forty cents, almost triple the price. Throughout the decade, DC tried different pricing to try to find something that worked. With *Detective Comics*, DC went for quantity over quality, hiking the price while upping the page count and filling the book with only one new story and a variety of reprints.* Many of Catwoman's appearances in the 1970s were old tales in these reprinted stories.

By the mid-1970s, nothing was working for DC. They had to cancel several books, including *Detective Comics*, its longest running series. It was rolled into *Batman Family* with a few other Bat-character features for a year before they brought back *Detective Comics*. There were many creative and editorial shake-ups as DC tried to find something that would connect with readers. Catwoman got lost in the midst of all this shuffling, leading to further sporadic and disconnected appearances.

*The Brave and the Bold* #131 from December 1976 was a good example of this chaotic approach to Catwoman. The story was a Batman and Wonder Woman team-up and Catwoman was the villain, but everything about the character was wrong. She was referred to as Selena instead of Selina, and she wore her black-and-red costume after her old purple-and-green outfit had been reestablished as the norm. Most shocking of all, Catwoman murdered several people throughout the story, actions antithetical to every past comic book portrayal of the character. Catwoman was a thief, not a murderer, and the story had her cross that line without a good reason.

DC received a lot of letters about the issue, many of them outraged and confused about the depiction of Catwoman. One letter began, "**NO! NO! NO!** That is most definitely **not** the **Catwoman!** It must be some kind of feline impostor, for she bears no resemblance to the Princess of Plunder that I have loved for so long." Despite her lack of appearances, Catwoman had a sizable fan base, and even during her many story absences she appeared frequently in ads for comic book merchandise, including dolls, posters, and shirts. There was a

---

* In 1974, *Detective Comics* was upped to one hundred pages for fifty cents and then sixty cents. They tried again in 1979 with more new material, this time charging a dollar for only sixty-eight pages. Neither really caught on.

clear desire from the readership for more Catwoman, but throughout the decade no one at DC seemed able to meet it.

## Sudsy Drama

Catwoman's run of sporadic and contrary guest spots came to a close in 1979 when Selina Kyle walked into Bruce Wayne's office at the Wayne Foundation in *Batman* #308. Bruce was shocked, but Selina was in plain clothes and told him, "I am the Catwoman **no longer!**" She elaborated, "I've been **paroled**, Bruce—and I intend to do something **positive** with my life. That's why I've come to you . . . because I have some **money** I'd like to invest in **Wayne Enterprises.**" While Bruce was suspicious, Selina explained that the money was an inheritance, not stolen, and that now that her debt to society was paid she was determined to go straight. Bruce decided to give her a second chance, and the duo made plans to discuss potential investments over dinner the next week.

This issue was the beginning of a story line that ran off and on for the next seven years, as well as the first step toward romance for Bruce and Selina. When DC moved to serialized storytelling in the late 1960s, leaving behind self-contained tales for lengthier multipart narratives, romance became a key feature in the background of many series. The main plots involved short arcs that focused on the hero battling a particular villain, while their personal lives and often their romantic entanglements became running plotlines that could stretch on for years. The books turned into a sort of soap opera as various romances flared and conflicted.

In male-led series, female characters were often relegated to these soap opera plots. Lois Lane and Lana Lang were given little to do in *Action Comics* and *Superman* other than fight over the Man of Steel in a constantly shifting love triangle.* Superman had only two women on the line, but Bruce Wayne had a string of romances through the 1970s and into the 1980s. The era has been described

---

* It turned into a love square for a while when Superman dated Lois while Clark Kent dated Lana. That ended poorly for everyone involved.

as his lothario period; Bruce took his playboy disguise to heart and Batman got in on it as well. At one point or another, he attempted to romance nearly every female character who appeared in the Bat-books.

Before things began with Selina, Batman had been involved in two long-term relationships. Talia al Ghul entered his life in the early 1970s, and then never left for long as she frequently returned to stir up more drama. She was followed by Silver St. Cloud, who dated Bruce for a year before she discovered that he was Batman. They soon broke up because she couldn't bear worrying about him every night. As Selina prepared to go straight, Bruce was single again, and a new love was soon kindled. For the next seven years, the majority of Catwoman's appearances revolved around this romantic relationship.

The first act of the saga ran for a year and a half in *Batman*, in a story primarily written by Len Wein with art by Irv Novick. After their initial meeting, Bruce got one of his most trusted employees to investigate Selina and ensure that she'd gone straight. In the meantime Bruce and Selina began to see each other, but then Selina found out about the investigation. She angrily confronted Bruce and threw a drink in his face, then stormed off as she raged, "I may not be **the Catwoman** any longer, mister—but **Selina Kyle** still knows how to use her **claws!**" Selina later forgave Bruce after he apologized profusely, and the two started to date publicly.*

But then things took a dark turn. Bruce began to read into Selina's innocent comments, like her interest in Egyptian cat artifacts or her appreciation of fine jewelry, and worried that she would be tempted to return to her former life. At the same time, Selina began to complain of headaches and was diagnosed with an exotic disease that gave her only a month to live. The only cure was rare Egyptian herbs, some of which were on display at the Gotham City museum, and Batman instantly blamed Selina when the museum was broken into. She swore that she didn't do it and went to Bruce for help,

---

* Somewhat ominously, one of their first outings was at a costume ball where they dressed as Henry VIII and Catherine of Aragon.

not knowing that he and Batman were one and the same. He didn't believe her, either.

Bruce's secret identity added a one-sided power dynamic to the relationship. He knew that Selina was Catwoman, and saw her through that lens, while she only knew part of who he was. He could also use his Batman identity to do things Bruce couldn't, like surveil and confront her, manipulating Selina without her knowing that her boyfriend was behind it. It was dishonest and controlling and kept them on an unequal footing.

When Batman learned that the real culprit of the museum robbery was Catman, he apologized to Selina and, in her Catwoman guise, she helped Batman catch him. Although her disease was cured through magical means, the pain of Bruce not believing her after the museum incident led to the end of their relationship. Selina decided to leave Gotham City, and Bruce was heartbroken.

After the break-up in 1980 Catwoman returned occasionally over the next few years. Robin brought her in to help Batman when Talia got him embroiled in a conflict with Ra's al Ghul, and Catwoman was motivated to lend a hand because of her old affection for Batman. She even recognized that romantic envy was behind her involvement when she mused, "I'm wondering if seeing Batman with Talia made me . . . **jealous** in some stupid manner! Blast! Am I really that **petty?**" Selina was back after Bruce a few months later, telling him that she still loved him, but their romantic moment turned sour when she mentioned Catwoman and Bruce tensed up. She left Gotham again, unwilling to be in a relationship haunted by her past as Catwoman.

This departure led to a new solo backup feature for Catwoman that debuted in *Batman* #345 in March 1982. It only ran for six issues, and the tone was very dark, even though the stories featured Catwoman fighting crime. The first issue began with a dream sequence in which Selina married Bruce. It was a joyful affair, officiated by Commissioner Gordon, and Selina said, "I've never been as happy as I am in this moment!" Then the dream became a nightmare. Selina turned into a cat monster, and Robin yelled, "She'll **always** be a cat!" while Gordon exclaimed, "**Yes,** kill the wretched creature."

Bruce just coldly stared her down. All the guests pulled out guns and surrounded Selina, and as they opened fire she awoke screaming.

The dream set the tone for the stories that followed. In the main text Catwoman solved crimes and the criminals ended up harshly punished; one villain was run over by a train and another was trampled by horses. Meanwhile, the subtext suggested that Catwoman was the one who deserved punishment for her failed relationship with Bruce. After the harsh dream that opened the first issue, the story's cliff-hanger had Catwoman hanging limp from a noose. The next two arcs focused on women; in the first a wife who betrayed her politician husband ended up falling and breaking her spine, and in the second Catwoman posed as a deceased stripper who looked just like her in order to track down the woman's murderous boyfriend. The constant images of dead or grievously injured women were compounded by the punitive nature of the stories, and having these stories follow Catwoman's bizarre, clearly guilt-ridden dream sent a message that Catwoman had wronged Bruce and deserved her own punishment. The brief run was oddly psychologically twisted.

It was also a forerunner for Catwoman's darkest soap opera episode yet. After Selina left Gotham again, Vicki Vale returned to the Bat-books and began dating Bruce. When Catwoman learned of their relationship, she turned into a crazed stalker. She called Vicki to try to scare her away, telling her, "Consider this call a warning. If you value your life—**stay away from Bruce Wayne!**" In the following issue, Selina had another disturbing dream in which she attacked Vicki and murdered her, tearing her apart with her claws. She was troubled by the dream, but it didn't stop her from later showing up at Vicki's home in her Catwoman regalia with her panther in tow to hit her with her whip and tell her, "I'm not **playing games**, Vale! My **life** and **sanity** are at stake! I **need** Bruce Wayne—he's my **compass!** YOU WON'T TAKE HIM AWAY!"

After neither of her threats ended the relationship, Catwoman took drastic action. When Vicki and Bruce were out on a drive along the coast one evening, Catwoman ran them off the road, sending them careening off a cliff and into the ocean. She jumped into the water to save Bruce, but he fought her off so that he could rescue

Vicki. Catwoman's stalking ended soon after with a cathartic fight with Batman, and she then disappeared from the Bat-books for another couple of years.*

When Catwoman returned in late 1985, Bruce was still in lothario mode and had moved on to a new flame. After things ended with Vicki, he became enmeshed in a complicated relationship with Nocturna, a villain who was also the adoptive mother of the new Robin, Jason Todd. Initially, Catwoman was just back in town to clear her name after she was falsely accused of a series of murders, but she quickly got tangled up in Batman's affairs. She needed Nocturna's help to prove her innocence but Nocturna refused, ultimately leading to a confrontation in which Catwoman was struck with a bolt of lightning and appeared to be dead.

This was no common fake-out. The lightning strike occurred in the middle of *Crisis on Infinite Earths*, a major event series designed to streamline DC's decades of convoluted continuity. Entire universes were destroyed, and several major characters were killed, sending shockwaves through the fan community. Notable heroes like Supergirl and the Flash had already died before Catwoman was struck by lightning, and readers writing into *Batman*'s letter column were beside themselves with worry. Elvis Orten asked, "What are you trying to do, give me heart failure?" and Phetsey Calloway wrote, "I don't think I can face Gotham City without the possibility of Selina's vivid presence." Bob G. Prat was more direct when he declared, "If Catwoman dies, I'll drop my subscription and never read another issue of *Batman* or *Detective* as long as I live."

Luckily for Bob and the rest, Catwoman recovered from her injuries. Furthermore, almost losing her led Batman to end things for good with Nocturna and pursue Catwoman instead. Thus began the final act of the soap opera, with Catwoman dating Batman instead

---

* Catwoman's dialogue during the fight suggested that she knew that Batman was Bruce Wayne, and he ended up apologizing to her for her past hurts as Bruce while wearing his Batman costume. This appears to have been a continuity error, because before this story Catwoman didn't know Batman's identity, and she again didn't know it when she returned two years later. It was probably an editorial slip-up, since the Bat-books changed hands several times in the early 1980s.

of Bruce. Things went well for a while. The duo double dated with Black Canary and Green Arrow, and Catwoman started to bond with Robin. Then Batman's mistrust returned yet again, this time in comical fashion: Batman thought that Catwoman was spending time with another man when she was actually training a new pet panther.

Batman pulled away, and Catwoman ended up breaking things off in a tepid conclusion to years of romantic drama. A few issues later, the Joker used a machine to alter Catwoman's brain and return her to a life of crime. It was her last appearance before the Bat-books were revised to fit the altered post–*Crisis on Infinite Earths* DC Comics universe. After years of romance-centric story lines and fighting crime to get a boy to like her, it was fitting that her final issue in this universe brought her back to her criminal beginnings.

## Another World

As *Crisis on Infinite Earths* tore through the world of DC Comics, one of the major casualties was Earth-Two, an alternate universe that regularly crossed over with DC's mainline titles. When DC brought back some of its abandoned superheroes in the mid-1950s, it altered several of their costumes, secret identities, and power sources without explaining the change. For example, the original Flash, Jay Garrick, was replaced by Barry Allen, and the original Green Lantern, Alan Scott, was replaced by Hal Jordan. Once the new heroes were established, fans began to wonder what had happened to the original heroes. DC's answer was Earth-Two, an alternate universe that continued the Golden Age continuity from when DC superheroes were at the height of their popularity in the early 1940s. The Flash discovered the universe in 1961, and soon the modern Justice League was teaming up with the classic Justice Society on an annual basis.

Earth-Two proved popular, and several series that continued the adventures of lesser-known Golden Age heroes ran throughout the 1970s and 1980s. More well-known heroes like Batman, Superman, and Wonder Woman, who never ceased publication, didn't play a big role initially, seeing as they'd never been replaced or erased, but they were eventually worked in. For the Batman mythos, they created a divergent point in 1954. Both universes shared Batman's Golden Age beginning, but the Earth-Two Batman took a different path after 1954 and his history was slowly filled in over the years across a variety of Earth-Two comics.

The primary vehicle for exploring this history was the Huntress, a new Earth-Two character who debuted in 1977. Her stories offered occasional glimpses into her past, particularly her early life with her parents, Bruce Wayne and Selina Kyle. Other Earth-Two features then picked up on the tidbits presented in Huntress comics and fleshed them out further. Through all of these tales, readers were able to cobble together the story of Earth-Two's Catwoman and Batman. Much like in the concurrent Earth-One comics, Catwoman's role was one of romance and drama, but it all started with her death.

Huntress's debut began with the wedding of Bruce and Selina. The flashback explained that after the criminal Catwoman reformed and surrendered to the police, "Batman was **watching** that night . . . and Bruce Wayne was **waiting** the day Selina Kyle emerged from prison a free woman." They were soon married and had a baby, Helena. The story's present was set years later, when Helena was a teen. Selina was the early focus of the tale; one of her old criminal associates blackmailed her into pulling one more job with evidence that she'd murdered someone as Catwoman. The evidence was forged, but Selina didn't know that and took the job to spare her family the shame of her supposed crime. The job was interrupted by Batman, who was unaware that Selina was involved. One of the goons tried to shoot Batman, but Batman kicked him first, causing the shot to go wild. It hit Selina, and she plummeted to her death. Bruce was shattered and retired from crime fighting, leaving Helena to don the mantle of the Huntress and catch the man who blackmailed her mother.

After her death, Catwoman was limited to flashbacks. *The Brave and the Bold* #197 told how Bruce and Selina got together while fighting off the fear-inducing toxins of the Scarecrow. Batman revealed to Catwoman that he fought crime to avenge the death of his parents, and she admitted that the amnesia story from the early 1950s was a lie. She had been in an abusive marriage and stole from her husband to get back at him. Stealing felt so good that she kept doing it and became Catwoman, but she eventually realized, "I was **thirty** years old and I didn't want to die without **love**, without **children**." The amnesia story was an attempt to escape her past. Ultimately, they both revealed their secret identities to each other and fell in love.

That was the extent of what readers learned about Selina. Bruce received a far more complete history over the years, with flashbacks detailing his philanthropic work in Gotham City and several team-ups with the Justice Society. He also had the benefit of being alive after the Huntress debuted, and his story continued with him becoming Gotham's police commissioner. Meanwhile, little was revealed about Selina's life after she retired from crime, apart from her getting married and having a child, and she was sacrificed as backstory for Huntress. Selina was domesticated, reduced to a bland, stereotypical wife-and-mother role that was completely at odds with her vivacious origins. The Bronze Age tamed Catwoman dramatically, across multiple universes.

This taming was also accompanied by a degree of shaming. Initially, Huntress drew inspiration from her mother. Her costume was an amalgamation of the blue and purple of her parents' costumes, and she combined their skill sets into one fearsome crime fighter. In an early issue of Huntress's regular backup feature in *Wonder Woman*, she even felt like she was gaining strength from her deceased mother as she battled Lionmane, one of Catwoman's old foes. But all of that quickly changed.

While her mother's death may have spurred her to become the Huntress, Helena was clearly trying to follow in her father's footsteps. She referenced him constantly, remembering old advice or wondering what he'd do in a given situation, while Catwoman was rarely mentioned at all. The regular introduction to her feature even read, "**Helena Wayne** carries on her father's mission by battling crime as . . . **the Huntress**," leaving Catwoman out entirely. In one story, Helena found her old diary and on the day that she learned her father was Batman she had written, "I do so want to spend my life being just as good as HE is!"

When Catwoman was mentioned, it was rarely positive. In *Wonder Woman* #307, Huntress was in the thrall of a powerful hallucinogenic and had a vision of her mother as a black cat creature. The creature told her, "You will **never** be without me . . . your **dark side** . . . ! **You** know what I was! **You** know you're **capable** of **following in my footsteps!** And nothing frightens you **more!**" Helena's conflicted feelings about her mother again came to the fore in a later issue, when she dreamed that a giant black cat was chasing her. When she woke up, Helena thought, "I can't go on thinking that someday . . . someday . . . my **heritage** will catch up with me!" She tried to console herself with the fact that she'd devoted her life to justice and standing for what's right, but noted, "Those are my **father's** traits. It's my **mother's** contribution to my makeup that has me worried!" Helena never resolved her feelings because her featured ended in the following issue, and she was then erased in *Crisis on Infinite Earths*.

Just as Batman constantly distrusted Catwoman on Earth-One because of her criminal past, Huntress distrusted her mother's influence on her life in Earth-Two. This perpetual shaming illustrated the no-win situation caused by Catwoman's criminal history. Although she reformed and became a respectable citizen, even the people she loved most couldn't let go of her past.

Catwoman's daughter, Helena, later returned in other projects, first as the protagonist of the WB's *Birds of Prey* television series in 2002, and then as part of DC's new Earth 2 lineup in 2012.* These new Helenas were different from the original in a variety of ways, but Catwoman was dutifully killed off at the beginning of each project.

---

* A new Huntress debuted in the 1990s, but she was an entirely different character named Helena Bertinelli who had no familial ties to Batman or Catwoman.

# 5

## Gone Astray

$\mathcal{F}$ ollowing the end of *Crisis on Infinite Earths* in 1986, DC Comics relaunched its entire comic book line. Instead of a multiverse with lengthy and often confusing histories, DC's superheroes would exist in one coherent universe. However, the relaunch wasn't equally applied. Some characters, like Superman and Wonder Woman, were rebooted entirely. Their histories were wiped away and new creative teams started from the beginning to build modern versions of the characters that, while inspired by the old, had no direct connection to their past incarnations. DC even relaunched their eponymous series with a new *Superman* #1 and *Wonder Woman* #1 to reinforce this clean slate.

Batman's relaunch was murkier. Both *Detective Comics* and *Batman* continued their numbering, and the broad strokes of the mythos carried on. The books didn't start fresh with a young Batman and a new Robin; by the end of the pre-*Crisis* continuity, the original Robin had grown up to be Nightwing and was a key member of the Teen Titans, a popular team that also continued into this new universe. Batman remained in the same place in his life that he had been before the relaunch, but there were tweaks. For example, the second Robin, Jason Todd, was changed from little more than a doppelgänger of the original Robin into a snarky street kid whom Batman found attempting to steal the tires off the Batmobile.* But while Batman remained roughly the same, writers and artists weren't beholden to the exact details of his five decades of comic book history and many minor characters were revised and updated.

Catwoman was one of them. Her pre-*Crisis* history was erased entirely. She was still Selina Kyle and was still a master thief, but her past adventures were no longer canon, nor was any aspect of her relationship with Batman carried over into the new universe. Catwoman was rebuilt from the ground up.

This began in "Year One," an arc that debuted in *Batman* #404 in February 1987. The story line explored the early days of Batman, fleshing out a period that hadn't yet been depicted in detail. "Year One" was also the line of demarcation between the pre- and post-*Crisis* era, and all the changes therein would carry over into the new universe. Written by Frank Miller with art by David Mazzucchelli, "Year One" presented an iconic take on Batman that still influences how the character is written today. Miller is arguably the most influential creator to work on Batman in the modern era, and his tough, gritty version of the Dark Knight set a new standard that was much lauded by fans and critics.

Miller's take on Catwoman was not as impactful. He radically altered the character, turning Catwoman from a playful criminal into a bitter prostitute/dominatrix. The change was so stark that she disappeared for years afterward because no one else quite knew what to do with her. This grim take on Catwoman was not out of character for Miller, who had a history of crafting iconic stories for male characters while his supporting female characters succumbed to his dark worlds. "Year One" changed how Catwoman was perceived going forward, sexualizing the character in ways that she has yet to fully move beyond.

## Frank Miller

Frank Miller began his comic book career as an artist in the late 1970s, drawing a variety of brief stories for several publishers before

---

* The revised Jason Todd didn't go over well with fans, and they were given the opportunity to vote on whether Jason lived or died in a special cliff-hanger event two years later. He didn't make it.

he ultimately landed at Marvel. After a few small jobs, he became the artist on *Daredevil*, a comic about a blind man, lawyer Matt Murdock, whose enhanced remaining senses allowed him to fight crime as the superhero Daredevil. The book's sales were struggling, but when Miller's editor let him take over the writing duties as well in 1981 the series quickly became a hit. Miller's preferred style was more film noir than superhero, and he steered *Daredevil* in that direction to much acclaim. Bigger gigs soon followed, and today Miller is a legend in the world of comics.

Every issue of *Daredevil* since Miller has been influenced by Miller. The same is true for every issue of *Batman* following "Year One" and Miller's classic miniseries *The Dark Knight Returns*. He's had a similar influence on every live-action adaptation of both characters since his tenure; the *Daredevil* movie and television show both have Miller's fingerprints all over them, while *Batman Begins* owes a great debt to "Year One" and *Batman v Superman: Dawn of Justice* was inspired by *The Dark Knight Returns*. In short, Miller redefined Daredevil and Batman in the 1980s, and his take on both characters still has sway today.

However, Miller's famous work on his male protagonists often came at the expense of each character's supporting female cast. Some critics call Miller's comics sexist, arguing that his female characters are little more than fodder to further the adventures of his male heroes. In her article "The Writer Who Made Me Love Comics Taught Me to Hate Them," pop culture critic Susana Polo notes, "I have never read a Frank Miller book with an original female character who didn't fall into two categories: sex worker—or victim of a brutal beating or murder." Women in Miller's stories were often defined by their sexual relationship with the hero and then hurt or killed in order to illicit an emotional response from said hero to cause him to take action. His books rarely went well for the women involved.

Case in point, *Daredevil*. Throughout his run, Miller brought in several female characters who followed this pattern. Miller's most famous creation was Elektra Natchios, a former love of Matt Murdock's from his college days who entered his current life as an assassin working for the villainous Kingpin. Although Matt already had a girlfriend, the return of Elektra rekindled his feelings for her, complicating his now adversarial relationship with his old flame. Elektra, a raven-haired ninja in a tight and skimpy red outfit, became an instant fan favorite, and as the story progressed she soon found herself on the wrong side of the Kingpin. Ultimately, she was killed by another villain, Bullseye, and her death haunted Daredevil for the duration of Miller's tenure. Resurrections were teased, furthering Daredevil's agony and adding drama to the book, but all the while Elektra remained dead.

Matt's girlfriend at the time, Heather Glenn, met a similar fate. After Elektra's death, Matt was erratic and unstable. He proposed to Heather, telling her, "There's a **hole** in me. A great, black hole that **you** could fill." At the same time, as Daredevil he began to tear apart Heather's family business. The company had criminal dealings, but the stress of it all affected Heather deeply and put her in a bad emotional situation. While she survived Miller's initial run on Daredevil, the die was cast and she ended up committing suicide in a story by the next creative team.

After a two-year hiatus, Miller returned to *Daredevil* in 1985 and reversed his formula somewhat. Rather than having the romantic interest spiraling down to her doom, this time her life improved, but only after she endured a series of horrible experiences. Karen Page had been a mainstay in *Daredevil* until the early 1970s, when she left her job as Matt's secretary to become an actress. Miller brought her back as a drug addict reduced to appearing in pornographic films to get a hit. She was so desperate for drugs that she sold away Daredevil's secret identity, which led to the destruction of Matt's entire life. Karen was out of the country, and she had to trade sex for passage back to America with an abusive man. Ultimately, Karen got away from her abuser, got clean, and ended up dating Matt, completing the reversal of the formula.*

Miller returned to Elektra in 1990's *Elektra Lives Again*, a mistitled tale that focused on Matt's grief over losing her. He was the protagonist, and Elektra appeared in a series of his dreams until the

---

* She also didn't die, at least not until many years later when, continuing the proud tradition started by Miller, she was killed off to cause more turmoil for Daredevil.

end of the book when she returned and was promptly killed again. She had barely any dialogue throughout the comic, except for once saying, "Matt," and then finally uttering "Good-bye" as she was murdered.*

Miller's track record continued when he moved to DC Comics. Before he revamped Catwoman for the new DC universe in "Year One," Selina Kyle played a small but pivotal role that followed Miller's usual formula in *The Dark Knight Returns* in 1986. *The Dark Knight Returns* was a lavishly produced four-issue miniseries that told the tale of an older, retired Bruce Wayne returning to his role as Batman to save Gotham City from anarchist punks, stop the Joker, and ultimately battle Superman. The series was a smash hit and, along with Alan Moore and Dave Gibbons's *Watchmen*, marked a major turning point in the superhero genre toward more dark and violent narratives.† Today it's widely considered to be one of the best Batman stories of all time.

Selina didn't appear in the flesh until the third issue of *The Dark Knight Returns*, but a panel in the opening issue set up the first step in the Miller formula: the romantic connection to the protagonist. In an answering machine message to Bruce Wayne, Selina simply stated, "**Selina**, Bruce. I'm lonely." This limited amount of information spoke volumes, communicating a sense of past romantic involvement and the potential for it to continue. Bruce was mostly in shadow in the panel as he listened to her message, but his sad eyes expressed loss and perhaps longing. The shadows also hid his wrinkles and haggard features, making him look younger in a way that harked back to his more virile, lothario days.

When Selina finally appeared later in the story, she was almost unrecognizable. She was older and heavier, her wrinkled face caked with bright makeup, and her hair was a frizzy pink mop. She also had a downcast look that was underscored by the drink in her hand and

---

* The graphic novel was also published through Epic Comics, Marvel's mature readers imprint, which allowed Miller to draw Elektra naked.
† Some like to call this a turn toward more realistic narratives, but *The Dark Knight Returns* featured a busty, bare-chested villain with swastikas covering her nipples, so it was all still very ridiculous. Darkly and often grotesquely so, but hardly a bastion of realism.

the shelf of bottles next to her. Selina was the madame of the Kyle
Escort Service Inc., a business that catered to Gotham's most exclu-
sive clientele, including high-ranking government officials. When the
Joker appeared in her office, she immediately told him, "You get the
**hell** out of—" but she was quickly interrupted. The Joker covered her
mouth and said, "The years have not been **kind**, Selina . . ." before he
kissed her while wearing a mind control lipstick. Under his power,
she arranged for one of her escorts to use the lipstick on a congress-
man client, causing him to jump off a building and kill himself.

The police quickly connected the death to Selina, but Batman
found her first. The Joker had left her hog-tied in a Wonder Woman
costume, a clear reference to the bondage fetishism that pervaded
Wonder Woman comics in the Golden Age. Selina was bloodied and
bruised, with her left eye blackened and nearly swollen shut and
trails of mascara-stained tears running down her face. The scene was
so disturbing that Batman's new, young Robin had to look away.*

This brutal assault of Selina fulfilled the last component of the
Miller formula: harming a secondary female character in order to
emotionally affect the male protagonist. Batman kissed Selina dramatically and rushed off to confront the Joker, leading to their final
battle and ultimately to the Joker's death. Serving as a tool to lead
to this fight was Selina's only role in the book, and she didn't appear
again until one panel during Bruce's funeral at the end of the story.†

When Miller returned to Catwoman in "Year One," rather than
playing off past incarnations of the character, he used only himself
for inspiration. His take on a younger Selina showcased the first
steps that would eventually lead her to becoming the Selina of *The
Dark Knight Returns*.

"Year One" was a dual narrative that alternated between Bruce
Wayne returning to Gotham City to become Batman for the first time
and Lieutenant James Gordon transferring to Gotham only to find
himself embroiled in the city's corrupt police force. Side characters
flitted in and out of the two main stories, and Selina was a small

---

* This new Robin was Carrie Kelly, a plucky teen girl, and she escaped *The Dark Knight
  Returns* relatively unscathed. Her later appearances took a darker turn, however.
† He wasn't really dead, of course. He's Batman.

component of the Batman half. When she first appeared, she was standing in a window overlooking a street in Gotham's sleazy East End. She was dressed in a leather bustier and leather pants with high-heeled boots, smoking a cigarette and holding a riding crop, her hair shorn almost to the scalp. She was a prostitute and a dominatrix, and when the unseen man on the bed behind her pleaded, "Selina . . . don't stop **now** . . ." she snapped, "Shut up, skunk. You know what I hate **most** about **men**, skunk?" The man moaned, "**Please**, Selina . . . **tell** me . . . why you **hate** us so . . . oh, **please** . . ." to which she replied, "Never met one."

Selina was watching a disguised Bruce as he hassled Stan, her pimp, and when they began to fight, the prostitutes on the street all ganged up on Bruce, including Selina's underage roommate, Holly. Selina leaped from her window to the street, saying, "**Damn** it—**nobody** hurts **Holly**." She came at Bruce with a high kick, but he blocked it and then punched her in the face. Everyone then scattered when the cops showed up.

Much like his depiction of Karen Page as a drug-addicted porn star, Miller's decision to turn Selina into a prostitute came out of nowhere. It wasn't rooted in any past versions of the character, save for his own. "Year One" was a fresh start for secondary characters especially, and Miller could have taken Catwoman in any direction he wanted, but his penchant for dark, gritty tales and his noir sensibility made her a dominatrix.

Using her sexuality to control a man wasn't anything new for Catwoman, but the context had shifted dramatically. From her earliest days as the Cat, she had used her feminine wiles to manipulate Batman and keep herself out of prison. However, she was an independent operator who dealt with men however she saw fit, on her own terms and to her great benefit. As "Year One" began, this independence was gone. She had to answer to an abusive pimp, and also pay off the cops to keep them out of her hair. Her sexuality no longer belonged to her; it was controlled and dictated by a series of men, and she lived in squalor in the worst part of Gotham City.

She soon struck out on her own. Explosions ripped through Robinson Park in the third issue of "Year One," waking up Selina and Holly. They went out to see what was happening, and watched Batman defeat Gotham's most elite police unit. Selina also lent a hand; her gray Siamese cat bounded through the building where the cops had cornered Batman, distracting the police and helping Batman escape. The cat then fled a massive firefight and ran right into Selina's arms. Inspired by Batman's example, Selina punched out her pimp and walked off with her young friend in tow, telling her, "We're changing our line of **work**, Holly. I got an **idea**."

The issue ended with Selina donning a gray costume with cat ears and whiskers. A confused Holly groused, "I don't know, Selina—I mean, you spent all our **mon**ey on that **costume**—I mean it's pretty **que**er." Selina replied, "It's **money**, Holly. Be a kick. Just **watch**," and she jumped out a window into the night. When she reappeared in the next issue, three months had passed and Selina had performed four high-profile cat burglaries, including her latest, in which she stole the police commissioner's pop memorabilia collection, valued at $40,000. The police were trying to pin the burglaries on Batman, so Selina set her sights higher. She planned to rob Carmine "the Roman" Falcone, the biggest crime boss in Gotham, and scratch him on the face so everyone would know it was her.

Batman stumbled upon her robbery but, perhaps out of repayment for the Robinson Park incident or perhaps because of his distaste for the Roman, took out Falcone and his armed goons with his Batarangs. This left Catwoman free to complete the job and leave her mark on the Roman. However, the evening news still connected Batman to the robbery, and called her Batman's assistant. In her last panel of "Year One," Selina mused, "I'll have to do something **really** nasty, next time."

Ultimately, every step of Catwoman's creation was influenced by Batman. He inspired Selina to don a costume, his reputation pushed her to break out from his shadow and establish herself, and he helped her pull off her signature heist. She was inextricably tied to Batman, a significant shift from her past independent incarnations.

The response to "Year One" was very positive, and the new Catwoman went over well in *Batman*'s letter column. Reader Kirk Chritton wrote, "The subtle, three issue build-up to the new origin of Catwoman is the most refreshing approach I've seen in years," while Robin Scott Lane said, "You've made her a dominatrix. Very reasonable. Much more likely than a victim of amnesia or a thrill-seeking abused wife."* The only contrary opinion came from John Craddock, who wrote that "Year One" was a "complete and dismal failure." In terms of Catwoman, Craddock opined, "This is the biggest insult to any character ever done in any art form. Selina Kyle is not a hooker. That is thoroughly out of character."

While Miller's prostitute-turned-cat-burglar origin was now canon for Catwoman, no one else at DC seemed to know what to do with this new take on the character. For the next six years she appeared sparingly. Her only semiconsistent outlet was *Legends of the Dark Knight*, a series that primarily featured out-of-continuity stories set in the "Year One" era; Catwoman was referred to as a "tough hooker" in the title's first issue and occasionally appeared in the stories that followed, often barely dressed. After several years as a regular in the Bat-books before the *Crisis*, the post-*Crisis* revamp severely diminished her presence in the main titles.

This wasn't an unusual situation for the Bat-books' editorial team, who established a pattern of letting high-profile creators tell a dark, edgy story about Batman that radically changed a female supporting character without putting any plans in place for what to do with that character afterward. In 1988 Alan Moore and Brian Bolland's *Batman: The Killing Joke* centered on a major conflict between Batman and the Joker, spurred by the Joker shooting Barbara Gordon in the spine and paralyzing her, as well as sexually assaulting her. The injury was a plot device that also ended Barbara's career as Batgirl, and the editors put no thought into how to use her moving forward.† Miller's changes to Catwoman similarly lacked forethought. The momentary gritty shock value of making Selina a prostitute was quickly followed by her near disappearance.

---

* Robin Scott Lane also added a warning that, because of Selina's distaste for men, people might think that she was a lesbian. He added, "I don't mean to make a guess, not having all the facts; I'm just telling you what it looks like so far."
† Barbara Gordon reappeared as the computer hacker Oracle years later in *Suicide Squad*, a series under a different editorial umbrella. The Bat-offices were content to leave her as the casualty of a bestselling book.

The first attempt at figuring out what to do with Catwoman came a year and a half after "Year One" in the pages of *Action Comics*. The series had switched to a weekly anthology format in 1988 and Catwoman starred in a brief four-issue arc written by Mindy Newell with art by Barry Kitson and Bruce Patterson. It was set in the present, and initially harked back to the pre-*Crisis* era as Catwoman, sporting a purple-and-green outfit and long hair, stole an ancient Egyptian brooch from a museum. The story then took a dark turn; Selina gave the brooch to Holly, now living in the suburbs of New Jersey, and Holly's philandering husband killed her and ran off with the valuable brooch. Catwoman tracked him down with uncharacteristic brutality that matched her new darker, grittier incarnation, killing two security guards and framing the husband for the murders and the theft of the brooch.

Responses to the story in *Action Comics*' letter column were mixed at best, but it went over well enough internally that DC launched a four-issue *Catwoman* miniseries in February 1989. Once again written by Newell, with art from J. J. Birch and Michael Bair, the book doubled down on the success of "Year One," going further into Selina's past as a prostitute as well as incorporating and expanding on scenes copied straight from "Year One." The first issue's cover tagline declared, "In the Ruins of Innocence, the Batman's Enemy Is Born . . ."

The book opened with a nun discovering the battered body of a prostitute who had been raped and beaten. It was Selina, and the cop who visited her in the hospital to investigate the incident told her, "You're pissing blood," before he informed her that she could press charges on her attacker because "even whores got rights." This was just the first of several scenes in the miniseries in which Selina was called a whore. Her attacker was her pimp, Stan, who gave her a leather dominatrix suit with cat ears for her next job when she returned from the hospital. This became her Catwoman costume at the end of the first issue, after she saw Batman escape the police in Robinson Park.

There was a degree of reclamation in Selina using the suit as her Catwoman outfit, turning something meant to keep her under the control of her pimp into something that set her free. Her first act in the costume was to confront Stan; Selina had been taking fighting lessons since her attack, and this time she was ready for him. She scratched him across the face and knocked him down, telling him, "Don't kick the cat again, Stan. **Ever.**" But after this first cathartic scene, Selina's Catwoman identity became more of a burden than a benefit.

The miniseries introduced Selina's sister, a nun named Sister Magdalene. The sisters were a literal virgin-whore dichotomy, and the story engaged in the usual moralizing patterns that accompany this trope. Selina, the fallen sister, pulled the innocent Magdalene into her dark, dangerous world when Stan, wanting to get back at Selina, kidnapped Magdalene and held her hostage. This eventually led to a tense battle on a high walkway, and Magdalene would have plummeted to her death if Batman weren't there to catch her. Stan wasn't so lucky, and he fell off the walkway to his death.

The incident left Selina shaken, and in a confessional moment with her sister she admitted what being Catwoman offered her. She said, "**I** can't take it. But **she** can. The **Catwoman—she** can stand it **all**. Everything **crummy** that life can throw at her, she just throws it right **back**—and it doesn't even **faze** her." Selina then cried, "**Nothing** hurts her—it's like she's **dead**. Oh, Maggie—it's so much **easier** being dead!" After Magdalene was almost killed, Holly was assaulted by a police captain because of her association with Selina, and the combined guilt was too much for Selina. As the series ended, she retreated into her escapist identity and left her adopted sister in the care of her biological sister at the convent, striking out on her own as Catwoman so that no one close to her would get hurt again.

When a fan of Newell's *Action Comics* run wrote in to request that she write a monthly Catwoman series, the book's editor responded, "If enough people buy the first issue of the **Catwoman** mini-series and the other issues as well, that would be a good way to get Mindy a regular gig." That audience failed to materialize, and the final issue of the miniseries in May 1989 marked Catwoman's last major comic book appearance for several years. Miller's take on the character, as expanded by Newell, wasn't what fans wanted from Catwoman.

The Bat-books followed up on the success of "Year One" with the less impactful arcs "Year Two" and "Year Three." Catwoman didn't play a part in either story. While DC's Batman line was sizable in the early 1990s thanks to the success of Tim Burton's *Batman* film, Catwoman was largely limited to rare cameos. Her only significant story was a two-issue arc early in 1991 that centered on a television news show essentially daring Catwoman to steal the Emerald Cat of Karnak from the Gotham Museum and Catwoman pulling off the job. The story was an obvious attempt to reintroduce the character; she had long hair and a new young friend to replace Holly, and she even engaged in some crime fighting of her own. The arc went over well in the *Batman* letter column, with many readers echoing the sentiment of Neil Ahlquist's enthusiastic reaction, "At long last, the Catwoman is back!" But no further stories followed, and Catwoman disappeared for another couple of years.

Frank Miller disappeared from superhero comics as well. After his string of Daredevil and Batman bestsellers, he wanted to create his own characters and tell stories in worlds of his own devising. His major project in this period was *Sin City*, a comic that opened with the murder of a female prostitute and tracked its impact on the first volume's male protagonist. Ultimately, the series' seven volumes featured a variety of female characters, almost all of whom were prostitutes, strippers, ninjas, assassins, or some combination thereof.

## Roman Holiday

The four issues of "Year One" were a big hit for DC when they were first published, and the story has been a perennial bestseller ever since. DC collected the issues as the graphic novel *Batman: Year One* in 1988, and it's been reissued several times over the years, along with all manner of deluxe and special editions. While "Year Two" and "Year Three" were quickly forgotten, *Batman: Year One* stayed so popular that DC decided to publish a new sequel nearly a decade later. Written by Jeph Loeb with art by Tim Sale, *Batman: The Long Halloween* was a thirteen-issue miniseries that depicted Batman's early career and picked up on the threads left by Miller. It went over well and spawned a follow-up miniseries, *Batman: Dark Victory*, and the collections of both books have remained in print since then, across a variety of editions.

*Batman: Year One*, *Batman: The Long Halloween*, and *Batman: Dark Victory* together constitute the bible of Batman's early years in the Modern Age of comics. Loeb and Sale built on the foundation of Miller's origin by continuing the focus on Batman and Gordon's relationship, incorporating the mob families established by Miller and exploring the corrupt world of his Gotham City. Their books were a continuation of *Batman: Year One* in every way.

Except for Catwoman. Loeb and Sale did away with the gray-costumed, short-haired former prostitute and her run-down apartment. Their Catwoman wore a purple costume and had long hair, and their Selina Kyle was a wealthy socialite who hobnobbed with Gotham's high society. Holly was gone, along with any mention of Selina's former life.

The only element that remained of Miller's Catwoman were the three scars that ran down the cheek of Carmine "the Roman" Falcone, which were displayed prominently when he first appeared in the debut issue of *Batman: The Long Halloween*. Loeb and Sale cultivated an air of mystery around their Catwoman and decided to give her a connection to the Falcones that was slowly teased throughout both books. The Falcones were key players in the first volume, and the book opened with the Roman's nephew's wedding. Selina and Bruce Wayne were both in attendance, and even danced together before going their separate ways.

Later that evening, the pair reunited as Catwoman and Batman when he interrupted her robbing the Roman's penthouse apartment. A chase ensued, and Catwoman escaped Batman with ease, but an irate Falcone put a $1 million bounty on both of their heads. In retaliation, Catwoman tracked down Batman and told him, "I **don't** want to help. But, I might be able to be **helpful**," and gave him the location of the warehouse where Falcone stockpiled his cash.

Thus began a dual narrative. As Selina, she dated Bruce in what was an entirely genuine relationship. Neither knew the other's secret identity, and dating Selina had Bruce contemplating what it would take for him to give up being Batman. As Catwoman, her role was more ambiguous. She was still a thief, but she was always near the Falcones and willing to provide Batman with information that would harm them. Her behavior left Batman completely flummoxed, and doubly so after she showed up in Wayne Manor to save Bruce from the hypnotic influence of Poison Ivy. At one point, Batman asked Catwoman, "Why? Why do you help?" Her answer was evasive: "In time. You'll see."

Ultimately, the story ended with Catwoman joining a team of villains who were against Falcone, and Two-Face killed him. Falcone's death led to fractures in both of Catwoman's relationships as *Batman: Dark Victory* began. Bruce was busy as Batman and had less time for Selina. Initially, she tried to reduce the new distance between them—quite literally so at Thanksgiving, when the duo were seated at opposite ends of a long, ornate table and she dragged her chair down to the opposite end to share Bruce's plate. But after Bruce stood her up on Christmas Eve and New Year's, she was getting annoyed.

Batman was standoffish with Catwoman as well. When she warned him that the Falcones were going to kill Two-Face, Batman didn't care. She slapped him across the face twice and growled, "I hope you'll show a little more **interest** when they come after **me**." In the book's fifth issue, Batman saved Catwoman from being burned alive in a crematorium, and she decided to try to clarify their relationship, suggesting, "Let's do it. Right now. Take off the masks. No secrets." After a brief pause, Batman replied, "What is your relationship to the Falcone crime organization?" Catwoman snarled, "Happy Valentine's Day. Your loss . . ." and then left town for the next several issues. At the end of the book, Selina visited the Roman's grave and said, "I **know** you are my **real** father, but I can never prove it." She'd spent her away time in Italy trying to find definitive evidence that she was his daughter, but was unable to do so.

Her Italian voyage was fleshed out when Loeb and Sale added a third book to the series, the six-issue *Catwoman: When in Rome*, in 2004. Selina traveled to Italy with the Riddler, and quickly got in trouble with the local mafia due to the Riddler's secret betrayal. When she later confronted him, Catwoman had to fight the Riddler and his allies: the Cheetah, the Scarecrow, and a mafioso armed with Mr. Freeze's ice gun. She defeated them with ease. While Selina didn't find any physical evidence to prove her parentage, a local gangster assured her that the Roman's first wife had a daughter who was supposed to be killed but was secretly sent to America to be adopted. In the end, Selina left Rome with that knowledge, the memories of a brief affair, and a valuable ring that she stole from the Vatican.

*Catwoman: When in Rome* hasn't proved quite as popular as Loeb and Sale's other Batman titles; their earlier books are jam-packed with every hero and villain in Gotham, while their Catwoman book is more of an enjoyable side story. Nonetheless, their take on Catwoman across all three titles reshaped the continuity of her early years away from "Year One." They provided an alternate version of her origins that other creators could build upon and influenced the way that the character was depicted in the regular monthly books. While other comics throughout the 1990s tried to move Catwoman away from "Year One," none have had the impact or staying power of Loeb and Sale's work. A high-class thief who had a complicated relationship with Batman became the dominant incarnation of the character throughout the 2000s in part because they had resteered the character so effectively.*

That Loeb and Sale felt the need to reorient Catwoman in such a way speaks to the unworkability of Miller's take on the character. They carried over so much of his work, but his Catwoman appeared to be a step too far into gritty, exploitative territory for them. Loeb and Sale found a way to make Catwoman strong and sexy without turning her into a prostitute, back-burnering that backstory for good.

## Frank Miller Strikes Again

In recent years, Frank Miller has gone Hollywood. He codirected a much-lauded film adaptation of *Sin City* with Robert Rodriguez

---

* Catwoman was a high-class thief in the influential *Batman: The Animated Series* cartoon throughout the 1990s as well, which may have inspired Loeb and Sale's depiction and also combined with it to reorient the character for good. For more on this animated incarnation of Catwoman, see chapter 7.

in 2005, along with its less lauded sequel in 2014. On his own he directed *The Spirit* in 2008, bringing Will Eisner's classic comic book character to the big screen for the first time, but it was panned across the board. Miller's graphic novel *300*, the tale of the Spartans' last stand at the ancient Battle of Thermopylae, was also turned into a hit film by Zack Snyder, and Warner Bros.' DC Universe Animated Original Movies line has released faithful adaptations of *Batman: The Dark Knight Returns* and *Batman: Year One*.

Miller also returned to superhero comics, starting with *Batman: The Dark Knight Strikes Again*. Originally released as a three-issue miniseries beginning in 2001, the book was a sequel to *Batman: The Dark Knight Returns* in which Batman, years after faking his death, reemerged from hiding to lead a team of heroes against America's evil, dictatorial regime. After the massive success of Miller's past Batman books, *Batman: The Dark Knight Strikes Again* was hotly anticipated and had strong initial sales. Then people read it. The art was crudely drawn and scratchy, the story was convoluted and violent, and the beloved superheroes that populated the book were unrecognizably harsh. Critics savaged the book almost universally, and it lacked the staying power of Miller's earlier work.

Selina Kyle wasn't a part of *Batman: The Dark Knight Strikes Again*, but Batman's lieutenant Carrie Kelly traded her Robin identity for a new code name: Catgirl. The name came with a new leopard-print suit made in the style of a typical Catwoman outfit, with cat ears and clawed gloves. Unfortunately for Carrie, the associations with Catwoman didn't end there. Just as Selina was brutally assaulted in *Batman: The Dark Knight Returns* to lead Batman to a major confrontation with the Joker, so too was Carrie savagely beaten by a Joker-esque character, a deranged and superpowered Dick Grayson, who now resembled the Joker, to dramatically build to Batman's climactic battle with Dick.

The attack was portrayed in a series of small panels, several of them close-ups of Carrie's injuries. Her internal monologue read, "He's **breaking** me. Bone by **bone**. He's **killing** me. Cut by **cut**. He cuts my **face**. He cuts my face **bad**." Dick taunted her, "So pretty. Sweet sixteen. I'm going to skin you alive." Ultimately, Batman defeated Dick while Carrie lay battered and bandaged in the Batmobile. One of her eyes was blackened and swollen shut: the left eye, just like Selina in *The Dark Knight Returns*.

Despite the poor reception for *Batman: The Dark Knight Strikes Again*, DC brought Miller back for another Batman story in 2005. *All Star Batman & Robin, the Boy Wonder* was the first title in DC's new line of out-of-continuity stories written and drawn by top creators. Miller wrote the book and was joined by superstar penciller Jim Lee and inker Scott Williams. Miller saw the series as part of his *Dark Knight* world, set a few years after *Batman: Year One*.

Again, the anticipation was massive, and the first issue sold 261,000 copies in its first month, over 100,000 copies more than the next title on the sales charts, but reviews were mixed. The book's Batman was somewhat unhinged; in an early issue, he introduced himself to a newly orphaned Dick Grayson by declaring, "I'm the goddamn **Batman**." The odd tone, combined with shipping delays due to Lee being behind on the artwork, eroded interest in the book. Ten issues were released between 2005 and 2008, and the story remains unfinished. A promised six-issue conclusion has yet to materialize.

Catwoman appeared in the series' eighth issue, reclining on a bed and surrounded by her cats. She wore a tight purple costume with high black boots and gloves, held a whip, and had a collar with a ring around her neck. Catwoman was visited by the Joker, but she told him, "Get **lost**. I've heard **rumors** on how you handle **women**—and even I don't play it **that** rough." But when the Joker replied that he was up to some mischief, she was intrigued.

When Catwoman returned two issues later, she lay collapsed in an alley, bloody and bruised. She'd been badly beaten by the Joker, her costume was torn up, and she was losing blood at an alarming rate. She gave a note to the police officer who found her, telling him to give it to Batman, and then she disappeared. The note simply read, "The first time."

In the middle of this grisly scene, Miller chose to reference the first time Catwoman and Batman had sex. When he got the note, Batman remembered their "sweaty, dirty, glorious mess" of an evening and went to Robinson Park, where he found Catwoman waiting for him, barely conscious. As he held her limp body, Batman told her, "Don't talk, baby. You're safe," and he thought, "She's soft and light and perfect. I always forget how small she is." What happened next is unknown because this was the last issue of the series that came out, but presumably Batman was off to confront the Joker.

Miller was still trapped in the same formula when it came to female characters, and this continued in his next outing with Catwoman. Technically, it wasn't actually Catwoman. In 2006 Miller announced that he was working on a book called *Holy Terror, Batman!* that pitted Batman against Al-Qaeda in a story reminiscent of World War II–era propaganda. Miller and DC parted ways midway through the project, and the book became just *Holy Terror* with a new lead hero, the Fixer.

Despite the change in publisher, *Holy Terror* was a Batman book at its core; some pages even had overlooked vestiges of its origin, like bat ears on the hero's shadow. The Fixer was joined by Natalie Stack, an obvious analogue of Catwoman. She described herself as a "cat burglar," wore a leather costume with claws, and even mentioned that she had "nine lives and all that" after a close scrape with death. The book began with the Fixer pursuing Natalie across Empire City after she stole a diamond bracelet. The fight that followed quickly turned into sex, near Robinson Park, no less, but their amorous activities were interrupted by a series of terrorist bombings that blasted shrapnel through the city, causing massive death and destruction. Appalled by the attacks, the Fixer and Natalie immediately committed themselves to finding whoever was behind it.

The book was narrated by Natalie, and the text made her subordinate role clear. Immediately after the first bombing, she noted, "[The Fixer's] got a tremble running through him, too. But his is angry. Like he wants to start killing people. Me, I'm just plain scared." As they chased down the terrorists, the Fixer took the lead while Natalie followed, saying, "Right behind you, boss."

In true Frank Miller fashion, the book ended with Natalie in peril. She was captured by the jihadists in their secret base hidden deep underneath a midtown mosque, and hog-tied in a familiar pose. As her captor contemplated whether she should be nude for her beheading, the Fixer arrived. He killed the jihadists, saved Natalie, and blew up the base as Natalie thought, "Okay. So maybe I'm in love, too."

*Holy Terror* went over poorly. The book was blasted for its Islamophobia, with reviewers calling it "one of the most appalling, offensive and vindictive comics of all time" and "a hateful, ill-considered, simplistic, ugly, nasty little book." But while the racist angle was fairly new for Miller, the sexism was par for the course.

Despite the universal disdain for *Holy Terror*, DC recently brought Miller back to Batman yet again, for the unfortunately titled *Dark Knight III: The Master Race*. They didn't let him do it on his own this time, though; Miller was joined by cowriter Brian Azzarello, an Eisner Award winner best known for his crime series *100 Bullets*, and artists Andy Kubert and Klaus Janson, both legends in the business. The story saw Batman and the rest of DC's heroes facing off against a sinister group of Kryptonians who had been freed from the bottle city of Kandor.*

While Selina Kyle isn't a factor in the book, the first issue revealed another promotion for Carrie Kelly: she was now Batman. For a few pages, at least. The police were after Batman and finally caught up with her at the end of the issue. A gang of officers surrounded her and began to attack her with their batons, and the "whack whack whack whack whack" sound effects were punctuated by blood spatter. Carrie fought back valiantly but was eventually subdued, and when the commissioner pulled off her mask to reveal her bloodied face, her left eye was blackened and swollen shut.

---

* DC also released an oversized special during *The Dark Knight III*'s run called *The Dark Knight Returns: Last Crusade*. Set in the past and cowritten by Miller, Selina Kyle appeared in only two pages, both featuring postcoital conversations with Bruce Wayne.

# 6

# Hear Me Roar

The campy legacy of the *Batman* television show cast a long shadow that made developing new Batman projects a difficult task. This wasn't helped by *Legends of the Superheroes*, a cheaply produced pair of specials that aired in January 1979. Adam West and Burt Ward reprised their roles as Batman and Robin and joined with several other DC heroes to defeat the Legion of Doom in the first episode. The second was a roast, hosted by Ed McMahon, in which the superheroes and villains cracked jokes at each other's expense. Both specials were a trainwreck on every possible level.

Perhaps because of this, producers Michael Uslan and Benjamin Melniker were able to purchase the film rights to Batman later that year. They wanted to go in the opposite direction of Batman's past live-action incarnation and present a dark, serious take on the character, but few studios were interested. Even after Warner Bros. got on board, the property languished for years as script after script was written and directors came and went.

Finally, director Tim Burton joined the project in 1986. Burton had been making quirky short films for years and recently helmed the hit film *Pee-wee's Big Adventure*. He brought in Sam Hamm to write a new script, and it went over well with Warner Bros. executives, but the project wasn't officially greenlit until Burton's second major feature, *Beetlejuice*, made a big splash with moviegoers in 1988.

Production soon got underway on *Batman*. Michael Keaton starred in the title role, despite the outrage of many Batman fans when his casting was first announced. Jack Nicholson played the Joker, and Kim Basinger played Bruce Wayne's love interest, reporter Vicki Vale. Burton's Gotham City was bleak and gothic, protected by a stern Batman in an all-black suit. Accompanied by Danny Elfman's menacing score, the film was a highly stylized, dark approach to the world of Batman.

The film began with Batman taking on a pair of muggers. He knocked out one and let the other go free, instructing him to warn his criminal peers about Gotham's new protector. Soon after, mobster Jack Napier was knocked into a vat of acid during a fight with Batman and emerged as the criminally insane Joker. While Batman thwarted the Joker's various plans, Bruce Wayne fell for Vicki Vale as she researched Batman. After Batman revealed his true identity to Vicki, she was kidnapped by the Joker in the film's climactic scene. The hero and villain battled, with the Joker falling to his death, and the film ended with Gotham saved and the damsel rescued.

When *Batman* hit theaters in June 1989, it broke the opening weekend box office record, and it went on to gross more than $400 million worldwide. Warner Bros. immediately began production on a sequel, but Burton wasn't keen to return. He didn't love how *Batman* turned out and was down on the idea of sequels in general, so he went off to write and direct *Edward Scissorhands*. Warner Bros. eventually lured Burton back by promising him more creative control over the second film and work quickly began in earnest on *Batman Returns*. This time, Batman would face off against two classic villains: the Penguin and Catwoman.

## This Hit, That Ice Cold

Before Burton agreed to come back, Warner Bros. commissioned a script from *Batman* writer Sam Hamm. Then titled *Batman 2*, the script was a straight sequel to the original that followed up on its lingering story lines and expanded the world in familiar ways. Vicki Vale returned and was a key component of both Bruce and Batman's life, and Robin entered the mix as well. The main story centered on Catwoman and the Penguin teaming up to steal raven statues owned by the five richest families in Gotham City that, when put together, created a map to a secret treasure the families had hidden long ago.

Hamm's Catwoman resembled her pre-*Crisis* incarnation to a certain degree. He described her as "dark and elegant, fine-boned, regal of bearing" with "exotic, vaguely Eurasian features." But she was far more fierce. In her first scene, she scratched a young man and lapped up his blood. She then got into a firefight, mowing down her foes with an automatic rifle, and later she viciously sliced a man to ribbons with her long, razor-sharp claws.

The script also put Catwoman in sexual situations constantly. Before cutting the aforementioned man to shreds, she seduced him and tied him to his bed. Selina also tried to seduce Bruce throughout the film in her guise as the Fluegelheim Museum's curator of antiquities; catty encounters with Vicki Vale soon followed. Hamm described her Catwoman costume as "inky black leather from head to toe" with a "bondage mask" that was "studded, with openings for the eyes and mouth." During her first encounter with Batman, Hamm had her "POSING for him in a little private show—a strange, self-infatuated, AUTOEROTIC DANCE ROUTINE for BATMAN's benefit."

In the end, Batman defeated Catwoman and the Penguin in a brawl at Wayne Manor, and Catwoman's loss was especially ignominious. As Catwoman leaped off a high balcony onto a chandelier, Batman shot down the chandelier and Catwoman fell to the floor below. She landed on her back, her limbs splayed at "unnatural angles," seemingly paralyzed from the fall as she whimpered, "I can't move. I can't move." When Batman approached her, she pleaded, "Do me, baby . . . do me now . . . that's what I want. Please?" Batman wouldn't kill her, so she tried to slit her own throat with her claws, but Batman stopped her with knockout gas.

When Burton signed on to helm *Batman Returns*, he discarded this script entirely. Because of his disappointment with the first film, he wanted to start fresh; he saw the movie not as a sequel but as an entirely new film. Warner Bros. had kept all the sets from *Batman*'s shoot in London in storage for the sequel, but Burton decided to build brand-new sets and shoot in Burbank, California. Several elements of Batman and his world were redesigned to further underline the clear break that Burton aimed for. Hamm's script, with its many ties to the original film, was the complete opposite of what Burton wanted.

Burton brought in Daniel Waters to write the new script. Waters had penned the dark comedy *Heathers*, and Burton thought that his sensibility would fit his vision for the film. Catwoman and the Penguin stayed on as villains, but their stories were completely changed, while Vicki Vale and the debut of Robin were cut out entirely. The end result was a twisted Christmas fairy tale with a plot partly inspired by an old episode of *Batman* in which the Penguin ran for mayor of Gotham City. Michael Keaton returned as Batman, while Danny DeVito played a grotesque Penguin; he'd been abandoned by his parents as a baby because he was deformed, and was subsequently raised by circus folk and lived in Gotham's sewers. When the Penguin kidnapped wealthy industrialist Max Shreck, played by Christopher Walken, Shreck saw an opportunity and turned the Penguin into his pawn candidate for the city's mayoral election.

For Catwoman, Burton and Waters went for a brand-new origin. Waters later said of his approach to Catwoman, "Hamm went back to the way comic books in general treat women, like fetishy sexual fantasy. I wanted to start off just at the lowest point in society, a very beaten down secretary." Selina Kyle was Shreck's mousy assistant, but Shreck pushed her out a window when she learned the nefarious secret behind his new power plant. Through vague, perhaps supernatural means, Selina survived the long fall and returned as the newly empowered, fierce Catwoman. She then set about vexing all the men who were vying for control of Gotham.

After the massive success of *Batman*, interest was high for the sequel's only substantial female part. According to producer Denise Di Novi, "Every major movie star from 17 through the late 40s got in touch about the role." After considering and auditioning a wide array of actors,* Burton decided to cast Annette Bening but she got pregnant just before shooting began and bowed out of the part. The search reopened, and Burton ultimately chose Michelle Pfeiffer to portray his ferocious Catwoman.

Michelle Marie Pfeiffer was born in 1958 in Santa Ana, California. She won the Miss Orange County pageant in 1978 and after finishing sixth in Miss California she parlayed her pageant success into an acting career. She quickly found work in a variety of gigs, including a lead role in the much-maligned *Grease 2*, but her big break came with *Scarface* in 1983. Pfeiffer was nominated for two Academy Awards in the late 1980s for *Dangerous Liaisons* and *The Fabulous Baker Boys*; she also won a Golden Globe for the latter, which was the first in a series of five straight years of Golden Globe nominations for Pfeiffer.

Pfeiffer had low expectations when she first got the script for *Batman Returns*, and she later recalled, "I thought it would be a couple of scenes and probably, you know, not a fully developed character." To her surprise, "I read the script and I found her to be very interesting and very complicated and actually quite a challenge." That the character was well written was a bonus for Pfeiffer, who admitted, "I didn't care, I would've done it anyway because it's a kind of idol from my childhood." She grew up watching Julie Newmar's Catwoman and absolutely loved the character. Pfeiffer said of Newmar, "She just broke all of the stereotypes of what it meant to be a woman. I found that shocking and titillating and forbidden [. . .] I just found Catwoman thrilling to watch."

Owing to her late casting, Pfeiffer had little time to train for Catwoman, but she threw herself wholly into it. In the month before shooting began, she spent four hours a day doing martial arts, yoga, and gymnastics. She also trained with a professional whip master to be able to properly use Catwoman's signature whip. The results were

---

* The long list of women who were considered or campaigned for the part included Ellen Barkin, Kim Basinger, Jennifer Beals, Lorraine Bracco, Cher, Geena Davis, Bridget Fonda, Jodie Foster, Nicole Kidman, Jennifer Jason Leigh, Madonna, Demi Moore, Lena Olin, Susan Sarandon, Brooke Shields, Meryl Streep, Sigourney Weaver, Raquel Welch, and Sean Young.

impressive. Burton was blown away by her abilities and declared, "She really did something incredible, and she's doing things that even the stunt people couldn't do in terms of beauty and movement." As filming progressed, Pfeiffer was able to kickbox in high heels on the set's sloped roofs better than her stunt doubles could.

Throughout the shoot Pfeiffer was completely dedicated to the role, even when it was unpleasant. She described her skintight costume as an "ordeal"; it took an assembly line of people to get her powdered down and into the suit. Once she had it on, it was so tight that she could only wear it for a limited amount of time before she started to feel light-headed because it constricted her breathing. The thin costume was no protection against the elements, either. Burton kept the set so cold in the Penguin's ice palace that Pfeiffer nearly froze, and she had trouble emoting in her scenes because her face was numb. But Pfeiffer toughed it out and embraced the difficulties even when she didn't have to. One scene called for Catwoman to put a bird in her mouth, and while there were several fake birds available, she opted to use the live bird so that the scene looked as realistic as possible.

*Batman Returns* broke the opening weekend box office record when it debuted, but Warner Bros. was disappointed with its overall earnings, and the film premiered to mixed reviews. However, one constant positive in the reviews was praise for Pfeiffer's take on Catwoman. Owen Gleiberman of *Entertainment Weekly* wrote, "The runaway star here is Pfeiffer, whose performance is a sexy, comic triumph." Peter Travers of *Rolling Stone* agreed, writing that "Catwoman is no bimbo in black leather. Pfeiffer gives this feminist avenger a tough core of intelligence and wit; she's a classic dazzler." Catwoman completely stole the show in *Batman Returns*, sticking it to all the boys in the process.*

## Whipping the Patriarchy

In *Batman*, Vicki Vale's role followed the typical formula for a female character in an action film. Though she was a skilled reporter

---

* Pfeiffer's Catwoman proved so popular with fans that her solo posters were regularly stolen all across America.

who helped Batman, she was his romantic interest first and foremost. Case in point, she landed the story of the century when she learned that Bruce Wayne was Batman, but kept it to herself because of their romantic relationship. Batman wasn't the only one attracted to her; the Joker fell for her as well, an infatuation that culminated in him kidnapping Vicki and setting up the film's final confrontation between Batman and the Joker. Vicki's only contribution to the fight reflected her role: she tricked the Joker into thinking she was going to fellate him, thus distracting him from Batman's approach. In the end, Batman saved Vicki, and in her final scene Alfred drove her to Wayne Manor to await the return of her hero.

*Batman Returns* was different. Selina dated Bruce throughout the film, and Catwoman and Batman had a flirtatious dynamic, but she wasn't defined by her relationship with him. Catwoman was focused on herself. Her sexiness was a tool she used for fun or to further her own agenda, always for her own pleasure. Catwoman wasn't just a departure from a conventional female role; she embodied a ferocious critique of this role and the sexist values it represented.

Initially, Selina was a stereotypically helpless, downtrodden woman, bespectacled and frumpy and a failure at every aspect of her life. She came to Gotham looking for a good job and big city excitement, but she was in a rut. At work, her boss demeaned her; when she tried to ask a question during a business meeting, Shreck dismissed her and told his guests, "I'm afraid we haven't properly housebroken Miss Kyle. In the plus column, though, she makes a hell of a cup of coffee." After the meeting, Selina chastised herself, "You stupid corndog!"

Out on the streets, she was helpless. When the Penguin's circus goons attacked the city during the annual tree-lighting ceremony, Selina was bumped, her papers went flying, and she lost her glasses. A clown used her as a human shield when Batman approached, and she just stood there whimpering in fear until Batman saved her.

At home, she had nothing but her pet cat. As Selina entered her apartment, she shouted out, "Honey, I'm home!" before sarcastically adding, "Oh, I forgot, I'm not married." The messages on her answering machine only brought more grief; her mother was disappointed in her, a regular sentiment as indicated by Selina's annoyed response, and her boyfriend broke up with her. The apartment itself was stereotypically girly in a childish way, pink all over and brimming with stuffed animals, a dollhouse, and a neon sign that read HELLO THERE. While feeding her cat, Selina asked herself, "How can anyone be so pathetic?"

Then Selina was pushed out a window by her boss, and her old life ended. Her transformation into Catwoman was a form of rebirth, marked by the destruction of the vestiges of her past self. She returned home after her "resurrection" and went on a tear: she covered her pink walls with black spray paint, fed her stuffed animals to the garbage disposal, smashed her old pictures and her dollhouse, and knocked out a couple of the letters in her neon sign so it now read HELL HERE. The symbolism was a tad on the nose, the eradication of everything traditionally feminine in favor of a new path, but Pfeiffer sold it well. Selina completed her rebirth by donning her newly sewn Catwoman outfit; the white stitching down her torso resembled the Y incisions on an autopsied cadaver.

A key component of Catwoman leaving behind her childish, dowdy past was her newfound sexuality. When she put on her costume for the first time, she posed in her window, backlit by her neon sign in a shot reminiscent of Amsterdam's red-light district and said to her cat, "I don't know about you, Miss Kitty, but I feel so much yummier." But unlike Amsterdam, Catwoman's posing wasn't for anyone but herself.

There was a kinky bondage feel to her black vinyl outfit that gave her a dominatrix vibe, and Catwoman quickly established that she was in control during her first outing. She interrupted an attempted rape in an alley, taunting the attacker, "I just love a big strong man who's not afraid to show it with someone half his size." She then purred, "Be gentle, it's my first time," before she kicked him repeatedly, scratched a bloody tic-tac-toe board across his face, and punched him out. The same dynamic continued in her second outing; as a pair of guards watched her skip with her whip through Shreck's department store, one observed, "I don't know whether to open fire or fall in love." Catwoman responded, "You poor guys, always confusing your pistols with your privates." She then whipped the guns out of their hands and sent them running.

Catwoman was as harsh with women as she was with men, but with a twist. After she stopped the would-be rapist, the woman he attacked tried to thank Catwoman, but she interrupted, "You make it so easy, don't you? Always waiting for some Batman to save you. I am Catwoman. Hear me roar." But this was less a rebuke of the woman and more a rebuke of the person that Catwoman used to be. As Selina, she'd been attacked and needed Batman to save her, but now she'd left that life behind and figured out how to save herself. The reference to an iconic women's lib anthem underlined the feminist empowerment behind her Catwoman persona.

Later in the film, Catwoman and the Penguin kidnapped the Ice Princess, a beauty pageant winner, framing Batman for the crime and her subsequent murder after Penguin caused her to topple off a tall building. The Ice Princess represented what Catwoman could have been: a vapid character in a small outfit paraded around for men to ogle, ultimately captured so that Batman could try to rescue her in typical action film style.*

Ultimately, Catwoman's primary conflicts were with the Penguin, Shreck, and Batman, and the forms of patriarchy that they represented. Each man "killed" her at some point in the film; Burton was intentionally ambiguous about whether she actually died and had nine lives or was just prone to lucky scrapes. But after each "death" she only came back stronger and, by the end of the film, had defeated them all.

The Penguin represented an old form of patriarchy, the aristocracy. He was born in an ornate mansion before he was abandoned, and his entire look, from his top hat to his waistcoat to his monocle, harked back to his patrician origins. In his interactions with Catwoman, the Penguin exuded an air of entitlement and sexual expectation. As a woman, she was there to please him and do what he wished, a dynamic that didn't sit well with Catwoman.

---

* While Catwoman wasn't much for the sisterhood aspect of feminism, she wasn't pleased with the Ice Princess's death and her anger at the Penguin for murdering her quickly led to them falling out.

Her introduction to the Penguin was telling. She wanted to team up with him to defeat Batman, and as the Penguin entered the room to meet with her, his organ grinder assistant informed him, "There's some*body* here to see you," putting a very clear emphasis on "body." In the interactions that followed, it was obvious that the Penguin viewed her as little more than that. When he first saw Catwoman, he remarked, "Just the pussy I been looking for." Soon he was crawling toward her and talking about their shared "naked sexual charisma." After she suggested that they ruin Batman instead of killing him, the Penguin dismissed her as a "screwed-up sorority chick who's gettin' back at her daddy for not buying her that pony when she turned sweet sixteen." He only really got on board Catwoman's plan when she told him, "The thought of busting Batman makes me feel all . . . dirty," and she gave herself a "cat bath" in front of him, licking her hand and rubbing it on herself as he grunted appreciatively.

After manipulating the Penguin into helping her take on Batman, Catwoman dismissed the Penguin when he suggested that they "consummate their fiendish union." He offered her the trappings of aristocratic life, and the subordinate role for women therein, painting a picture of them living together in the mayor's mansion: "Here you come, into the bedroom, twitching your little tail, my slippers in one hand, a dry martini in the other." When Catwoman replied, "Oh, please. I wouldn't touch you to scratch you," an irate Penguin exploded, "You lousy minx! I oughta have you spayed! You sent out all the signals, and I don't think I like you anymore!"

He thought he was owed something because of her flirtatious maneuvering, and when he didn't get it he attached his helicopter umbrella to her neck and sent her flying through the Gotham sky. This resulted in one of Catwoman's many "deaths," as she fell from the umbrella and smashed through a glass solarium. But she survived, and because she'd directed the Penguin's attention toward Batman, Batman took him out soon after.

Max Shreck represented a newer form of patriarchy, that of an industrialist in the male-dominated business world. Everything he owned bore his name, and he was wholly concerned with ensuring his legacy for his male heir, Chip.* Shreck had no respect for his female assistant. He constantly belittled her and his attempt to murder her was cavalierly dispassionate; she potentially stood in the way of him expanding his power, and thus she had to go. But after her resurrection, destroying Shreck became Catwoman's primary purpose.

She went after him where it mattered most, in his place of business. As Catwoman, she ransacked and then blew up his department store, taking away one of his sources of income. As Selina, she returned to work after her fall to taunt Shreck with the fact that she was still alive, sauntering into his office with her newfound confidence as he stared at her, mouth agape. She claimed to have no memory of what caused her lingering injuries, saying that the previous night was all a blur before concluding, "Couldn't you just die?"

Ultimately, Catwoman killed Shreck, electrocuting him to death in a grisly act that left nothing but a charred corpse, but before she did so he tried to buy his way out in typical industrialist fashion. As she cornered him, he pleaded, "I don't know what you want, but I know I can get it for you with a minimum of fuss. Money, jewels, a very big ball of string." But Catwoman couldn't be bought.

To a certain degree, Bruce Wayne represented a combination of the Penguin and Shreck's patriarchal foundations. As the inheritor of his family's manor and vast fortune, he had a foot in the world of the aristocracy, and as a businessman himself, his other foot was in the world of industry. But the core of his patriarchal values was far subtler and rooted in his Batman persona. Batman represented the shining knight, the hero who decided that the woman he was attracted to was a damsel who needed to be saved without ascertaining whether she wanted his help or not.

Catwoman played off this chivalrous impulse during their initial encounter. Soon after their fight began and Batman landed his first blow, she exclaimed, "How could you? I'm a woman!" Taken aback, he began to apologize before he was interrupted by a sharp kick and

---

* The film hints that Shreck may have killed his wife. Murder or not, her absence ensured that all the power he accrued was for him and his son alone.

some whip work that sent him backward over the ledge of a building. As Batman hung from the whip, Catwoman concluded her thought: "Like I was saying, I'm a woman and can't be taken for granted. Life's a bitch, now so am I."

Later in the fight, Catwoman preyed on Batman's obvious desire for her. She ran her hand along his chest and mused, "Who's the man behind the bat? Maybe you can help me find the woman behind the cat." It was all a ruse so that she could locate a weak spot in his costume, after which she jabbed him with her sharp homemade claws. In response, Batman hit Catwoman and sent her flying off the building, leading to another escaped "death" when she landed in a passing truck full of kitty litter.

In a line from the fight scene that was in the script but ultimately cut from the film, Catwoman highlighted the sexist imbalance between the two characters: "The world tells boys to conquer the world, and girls to wear clean panties. A man dressed as a bat is a he-man, but a woman dressed as a cat is a she-devil. I'm just living down to my expectations." The characters weren't all that different, motivated by tragedy to don costumes and work out their issues, but Batman was a hero while Catwoman was a woman gone astray. She refused to be seen in such a way.

She also refused Batman's attempts to save her. To counter his savior complex, she teamed with the Penguin to frame Batman as a criminal, explaining, "He knocked me off a building just when I was starting to feel good about myself. I want to play an integral part in his degradation." When the plan succeeded and the police shot Batman off the ledge of another roof, Catwoman perched on top of the stunned hero, licked his face, and informed him that she didn't want his help: "It seems like every woman you try to save ends up dead, or deeply resentful."

As Selina, she again flipped the script and refused to conform to a typical passive girlfriend role while dating Bruce. She was the aggressor in the relationship, strongly coming on to Bruce when they first met in Shreck's office. She kissed him first during their date at Wayne Manor, pouncing on top of him before they both had to make a hasty exit to become their alter egos. When they met at a ball the next night, after Bruce apologized for leaving he asked, "So no hard feelings, then?" and Selina pulled in close to him and purred, "Actually . . . semi-hard, I'd say," before suggesting that they go find a bed. She knew what she wanted and she went after it. It wasn't an act, either; she was a complicated character, and was genuinely attracted to Bruce, and to Batman to a certain extent as well.

However, in the end Catwoman's independence trumped everything else, and she rejected Batman's attempt to save her and sway her from her goals. Before she killed Shreck, Batman tried to stop her. He ripped off his mask and delivered an impassioned speech, telling her, "We're the same. Split down the center." She appeared to consider his offer to leave Shreck to the police and go home with him as she said, "Bruce, I would love to live with you in your castle, forever, just like in a fairy tale." But the second he touched her, she scratched him and finished, "I just couldn't live with myself, so don't pretend this is a happy ending." Catwoman wasn't a damsel in some traditional tale, meant to be saved by a brave knight. She was forging her own new brand of story in which her narrative and desires were paramount and she was the hero.

## The Real Protagonist

Despite the film's title, Catwoman stealthily took over the show and became the main character of *Batman Returns*. The film's early moments focused on the three male leads, seemingly setting up the epic battle to come. The opening scene was the Penguin's origin, in which the aristocratic Cobblepots threw a bassinet containing their deformed infant into a river on a wintry Christmas night. The bassinet's journey through Gotham's sewer system then served as the backdrop for the film's opening credits. When the film moved to the present day, it did so with a paperboy pitching passersby on the day's headline story, "Penguin—Man or Myth or Something Worse?" Next up was Max Shreck in an important business meeting with the mayor, after which he and the mayor went down to the city square to oversee the city's Christmas tree–lighting ceremony. The Penguin's circus associates interrupted this ceremony with an attack that brought out Batman, who easily fought his way through the nefarious clowns, fire-breathers, and organ grinders. Penguin kidnapped Max Shreck, and they quickly teamed up, appearing to set the table for the rest of the film.

Selina was peripheral in these early scenes. The camera work in Shreck's office illustrated her lack of importance; she was either deep in the background, creeping in from the side of the screen, or shot with her back to the camera. Shreck was front and center. But once Selina transformed into Catwoman, she quickly took control of the film. By the end of the movie, all the men who stood in her way were either destroyed or demoralized.

Meanwhile, the goals of the three male leads were vague. The Penguin wanted revenge against the city that he felt had abandoned him, but his plans weren't specific as he vacillated between attacking the city and running for mayor. He was just an overgrown child, easily led and prone to outbursts. Shreck wanted power, but he also lacked a focused plan. He had his power plant scheme, but quickly got caught up in the mayoral race and the power plant faded into the background. Batman wanted justice, but his role was purely reactionary. He had no larger plan other than responding to the actions of the other characters. Only Catwoman was on point, moving ever forward to her goal.

The film also geographically cordoned off the male leads into distinct districts. The Penguin was relegated to the sewer and his interactions with Shreck. Shreck was confined to his company with its boardroom, offices, and campaign headquarters. Batman was at home for the bulk of the movie, lounging in Wayne Manor or eating Alfred's vichyssoise while working in the Batcave. Bruce watched most of the film's major events unfold on his television before leaving to join the fray. All three men met in the city, mainly for action sequences, before returning to their respective corners, and there was only momentary crossover elsewhere.

Catwoman was everywhere, playing a substantive role in each zone. She teamed up with the Penguin, entering his domain to unite against the Batman. As Selina, she worked for Shreck and was a familiar presence in his offices. Selina also dated Bruce Wayne, which took her to Wayne Manor. Then, when the men came together to fight, Catwoman was always in the thick of it. She united the disparate realms of the film.

Catwoman also brought about the downfall of each main character. When she joined with the Penguin to ruin Batman, the egotistical Penguin took the lead, drawing all of the Dark Knight's ire. His mayoral plan was on the level and had a chance to succeed, but because Catwoman convinced him to go after after Batman, Batman in turn went after him and ruined him. Shreck then abandoned him, and the Penguin ultimately died after his retaliatory final attack was thwarted. With Shreck, Catwoman just killed him. She taunted him and messed with his business a bit first, but ultimately she ended him despite Shreck shooting her four times as she approached. There was no stopping her.

She also defeated Batman in the process. When Batman arrived to dissuade her, he was there in two roles. Initially he was the just and lawful Batman, trying to prevent a murder, but when he took off his mask he became Bruce Wayne, trying to save the woman he loved from a dark path. Then Catwoman scratched him and rejected him on both fronts, killing Shreck in a dual failure for the Dark Knight; Bruce didn't get the girl, and Batman didn't stop the murder.

In the end, Catwoman was the only character who won. She was also the only character in *Batman Returns* with a consummated story arc. Penguin tried to take his revenge but died. Shreck tried to gain power over the city but died. Batman tried to fight for justice but failed. Catwoman had an origin story, set a clear goal, dispatched the adversaries that stood in her way, and ultimately completed what she'd set out to do. It was her movie.

There's no better evidence for this than the film's final scene. Years earlier, *Batman* had ended with the Bat-Signal lighting up Gotham's sky as Batman looked on heroically, but Batman wasn't around for the end of *Batman Returns*. Instead, a downcast Bruce Wayne thought he'd spied Catwoman as he drove down a snowy street, so Alfred stopped the car and Bruce ran into an alley to look for her. He was mistaken; it was Selina's pet cat, whom Bruce then took in. As the car drove off, the shot rose up to the night sky and the Bat-Signal was again emblazoned across the clouds as Elfman's stirring theme began to play, but this time Catwoman rose into the frame to close out the film.

The Catwoman shot was a late addition to *Batman Returns*, shot just weeks before the film's release. Originally, Burton had left her ending ambiguous; Batman didn't find Catwoman in the wreckage surrounding Shreck's death, so the viewer was unsure whether she'd finally run out of lives. But as buzz began to build around the film and the enthusiasm for Pfeiffer's Catwoman grew, Burton decided to add her to the final shot. He had to use a body double for Pfeiffer and shoot it on a weekend at a cost of $250,000 for the simple single shot, but the change suggests that Burton had realized Catwoman was the true star of his film.

*Batman Returns* was an unusual movie, to say the least, and for the third film in the franchise, *Batman Forever*, Warner Bros. decided to part ways with Burton in favor of a more conventional, commercial approach. There were rumors that if Burton had returned, Catwoman would have been part of the film, but new director Joel Schumacher went with another pair of villains and a new female lead in Nicole Kidman's Dr. Chase Meridian. Nonetheless, the studio knew that Pfeiffer's Catwoman was a hit, and began to work with Burton and Waters on a spin-off film. While that project ultimately took more than a decade and the end result was far removed from what Burton and Pfeiffer had created, their Catwoman spurred a renaissance for the character in the early 1990s in both comic books and animation that has made her a mainstay in both worlds ever since.

# 7

# *Leaping into Animation*

$\mathcal{B}$atman has had a considerable presence in animation over the last fifty years, and Catwoman has been with him for most of his cartoon outings, starting with his first animated series in 1968. The live-action *Batman* television show was so popular that Filmation decided to add Batman and Robin segments to its already running DC superhero cartoon *The Superman/Aquaman Hour of Adventure*. With the Dynamic Duo now in the mix, Filmation renamed the series *The Batman/Superman Hour*.

Catwoman made her animation debut in the show's fourth episode on October 5, 1968, "The Nine Lives of Batman," and was voiced by Jane Webb, a voice-acting veteran who played a slew of roles in cartoons of the 1960s and 1970s. She sported a green outfit with a white mask, gloves, and boots, a costume that was reminiscent of her new, short-lived look when she returned to the *Batman* comic in 1967. Catwoman ensnared Batman and Robin in a series of nine deadly traps that she'd spent years devising. They escaped, of course, but not before Catwoman sprayed them with a radioactive chemical that made them glow; if she couldn't kill them, she could at least track them down and find out their secret identities. That plot also failed, as did another in which she kidnapped Robin and put him in a death trap. Batman's utility belt had just the tool necessary to free his chum, prompting Catwoman to gripe, "He carries a hardware store in that belt of his!" Ultimately, Batman nabbed her during a heist at the Gotham Diamond Exchange. It was an action-packed fifteen-minute outing.

Over a handful of appearances throughout the show's one-year run, Catwoman proved to be as troublesome to her fellow villains as she was to the Caped Crusader. She stole from the Penguin in one episode, refused to work with the Joker in another, and when the Penguin and the Joker later teamed up with the Riddler, she ratted them out to Batman and declared, "Now Catwoman shall reign as queen of the underworld!" Cartoon shows in the 1960s rarely offered much for female characters, but Catwoman was a surprisingly fierce and defiant foe for all the men of Gotham City.

Catwoman was back again a decade later in *The New Adventures of Batman*. The show was loosely connected to the original Batman cartoon—Filmation still produced it, and it had a similar animation style as well as several returning actors. However, Catwoman had a new sound and a new look. She was voiced by Melendy Britt, an actor who later voiced She-Ra, among many other roles. Her green outfit was replaced by an orange costume with a black mask and white gloves, along with brown hair instead of black; she looked more like Catman than any previous incarnation of Catwoman.

The new show was even sillier than its predecessor, owing to the constant mishaps of Bat-Mite, that mischievous imp from another dimension who had plagued Batman during the Silver Age of superhero comics. Catwoman hatched bizarre plots that involved cat rockets and cat robots, stole heating oil with a tractor beam and somehow stored the tons of liquid in an abandoned apartment building without it leaking out, and was forced to work with the Joker, Penguin, and Clayface when an alien from Bat-Mite's dimension wanted to team up "the four vilest villains planet Earth has to offer." There was one interesting change to her exploits in the new series: for the first time, Catwoman had female goons, even though the girl power proved ineffective as Catwoman ended up captured at the end of each episode.

*The New Adventures of Batman* also ended after a year, and Catwoman entered an animation drought. She didn't appear in *Super*

*Friends*, the long-running cartoon that teamed up a variety of DC heroes,* but Warner Bros. began to develop a new Batman cartoon after Tim Burton's *Batman* film became a hit in 1989. The result was one of Catwoman's most iconic incarnations, a depiction fueled by her breakout in *Batman Returns* that ultimately proved to be something new and different yet simultaneously classic.

## Batman: The Animated Series

When Warner Bros. Animation president Jean MacCurdy mentioned that the studio was thinking about developing a Batman cartoon at a staff meeting in 1990, Bruce Timm couldn't believe his ears. Timm worked in animation throughout the 1980s, including stints with Filmation and DiC, and his current gig was at Warner Bros. as a storyboard artist for *Tiny Toon Adventures*. After the staff meeting, Timm returned to his desk and immediately churned out a series of sketches; he was a longtime comic book fan, and a Batman cartoon was his dream job. When he submitted the sketches to MacCurdy later that day, he was hoping to become the program's main model designer. Instead, MacCurdy asked Timm to produce the show along with his *Tiny Toon Adventures* colleague Eric Radomski. Neither of them had produced an animated series before, but MacCurdy was sold on Timm's passion and style. Along with writers like Paul Dini and Alan Burnett, Timm began a program that would eventually grow to include the entirety of the DC Comics universe.

The show was heavily influenced by Burton's *Batman*, but Timm later revealed, "We had a love/hate thing going on with the Tim Burton movies." While the success of the films made the series possible, Timm wanted the show to be more than just a spin-off. What inspired him the most was the stylized, timeless quality of Burton's Gotham City. Timm took a similar tack, mixing the modern day with inspirations that included old pulp novels and the 1940s Fleischer Studios Superman cartoon shorts. The result was a show in which

---

* Artist Alex Toth did design a Catwoman model sheet for *Super Friends* in 1978, but she couldn't appear because her rights were tied up in *The New Adventures of Batman*.

Batman had high-tech computers and gadgets, but Gotham City was patrolled by police blimps and the villains used tommy guns.

For Catwoman, the studio wanted her to look as much like Michelle Pfeiffer's version of the character in *Batman Returns* as possible. Timm wasn't on board. "At the time," he said, "I was kind of put off by all the stitches. I thought it was a morbid way to go with the character, and I didn't really see the character that way." A black suit also worried him from an animation standpoint; filling her in all black could make the character look flat, and trying to add in highlights to counter that would be a precise, time-consuming task. Timm envisioned the character in an all-gray suit, like the one David Mazzucchelli gave her in "Year One." In the end, he found a compromise. Catwoman wore a gray catsuit, but with long black gloves and high black boots, along with black on the face of the mask; the studio deemed it "close enough." Timm also stayed true to Pfeiffer's incarnation by making Selina Kyle a blonde.

To voice Catwoman, the show's casting director Andrea Romano brought in Adrienne Barbeau, an actor and singer with a varied career. Barbeau was the original Rizzo in the first Broadway production of *Grease*, had a recurring role on *Maude*, and appeared in several horror films in the early 1980s. When Barbeau came in to read for Catwoman, she had nothing more than a passing familiarity with the character. Her audition was just five or six lines and only took about thirty seconds, and she simply read her lines without doing anything flashy or overstylized. Romano liked what she heard, and said of Barbeau's take on Catwoman, "She does not play the part sexy, she just has a natural sexiness to her voice and I thought it would lead to an interesting energy between Batman and Catwoman."

When *Batman: The Animated Series* debuted on Fox's Saturday morning cartoon block on September 5, 1992, Catwoman was the premiere's main villain.* After the show's iconic opening credits, featuring a theme song adapted from Denny Elfman's *Batman* film score, "The Cat and the Claw" began with Catwoman scaling a

---

* While "The Cat and the Claw" was the first episode of *Batman: The Animated Series* that aired, it was actually fifteenth in the production order and usually appears in that spot in collections of the series.

brick building, using her sharp claws to cut a hole in the glass of a window, and sending her pet cat Isis in to nab a pearl and diamond necklace. Batman soon gave chase, but Catwoman escaped when Batman stopped to save Isis from an oncoming car. After Isis ran back to Catwoman, who was waiting atop a nearby building, Catwoman blew Batman a kiss before she disappeared into the night. A clearly impressed and attracted Batman responded with a whistle of admiration.

Later in the episode, a date with Bruce Wayne was on offer at an auction for an animal rights group. The enamored ladies of Gotham had bid back and forth, building the price up to $1,000, when a green-eyed woman in a fuchsia gown topped them all with a bid of $10,000. Bruce Wayne was going on a date with Selina Kyle. He was intrigued and told her he was flattered, but Selina scoffed and replied, "Please understand, it's purely for the animals, Mr. Wayne. You're off the hook." A blushing Bruce insisted that they keep the date, and Selina agreed. While she'd rather have been out with Batman, Bruce soon made himself useful; Selina had been working on securing land for a wildcat reserve, and when a corporation bought the land out from under her to build a resort and then refused to talk to her, Bruce was able to land her an appointment with the CEO.

The appointment didn't go well, but Selina soon returned, this time as Catwoman. She broke into the corporation's headquarters to learn what they really wanted the land for, and was almost killed by their hired gun, the Red Claw.* Batman saved her and she kissed him, telling him, "You can't deny there's something between us." Batman grimly responded, "You're right, and I'm afraid it's the law." Catwoman pretended to be hurt by Batman's reply, and when he reached out to comfort her, she grabbed him, threw him off a roof, and made her escape.

The story continued in the following episode, with Catwoman and Batman learning that the resort was a cover for a terrorist group's weapons cache. They were captured by the Red Claw and nearly killed, but Catwoman freed them by cutting their ropes with

* The Red Claw was voiced by Kate Mulgrew, using the Russian accent she would later make famous as another Red on *Orange is the New Black*.

her claws as she noted, "What this situation needs is a woman's touch." In the end, Catwoman and Batman blew up the facility and stopped the Red Claw, and Catwoman fled the scene after blowing Batman another kiss. But Batman had figured out her secret identity, and the show ended with him waiting for her at her apartment and arresting her.

This animated incarnation of Catwoman was an animal rights advocate at her core. She liked to steal things, but did so to finance projects that would help animals, cats in particular. Catwoman clearly liked cats more than people, and was perfectly fine with violating the laws of human society if it meant she could help preserve feline wildlife. Timm explained, "The Catwoman of the animated series is neither hero nor villain, but combines aspects of both—depending on which works to her best advantage at the time." Barbeau saw the character in the same way: "In order to play Selina Kyle, she doesn't think she's doing something bad or mean, [. . .] obviously maybe she knows she's doing something illegal but, you know, there is a justification in her mind of why she behaves that way."

The attraction between Catwoman and Batman was also at the forefront of *Batman: The Animated Series* from the very first scene. There was a hint of the sharper, more manipulative dynamic of their relationship in *Batman Returns*, but the show also captured the amusing playfulness that had been key to Julie Newmar's Catwoman in the 1960s. Even though Batman arrested her in the end, he was upset about doing so and was clearly drawn to both sides of her persona. Romano said of their bizarre relationship, "Part of us, I think, as women viewers of the show, want to see her succeed at seducing him. You want to see both Batman and Bruce Wayne succumb to her charms because she's beautiful, she's rich, she's smart; she just has this one main character flaw, which is this mad desire to steal."

The first season of the series consisted of sixty-five episodes that aired on Saturday mornings and weekday afternoons, but Catwoman wasn't given a lot to do after the debut two-parter.* All told, she

---

* The episodes aired completely out of production order, which regularly interfered with the show's continuity, especially for Catwoman. We'll discuss the shows by production order instead of air date so as to reflect the intended story flow.

appeared in only six episodes of this initial run, half as many as other villains like the Joker and Two-Face. When she next appeared, it was only as Selina Kyle; the Mad Hatter had Batman trapped in a dream where his parents never died, he didn't become Batman, and he was engaged to Selina.

Her next actual appearance followed up on her Red Claw adventure, with a judge sentencing Selina to five years' probation as she warned, "If you ever don your Catwoman costume again to violate the law, I'll not only revoke probation, I'll throw the book at you." But Selina didn't listen. Isis was missing, and after searching the city Selina suspected that her pet was trapped in an animal testing lab. She broke in as Catwoman and found Isis but was infected with a toxin. Batman found her and saved her, shut down the lab, and returned Isis to her while she sat out the second half of the episode.

Batman was less helpful in Selina's next outing, in which she was kidnapped by a mad scientist and turned into a half-human, half-cat creature. Batman did come to rescue her, but in the end the scientist's other pet, Tygrus, ended up saving them both. It was only in her final appearance of this initial order that she got the chance to be the hero. When the Joker and Harley Quinn had Batman strapped in an electric chair, Catwoman arrived and fought the duo, giving Batman enough time to free himself. Batman immediately returned the favor, though; later in the episode, Harley captured Catwoman and was about to get her revenge by grinding her into cat food at a local factory, but Batman swooped in just in time.

As work on the series' initial order wound down, Timm began developing a potential Catwoman spin-off series. The character was wildly popular after *Batman Returns*, and fans responded positively to her animated portrayal as well, but the idea never got off the ground apart from a few sketches and a rough outline of a premise. It wasn't pitched to any executives, and Timm and his cohorts instead began work on an order of twenty new episodes of *Batman: The Animated Series*.

Nonetheless, this brief time spent focusing on Catwoman may have led the producers to reorient the character in their second run and return her to her cat burglar roots. In her first appearance in the new episodes, Selina was bored with civilian life and thought to herself, "I prowled through Gotham each evening, going where I liked and taking whatever I wanted, until I met him." When the Ventriloquist offered her a robbery job, she couldn't resist, but it was a setup. The police saw her, making her a wanted criminal again. After a judgmental speech from Batman, Catwoman told him, "I have to be who I am. I realize now I can't change that." She then escaped capture, while Batman looked on disappointedly.

Catwoman teamed up with Batgirl in her next outing as the pair worked together to track down a stolen jade cat statue. The team-up had conditions; if Catwoman lied to Batgirl, she had to turn herself in to the police. They found the statue, but instead of returning it to the museum like they'd planned, Catwoman tried to make off with it herself. Batgirl caught her and Catwoman dutifully let the cops arrest her. Before the police car made it half a block, though, both officers were thrown out and Catwoman drove off on her own, calling back, "I said I'd let them take me, but I didn't say how far."

That was Catwoman's last appearance in the initial run of *Batman: The Animated Series*, and while she capped it off in criminal fashion, the series as a whole was light on villainous antics for her. The show's tie-in comic book, *The Batman Adventures*, proved a much better outlet for Catwoman to engage in felonious fun. She stole the British Crown Jewels in the series' second issue, took out Batgirl, Harley Quinn, and Poison Ivy to steal a priceless diamond in another, and in a three-part arc in which Batman had amnesia she convinced him that they were partners in crime and the duo tore through Gotham. But she wasn't all bad; when Batman regained his memory, she kissed him on the cheek and told him, "I can't believe I'm going to hear myself say this, but . . . I wouldn't have it any other way."

After a few years on Fox, Warner Bros. Animation moved Batman to its own network, the WB, as part of its Kids' WB animation block starting in the fall of 1997. The move came with some big stylistic changes, as the renamed *The New Batman Adventures* took a slightly darker angle. All the animation was streamlined, with the characters drawn more simply and slightly more ominously: Batman lost the yellow oval on his chest logo and just sported a black bat, while the Joker moved from bright colors to a grimmer guise and his eyes turned completely black. The Kids' WB censors were far more amenable than those at Fox, who had always sent pages upon pages of notes, and Timm made the most of the lessened restrictions.

The dark turn led to a major shift for Catwoman. Visually, Timm had figured out how to make a black costume work, so now she was black from head to toe. The new animation made Catwoman look almost otherworldly; when in costume, her skin was colored so pale that it had a blue tinge, and she was more angular and thin, all sharp corners instead of soft curves. Her cowl added to her ghostly look by closing in the openings for her eyes, replacing her emotive green eyes with solid white triangles. Selina's look changed as well, as she left her blonde locks behind for a shorter black hairstyle.

Catwoman appeared in two of the twenty-four new episodes, with a more nefarious bent. In the first, she teamed up with Nightwing to stop a smuggling ring after flirting with him shamelessly and trying to convince him she'd gone straight. The team-up was a ruse so that Catwoman could get to a cat's-eye emerald hidden in a shipment of smuggled goods, but it was a ruse from Nightwing's end as well; he had Catwoman lead him to the emerald, and then Batman and Batgirl showed up to take her in. In her second episode, Catwoman tried another double cross, this time successfully. She'd run afoul of a cat-themed cult, and promised Batman that she'd return all of her stolen goods if he helped her out. The duo took down the cult and escaped their lair, but Catwoman ran off in the chaos. The episode ended with Selina in Paris, sharing caviar with Isis. She'd looted the cult before she left, and her apartment was filled with gems and jewelry.

The series' tie-in comic book, *Batman: Gotham Adventures*, fleshed out the origin of this new take on Catwoman.* While in her old gray suit, Catwoman broke into a cosmetics lab that was testing its products on cats, including the hair dye that Selina used. She rescued all the sick cats, and then, enraged, she kidnapped the

---

* DC Comics wasn't very good at having the titles of its tie-in comic books match the titles of its cartoons.

company's owner, Amy Mercedes, and told her, "If one of them dies
. . . you're next!" Mercedes was unrepentant, and Catwoman was
about to scratch her when Batman showed up to tell Catwoman
that she had to let Mercedes go so that she could face prosecution.
Catwoman reluctantly agreed, but when Mercedes slapped away a
cat as she left, Catwoman was furious. She leaped on Mercedes and
scratched her face until Batman stopped her. Catwoman knew that
she'd crossed a line, that "he'd finally seen the real me. The kind of
cruelty I'm capable of." Ashamed but defiant, Catwoman embraced
her darker side and donned her new, black costume.

Batman moved on to *Justice League* in 2001 to team up with
his fellow superheroes in a new series that continued in the same
animated universe but left most of Batman's supporting cast behind.
Catwoman was mentioned once or twice on *Justice League*, as well
as *Batman*'s futuristic spin-off *Batman Beyond*, but she didn't appear
in either series. However, she lived on via the Internet alongside
Harley Quinn and Poison Ivy in a series of animated shorts called
*Gotham Girls*.

The series began in 2000, and lasted for three ten-episode seasons. The first two seasons were comedic, composed of slapstick-
heavy one-shots. Adrienne Barbeau returned as the black-suited Catwoman, and the episodes involved hijinks like a statue that turned
Batgirl into a cat, the gals entering the Miss Criminal Mastermind
competition, and Catwoman hiring Harley Quinn to find her cat in
a noir spoof.* The show had very few male characters; Batgirl was
their primary foe, and men appeared only in passing.

The third season of *Gotham Girls* took this female-centrism even
further. It was a serialized story and the first episode, "Ms.-ing in
Action," ended with the disappearance of all the men in Gotham;
someone had triggered a device that transported away all the city's
biological males. The police blamed the disappearances on Catwoman, Harley Quinn, and Poison Ivy even though they had nothing to do with it, leading Batgirl to team up with the villains to prove
their innocence. The season expanded the scope of the series, bringing

---

* The Flash-animated episodes also included a game that viewers could play while watching
each short.

in established female characters like Officer Renee Montoya, along with new characters like the interim mayor and commissioner.

Catwoman's story line was particularly significant because it involved a transgender character, a rarity anywhere in 2002, much less in children's entertainment. Detective Selma Reesedale was missing along with all the men in Gotham, and the police force believed that Catwoman had kidnapped her. She hadn't, but Catwoman broke into Reesedale's apartment after she was accused of the crime to see what she could learn. After feeding Reesedale's cat, she learned that the officer, while biologically male, lived as a woman. *Gotham Girls* was fairly progressive with its treatment of Reesedale; Catwoman was unfazed by this revelation and continued to refer to her with feminine pronouns.* When Reesedale returned later in the season, she gave Batgirl key evidence that helped her find the culprit behind the disappearances.

After *Gotham Girls*, Catwoman's final appearance in this universe was "Chase Me," a six-minute short that was an extra on the direct-to-DVD release of the animated film *Batman: Mystery of the Batwoman*. Written by Paul Dini and Bruce Timm, the short had no dialogue, only a musical score. It began with a bored Bruce Wayne ducking out of a party only to find Catwoman in her black suit, breaking into his safe. After Catwoman pinned him to the wall by throwing her claws at him and made her escape, Bruce gave chase as Batman. She took him on a mad dash through Gotham, swinging from buildings, jumping on moving cars, and battling on top of a train.

They ended up at the zoo, where Catwoman let out all the big cats to try to slow down Batman. He eventually caught up with her, cornering her against the zoo's fence. She expressed remorse over the cuts that Batman had sustained while fighting his way through the zoo, and the two kissed as the police arrived on scene. Batman made a hasty retreat, but he left Catwoman handcuffed to the fence so that the police could arrest her.† It was a sad end for Catwoman, but one that captured the flirtatiousness yet impossibility at the core

---

* Batgirl did refer to her as "he" a few episodes later, however.
† Some argue that when Bruce returned to the party after the chase, the blonde woman he met was Selina. This is unlikely; she was a brunette at the time, and the blonde woman lacked the green eyes typical of Selina's earlier look.

of her relationship with Batman that had been established over the past decade.

## Animation Duplication

*Batman: The Animated Series* was a behemoth and established a new version of Catwoman for a generation of children. While comic books regularly sold in the tens of thousands, millions of kids watched the various incarnations of the Batman cartoon on Saturday morning and every afternoon for years. Catwoman appeared in only ten televised episodes, but they were rerun so often that Barbeau's version of the character had a massive impact.

Today, the show is considered to be one of the best animated series of all time, and Warner Bros. Animation's subsequent attempts at new Batman cartoons haven't yet been able to match the influence of their iconic predecessor. Nonetheless, their audiences still topped the comics with ease; the lowest-rated and most poorly received new Batman series, *Beware the Batman*, brought in nearly two million viewers every week. The incarnations of Catwoman that populated these series still had a considerable reach.

The first new series was *The Batman*, which premiered on the Kids' WB Saturday morning lineup in September 2004.* The show was designed by Jeff Matsuda, a former comic book artist who'd worked on some X-Men titles and Image series before moving into animation. His designs were broad and cartoony, and very outside the box, especially the villains; many of his characters bore only a passing resemblance to their past incarnations as he took them in new, somewhat crazed directions. Matsuda's Batman was fairly standard, though sleeker than previous versions. This Batman was younger and inexperienced, meeting a lot of his villains for the first time, and so Matsuda's take on the character reflected his youth. All told, *The Batman* ran for five seasons and aired sixty-five episodes.

---

* Some of the early advertising for the show highlighted its theme song, penned by U2's the Edge, but the response to the song was generally ambivalent and it was replaced after a couple of years. The song marked U2's second team-up with Batman; their song "Hold Me, Thrill Me, Kiss Me, Kill Me" was featured on the *Batman Forever* soundtrack and became a moderate hit.

Catwoman appeared in five of those episodes, in a costume that combined elements of the old with several new tweaks. She was clad all in black, but her collar was open wider and raised, the ears of her cowl were large and lined in pink, and she sported yellow goggles shaped like cat eyes. Catwoman was voiced by Gina Gershon, an actress best known for her work in films like *Cocktail*, *Showgirls*, and *Face/Off*. Gershon had always been a big fan of Catwoman and was thrilled to get the role, and said of her take on the character, "I'm not really a villain in this; I'm just kind of mischievous. I'll go off and steal something, but I'm not out to ruin or take over the world. I'm not trying to destroy things."

In Catwoman's first episode, she was after a Japanese jade lion statue. *The Batman* was known for its dynamic action sequences, and her lengthy chase and fight with Batman highlighted the show's strengths. Catwoman won the fight and took his utility belt as a prize, inadvertently wreaking havoc in the Batcave while she explored its circuitry before using the belt's gadgets to steal the statue. A horde of ninjas descended on her immediately after, but Batman showed up to help her out. While Catwoman could have escaped with the statue at one point, Batman was in trouble so she came back to save his life, taking out the final ninja but breaking the statue in the process. She wasn't too upset about it, though; this Catwoman was more into the thrill of the heist than the prize.

Subsequent episodes continued in this thieving vein, including attempted robberies of Egyptian artifacts, animation cels, and leopards.* Catwoman often found herself at odds with both Batman and the criminal community, fighting over stolen goods with villains while trying to avoid arrest. Not that Batman was much of a threat; she outclassed him and always escaped capture. Plus this younger Batman was less straitlaced, and enjoyed the flirtatious Catwoman and their cat-and-mouse games. After a few years, *The Batman* expanded to include members of the Justice League, and small-time criminals like Catwoman fell by the wayside. She was limited to just one brief cameo appearance over the show's final two seasons.

---

* The show's tie-in comic book, *The Batman Strikes!*, followed a similar tack with a variety of heists over Catwoman's several appearances; she even stole Wonder Woman's lasso in one issue.

*The Batman* was followed by *Batman: The Brave and the Bold*, which debuted on the Cartoon Network in 2008. The show aimed to capture a Silver Age sensibility, with classic costumes and over-the-top antics, and the stories were played for humor. The silly fun appealed to younger viewers, while the show was full of sly comic book references for older, knowledgeable fans. Catwoman appeared in a handful of episodes over the program's three seasons, donning the purple-and-green costume she wore back in the early 1950s, and was voiced by Nika Futterman, a veteran voice actor.

Her episodes captured the romantic follies of her 1950s appearances. In one, Catwoman had Batman and Green Arrow caught in a death trap, and Batman told her, "You've let larceny taint your loveliness, Catwoman." Intrigued that he thought she was lovely, the two began to flirt, giving Batman enough time to escape. Catwoman later fled the scene, but left Batman a note with her phone number and "XOXOX, call me." In another episode, Catwoman had Batman and Robin trapped in a jungle hunt, just like her final appearance before her lengthy *Seduction of the Innocent*–imposed hiatus. When Batman escaped her grasp, she fled on her panther and melodramatically lamented, "The most dangerous game, Batman . . . is love."

Catwoman's biggest role came in a team-up with Black Canary and Huntress. Batman had saved her life earlier in the episode after Two-Face interrupted her robbery, so she promised to help Batman stop the villain. Then a blow to the head turned Batman into a criminal as well, and Catwoman worked with Black Canary and the Huntress to fix him. The women posed as lounge singers to infiltrate a club, and sang a song that poked fun at male superheroes: "While all the boys can always save the day, / No one does it better than the Birds of Prey!" In the end, they defeated Two-Face and saved Batman, with Catwoman delivering the decisive blow that brought him back. She then made off with the Egyptian cape she was trying to steal at the start of the episode.

While Catwoman was never a big part of any of these animated series, she was a consistent and iconic element of the Batman mythos and often a fan favorite. The latest Batman cartoon, *Beware the Batman*, quickly failed by consciously avoiding Catwoman and the other familiar trappings of Gotham City. Premiering in 2013 on Cartoon Network, *Beware the Batman* was computer animated with a slick style. While Batman was his usual self in most ways, kindly butler Alfred became a tough brawler, and instead of Batgirl or Robin, Batman teamed up with the martial arts heroine Katana. He faced obscure villains like Professor Pyg and Anarky; classic foes like the Joker, the Penguin, the Riddler, and Catwoman never appeared.* The show went over poorly with critics and fans, and viewership was low. After airing eleven episodes Cartoon Network pulled *Beware the Batman* from its schedule and burned off the remaining episodes a year later.

Batman's been noticeably absent from the cartoon world ever since the unceremonious end of *Beware the Batman*, but Catwoman has a small role in an innovative new venture from DC Entertainment.† *DC Super Hero Girls* reimagines DC's heroes as students at a special high school for superheroes, and their adventures span webisodes, toys, books, and comics, all of them aimed at young female fans. While Catwoman isn't part of the core cast, she's a student at the school and is fittingly friendly with the Cheetah, the classic Wonder Woman villain turned into the school's mean girl. With such an expansive multimedia plan, a closer focus on Catwoman seems inevitable, introducing the character to yet another generation of fans.

---

* The show had something of a Catwoman analogue with Magpie, a kleptomaniac villain with romantic feelings for Batman. She had a black outfit and claws, liked to steal, and was voiced by Grey DeLisle, who also voiced Catwoman in the *Batman: Arkham* series of video games.

† Batman recently returned alongside Superman and Wonder Woman in the new *Justice League Action* cartoon, but Catwoman has yet to appear on the show.

# 8

# *Glaring Fixations*

*A*fter *Batman Returns* hit theaters, DC Comics moved to capitalize on the film's breakout star. The editors of the Batman line
decided to test the waters for a Catwoman series with a feature in
an anthology book, *Showcase '93*. The four-part "Sorrow Street,"
written by Doug Moench with art by Ed Hannigan, debuted in
January 1993, and the arc marked a new direction for Catwoman.
It was an action-packed adventure; after a new gang took over her
neighborhood and stole a painting that she was after, Catwoman
investigated and then defeated the group to regain control of her
turf. She was the center of the story, and Batman didn't appear at
all. At times Catwoman worked with the police to stop the gang,
but she also let the gang leader leave Gotham in exchange for the
aforementioned painting. Her allegiances varied, and ultimately the
book presented Catwoman as a morally ambiguous thief who pursued her own interests above all else.

This take on Catwoman didn't have a specific antecedent, lacking
the exploitative grit of Frank Miller's "Year One" or the empowered sensuality of Michelle Pfeiffer in *Batman Returns*. When DC
launched a solo *Catwoman* series a few months later in August 1993,
it continued in this vein. Originally written by Jo Duffy with art by
Jim Balent, the new series specifically went out of its way to distance

itself from "Year One." Balent left behind David Mazzucchelli's gritty artwork and drab gray palette for a flamboyantly curvaceous take on Catwoman with a bright purple costume. He also replaced her buzz cut with long, flowing locks. Duffy traded Miller's grim realism for over-the-top heists and action, and removed all of the trappings of her past life. In their first issue, Selina revealed that she spent "a fortune on a custom virus to wipe my real name from every press and law enforcement computer in the country," a sly hint that Duffy was moving on from past versions of the character.

"Year One" remained part of Catwoman's continuity, but it was downplayed and soon altered. *Catwoman* #0 in October 1994 told the story of how young Selina Kyle grew up to become Catwoman, and her dominatrix period took up only a third of one page. Moreover, the issue implied that she used prostitution as a ruse for robbing clients. In 1995 all of the Bat-books had "Year One" as the theme for their annuals, but *Catwoman*'s annual showed Selina using the information she gathered from her politician and businessmen clients to pull off big heists.* It also focused more on a new martial arts subplot in which Selina became involved with a mysterious group of ninjas.

The series was a new direction for the character, a clean break from her past incarnations that put Catwoman at the forefront of her own stories. It also firmly established her within DC's new universe; Catwoman headlined a series at the publisher for the next two decades. The only constant in the book was Catwoman. The book zeroed in on Selina and her own adventures, often taking her around the world for various heists involving an ever-changing cast of characters. *Catwoman* seemed to go out of its way to avoid Batman in favor of showcasing its feline star, even when the comic tied into the other Bat-books for special event crossovers.†

---

* Annuals are special oversized issues that typically present a self-contained story outside the main series' current plotlines. DC's annuals are sporadic at best, but for a few years in the mid-1990s the publisher was very committed to them, with a different theme each year.

† These events were all Superman's fault. After the "Death of Superman" crossover in 1992 became a global sensation, DC tried to replicate this success with a variety of "shocking" character-based events.

The first arc of *Catwoman* embodied this separation. In 1993 the Bat-books were in the middle of the "Knightfall" event, in which the steroid-fueled supervillain Bane defeated Batman by snapping his spine. *Catwoman* #1 debuted after Bane had taken control of Gotham's criminal underworld; he didn't trust the wily and defiant Catwoman, so he sent an assassin after her. The issue ended with the assassin shooting a rocket launcher into Selina's apartment. Selina survived, and over the next three issues she tracked the assassin to the Caribbean island Santa Prisca, saved the island's leader from assassination and a coup, and discovered that Bane was behind the assassin's hit on her before returning to Gotham to take revenge on Bane.

Catwoman was connected to the "Knightfall" event but also separate from it, literally so. It was a fun adventure without lasting effect. None of the story line was mentioned again, and Catwoman was the only character that carried over to the next story. *Catwoman* was light fun but erratic, an assortment of short arcs focused on thieving hijinks rather than prolonged character building.

There was also a deep contradiction at the core of *Catwoman*, centered on the book's creative teams. The story and the art were often at odds; the text presented strikingly feminist tales of Catwoman outsmarting and defeating her foes, but she was drawn in a glaringly hypersexualized manner. The end result was a mixed bag of bold heroism and blatant objectification, and this era remains a divisive period for fans of Catwoman even today.

## The Women Behind Catwoman

DC was remarkably progressive with the writers of *Catwoman*, employing several women to helm the series over its eight-year run. Mindy Newell had written minis for Catwoman in the late 1980s, but a woman writing an ongoing series was rare. When *Catwoman* #1 debuted, only two of DC's more than forty ongoing series were written by women, *Catwoman* included. Moreover, a book having more than one female writer in the 1990s was especially uncommon. Newell cowrote *Wonder Woman* from 1989 to 1990 and after she left, the book didn't have another woman regularly writing it until 2008. In the Superman line, Louise Simonson wrote *Superman: The Man of Steel* beginning in 1991, and after her tenure was done a Super-book didn't have a regular female writer again until 2005.*

*Catwoman* had five different female writers throughout its 1990s run, and the first was Jo Duffy. She was a veteran of Marvel who'd penned titles like *Power Man and Iron Fist*, Marvel's ongoing *Star Wars* book, and *Wolverine*. *Catwoman* was one of her first gigs at DC, and transitioning a secondary character into a solo star was a tough order. In the comic's letter column, many readers admitted to some initial trepidation about Catwoman headlining her own book, but the response was enthusiastic. Several fans drew a connection to another famed thief: Jeffrey DesRosiers noted, "It's Robin Hood with a selfish twist—rob from the rich, give to herself." The book brought in many female fans as well; Andrea wrote in, "Thank you for giving a female comic-book reader like myself someone to look up to. In this consistently male-dominated field I now actually have a comics hero. She's tough and feminine." The only pushback came from fans of Miller's tougher take on Catwoman, like a letter from Richard D. Stewart that concluded, "We don't need another bimbo."

Duffy didn't write Catwoman as a bimbo at all. In her next adventure after the assassination plot, she helped an environmental group steal a chemical that was being used by land developers to kill animals in the rain forest. When two members of the group took some of the chemical to murder the developers, Catwoman went after them. With Batman and the police on her tail for the initial robbery, she prevented the death of the developers but also ensured that they were taught a valuable lesson. She was similarly impressive in her next outing, breaking into a medical facility, battling armed guards, escaping the police, and ultimately kidnapping a corrupt businessman in order to steal a medical device to help her paralyzed friend walk again. Duffy's Catwoman could outfight or outsmart anyone who got her in way, and her fierce, clever take on

---

* The woman who ended both droughts, on *Wonder Woman* in 2008 and *Action Comics* in 2005, was Gail Simone.

the character cemented Catwoman's portrayal long after Duffy left the book fourteen issues in.

The next female writer to take over *Catwoman* was Deborah Pomerantz, who penned a three-issue arc beginning in July 1995. The story embodied the tone of the series; it was action-packed, self-contained, and showcased Catwoman's unusual moral code. It all began with Catwoman stealing a dagger owned by the Marquez cartel. She had no issues with the cartel and admitted a simple rationale for the theft, "I just want it because it's **pretty**. And because it's worth a **fortune**." But the cartel was upset with Catwoman and haunted her for the next six months, and when they started a war with a rival cartel, she decided to get involved. The arc was violent; each issue had at least one scene in which Catwoman defeated a gang of gunmen. She was given the chance to walk away from the war, but she stayed. While not a murderer herself, she wouldn't let their mistreatment of her go unanswered, and she manipulated the major players and exposed truths until they'd all each killed each other. The major lesson of most *Catwoman* arcs was "Don't mess with Catwoman"; she had a knack for revenge.

Pomerantz was followed by Joan Weis, who wrote *Catwoman Annual* #3 in June 1996. Weis was a writer and editor at NOW Comics, a publisher that specialized in licensed television adaptations, and the annual was one of her few comics writing gigs elsewhere. The theme for DC's 1996 annuals was "Legends of the Dead Earth," and creators were encouraged to tell stories set in alternate realities. Weis put Catwoman in a world where she and Batman were the villains of Gotham City, a criminal married couple pursued by the Joker, a cop bleached white after Catwoman kicked him into a vat of chemicals. The Joker finally cornered the couple with the help of their son, Dick, who was shocked to discover that his parents were murderous thieves. In the end, Dick shot his mother dead to prevent her from killing the Joker.

The book was a rare romantic outing for Catwoman and Batman in this era. The two were kept apart for most of the 1990s, and when confused readers used to their Bronze Age dalliances wrote into the letter column, the editor explained, "All those stories in which Batman and Catwoman were romantically involved, however much we may be fond of them, are not part of the 'official' Batman canon." In this new universe, the only place to find them together was in alternate-universe stories like Pomerantz's, collectively known as DC's Elseworlds line. The Catwoman-Batman connection was such a staple of earlier eras that creators brought it back any time they could get away from the mainline continuity; their romance included outings in which they were pirate lovers, paramours in a medieval fantasy, and monstrous cat and bat beasts.*

Devin Grayson became *Catwoman*'s next regular female writer when she took over the series with *Catwoman* #54 in February 1998. The book was one of Grayson's earliest writing gigs, and she went on to pen many DC series; she was also the first woman to be a regular writer on a Batman series when she launched *Batman: Gotham Knights* in 2000. Her first *Catwoman* issue brought some comedy to the series when Catwoman stole a massive diamond and was unimpressed with the museum's security system. So she returned it, forcing the museum to better protect it, and continued to steal the diamond and return it repeatedly until the security system was upgraded to her satisfaction. When the museum tried to play her by purchasing an expensive insurance plan on the diamond to cash in when she finally stole it for good, she decided to leave it there, telling the curator, "As long as I know you're suffering miserably for its upkeep, I think I'll keep my diamond **here**."

Gotham was rocked by an earthquake in the "Cataclysm" crossover event, and after the dust settled Grayson moved Catwoman to Manhattan and gave her alter ego something to do for a change. Selina Kyle blackmailed her way into becoming the vice president of a large industrial firm and was later named CEO. But that wasn't enough, and soon she was running for mayor of New York City. After the Trickster revealed her secret criminal identity, she faked her own death, sacrificing Selina to protect Catwoman. Her manufactured identity was far more important to her than her given name.

---

* Oddly enough, Batman remained Catwoman's main beau in this era, because all of these Elseworlds tales far outnumbered her fleeting romances in her regular series, with its constant cast turnover.

*Catwoman*'s final female writer, Bronwyn Carlton, added some depth to this given name when she took over the series in 2000. Carlton was an editor at DC with a handful of writing credits, and her time on *Catwoman* focused on the character's acrimonious relationship with Commissioner Gordon. But one of her issues added an interesting wrinkle to Selina's personal history. Selina's parents had been mentioned regularly throughout the series as part of her tragic backstory; when Selina was a girl, her mother committed suicide and her father then drank himself to death. Carlton added a new detail in a flashback in *Catwoman* #81 when she revealed that Maria, Selina's mother, was Latina.

The issue didn't get into the specifics of her heritage, but the small details made her Latina roots clear, if somewhat stereotypically. Maria was colored darker than her husband, referred to him as "papi," and cooked rice and beans; her husband also referred to her family as "refugees," and he told her to "speak English." This revelation made Selina half-Latina, continuing a tradition of recasting Catwoman as a woman of color. Eartha Kitt played Catwoman in *Batman* in the 1960s, and Frank Miller was ambiguous about Selina's ethnicity in his scripts for "Year One," calling her "exotic." When Miller was later hired to write a "Year One" screenplay that was never produced, he described Selina as a "long, lean black woman." Carlton's change was fitting for the character, and was an important counter to the startlingly white world of superhero comics.

Men wrote *Catwoman* in the 1990s as well. Chuck Dixon had a lengthy run after Duffy left the book; he sent Selina around the world after she was blackmailed into becoming a thief for a shady government agency, and also brought her back to Gotham for the "Contagion" event. Doug Moench took over after that and penned arcs in which Catwoman battled Cyber-Cat, a villain with feline-themed cybernetic armor; Catwoman later tangled with the criminal organization S.P.I.D.E.R. and stopped a serial killer. John Ostrander also had a brief run on the book in a crossover with the "No Man's Land" event, and several other male writers wrote an issue or two.

All told, the writing duties on *Catwoman* were split fairly evenly between women and men, with women writing forty-nine of the book's one hundred issues, including annuals and special issues. It was a remarkable split for the time, and remains so even by today's standards; women wrote only 15 percent of DC's books in 2016. When it comes to writing, *Catwoman* was impressively progressive. However, the writing was only half of the comic book.

## The Art of Jim Balent

*Catwoman* was drawn entirely by men, and one man in particular. Jim Balent drew the book for more than six years straight, a run that added up to over eighty issues, including the regular series and several specials.* Such a lengthy, uninterrupted tenure was a huge accomplishment, and was even more noteworthy because *Catwoman* was Balent's first regular comics gig. He'd done a variety of short stories for DC and smaller publishers over the years, but nothing with a steady monthly schedule until he launched *Catwoman* with Jo Duffy. Balent embraced the gig wholeheartedly and went the extra mile with fun details like hiding a cat on the cover of every issue.

Balent's artwork gave Catwoman her signature look for the decade, and it was a style somewhat at odds with the rest of the book. While the writing on *Catwoman* presented a clever, skilled, and complicated character, the art aimed for sexiness above all else. Balent gave Catwoman near-impossible proportions with lengthy limbs, a more than ample chest and rear, and a tiny waist. Her curvaceous figure was emphasized by a skintight costume that left little to the imagination, as if Balent drew her nude and had her colored purple. In fact, assistant editors often had to go through the line art and highlight all the nipples he'd drawn so that the production department could erase them before publication.

Sexy was Balent's forte. He laid out his comics in a manner that ensured Catwoman's assets were prominently featured, no matter

---

* Balent was the penciller on *Catwoman*, and his work was inked by seventeen different inkers during his tenure, starting with the legendary Dick Giordano for the book's first seven issues. Bob Smith was his most frequent collaborator; the duo worked together for twenty-five issues.

**TOP RIGHT:** *Batman* #1, cover by Bob Kane, DC Comics, 1940
The first appearance of Catwoman, originally known as the Cat. She tried to steal an emerald necklace and then successfully escaped from a lovestruck Batman.

**BOTTOM: Bob Kane and Catwoman model, ca. 1965**
For decades, artist Bob Kane received sole credit for creating Catwoman and writer Bill Finger went unrecognized. Kane was a fraud who rarely drew his own work; this piece is undoubtedly not his. IMAGE COURTESY OF PHOTOFEST (PHOTOFESTNYC.COM)

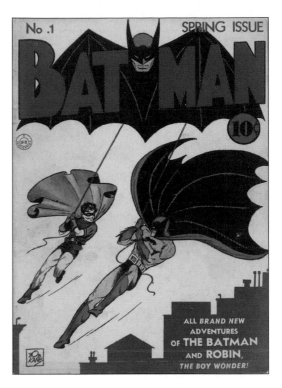

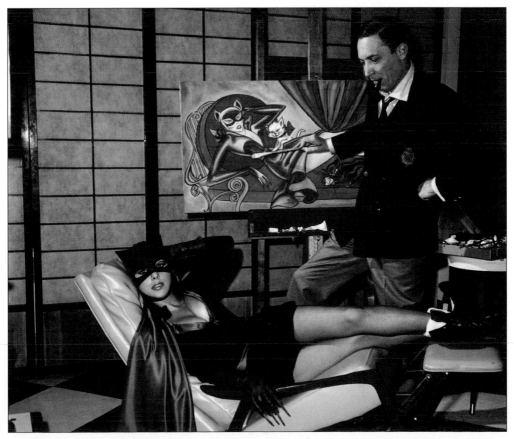

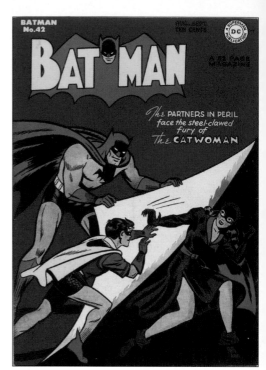

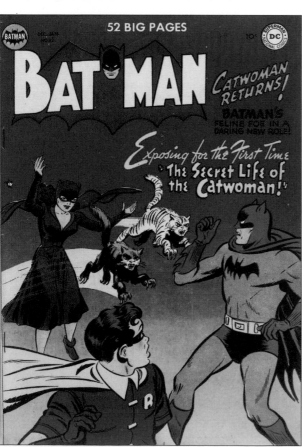

**TOP LEFT:** *Detective Comics* #122, cover by "Bob Kane" and Charles Paris, DC Comics, 1947

After starting the decade with a string of small robberies, Catwoman became a full-fledged supervillain in the late 1940s.

**TOP RIGHT:** *Batman* #42, cover by Jack Burnley and Charles Paris, DC Comics, 1947

Catwoman was a villain with panache, and she vexed the Dynamic Duo in this issue with a series of literary-inspired, feline-based crimes.

**BOTTOM LEFT:** *Batman* #62, cover by Win Mortimer, DC Comics, 1950

"The Secret Life of the Catwoman" revealed that she was actually an airline stewardess named Selina Kyle who became a criminal after a plane crash gave her amnesia.

**TOP LEFT:** *Batman* #65, cover by Win Mortimer, Lew Schwartz, and Charles Paris, DC Comics, 1951 Catwoman went straight after her memory was restored, but Batman and Robin remained suspicious of her nonetheless.

**TOP RIGHT:** *Detective Comics* #211, cover by Win Mortimer, DC Comics, 1954 Sick of the constant distrust, Selina Kyle returned to a life of crime with a vengeance. Catwoman then mysteriously disappeared for the next twelve years.

**BOTTOM RIGHT:** *Detective Comics* #318, cover by Dick Dillin and Sheldon Moldoff, DC Comics, 1963 Batwoman occasionally posed as a new Cat-Woman to trick the nefarious Cat-Man. The comics barely mentioned that there had been a different Catwoman previously.

**TOP LEFT: Publicity photo of Julie Newmar as Catwoman in *Batman*, ABC, 1966**
A former dancer and Tony Award winner, Newmar brought a feline physicality to Catwoman, beguiling Adam West's Batman for the show's first two seasons.

**TOP RIGHT: Publicity photo of Eartha Kitt as Catwoman in *Batman*, ABC, 1967**
Kitt took over the role for a handful of episodes in the third and final season, and was a purr-fectly fierce and fiendish Catwoman.

**BOTTOM LEFT: Publicity photo of Lee Meriwether as Catwoman in *Batman: The Movie*, 20th Century Fox, 1966**
Meriwether filled in for an absent Newmar in the *Batman* film produced between the show's first and second seasons, doing double duty as Catwoman and her Russian alias, Miss Kitka.

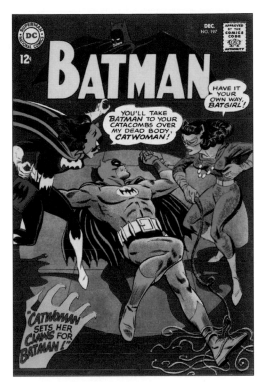

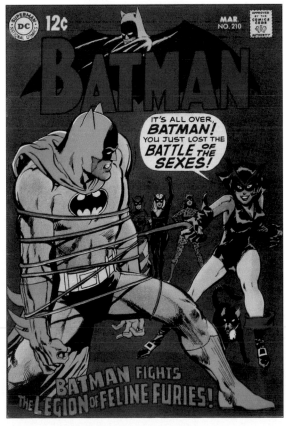

**TOP LEFT:** *Superman's Girl Friend Lois Lane* #70, cover by Kurt Schaffenberger, DC Comics, 1966
The success of the *Batman* television show led to Catwoman's comic book return. In her first issue back she faced off against Lois Lane instead of the Dynamic Duo.

**TOP RIGHT:** *Batman* #197, cover by Carmine Infantino and Mike Esposito, DC Comics, 1967
Catwoman returned to Gotham a year later in a new green costume, battling Batgirl for Batman's affection (even though Batgirl wasn't interested).

**BOTTOM RIGHT:** *Batman* #210, cover by Neal Adams, DC Comics, March 1969
Sporting another new outfit, Catwoman used the rhetoric of women's lib to recruit a team of "feline furies" to defeat Batman.

**Advertisement for Catwoman backup feature in *Batman* #345, artist unknown, DC Comics, 1982** | Catwoman appeared intermittently through the 1970s, then became a semiregular character in the early 1980s in romantic subplots. She even starred in her own backup feature for a few months.

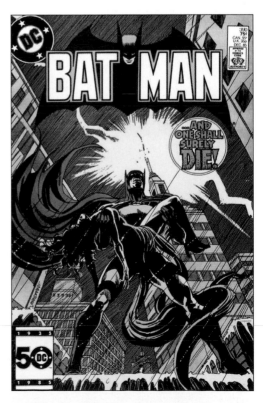

**TOP LEFT:** *Batman* #323, cover by Dick Giordano, DC Comics, 1980
Selina Kyle dated Bruce Wayne briefly, but the relationship turned sour when he suspected she'd committed a robbery in her Catwoman guise.

**TOP RIGHT:** *Batman* #355, cover by Ed Hannigan and Dick Giordano, DC Comics, 1983
Catwoman turned stalker when Bruce began dating Vicki Vale, making threatening phone calls and running the couple off the road.

**BOTTOM RIGHT:** *Batman* #390, cover by Tom Mandrake, DC Comics, 1985
This tease of the death of Catwoman was a frightening possibility given the major deaths occurring at the time in DC's *Crisis on Infinite Earths* event.

**TOP LEFT:** *Detective Comics* #570, cover by Alan Davis and Paul Neary, DC Comics, 1987
In Catwoman's final appearance before DC's line-wide reboot, the Joker returned a formerly reformed Catwoman to a life of crime.

**BOTTOM LEFT:** *Catwoman* #1, cover by J. J. Birch and Michael Bair, DC Comics, 1989
This first solo feature for Catwoman in DC's new continuity expanded on Frank Miller's recent "Year One" origin in which Selina was a dominatrix and prostitute turned cat burglar.

**BOTTOM RIGHT:** *Batman* #460, cover by Norm Breyfogle, DC Comics, 1991
Catwoman's new, dark origin led to her being shelved for several years. This issue was one of her rare appearances in this period.

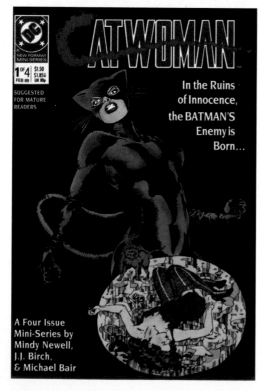

**TOP RIGHT: Michelle Pfeiffer as Selina Kyle in *Batman Returns*, Warner Bros., 1992**

Pfeiffer's Selina Kyle was a quiet secretary with a dull life in director Tim Burton's *Batman Returns* began. IMAGE COURTESY OF PHOTOFEST (PHOTOFESTNYC.COM)

**BOTTOM: Michelle Pfeiffer as Catwoman in *Batman Returns*, Warner Bros., 1992**

After her boss "killed" her, Selina became the sleek and powerful Catwoman and set out on a quest for revenge. IMAGE COURTESY OF PHOTOFEST (PHOTOFESTNYC.COM)

**TOP: Animation cel of Catwoman (and Isis) in "The Cat and the Claw, Part 1,"** *Batman: The Animated Series*, **Warner Bros., 1992**
Due to the popularity of Michelle Pfeiffer's Catwoman, the character became a major player in the new Batman cartoon. She was voiced by Adrienne Barbeau. IMAGE COURTESY OF JOHN D. ILES

**BOTTOM LEFT:** *Gotham Girls* **#1, cover by Shane Glines, DC Comics, 2002**
A recostumed Catwoman and several other female characters spun off into the *Gotham Girls* webseries and comics.

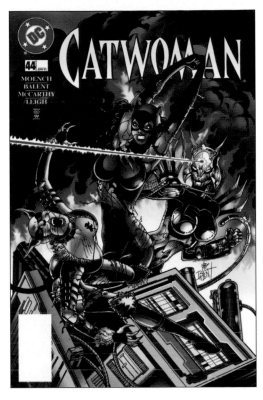

**TOP LEFT:** *Catwoman* #1, cover by
Jim Balent, DC Comics, 1993
Pfeiffer's popularity garnered Catwoman
a new comic book series as well. Balent's
exaggerated and sexualized art was a constant throughout the bulk of the book's run.

**TOP RIGHT:** *Catwoman* #44, cover by
Jim Balent, DC Comics, 1997
Catwoman's costars were often similarly
curvaceous women in tight outfits, including
these feline foes, She-Cat and Cyber-Cat.

**BOTTOM RIGHT:** *Batman: Dark Victory* #5,
cover by Tim Sale, DC Comics, 2000
Around the same time, Jeph Loeb and Tim
Sale presented a more elegant Catwoman
and moved away from her "Year One" origins.

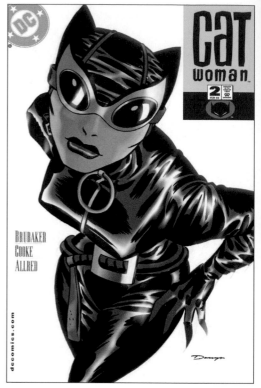

**TOP LEFT:** *Catwoman* #1, cover by Darwyn Cooke, DC Comics, 2002
Catwoman's series relaunched in 2002 with a new look, a black jumpsuit instead of a skintight costume and practical boots instead of heels.

**TOP RIGHT:** *Catwoman* #2, cover by Darwyn Cooke, DC Comics, 2002
Artist Darwyn Cooke completed the ensemble with a cat-eared cowl and cat-eyed goggles. The outfit has been her regular look ever since.

**BOTTOM LEFT:** *Catwoman* #73, cover by Adam Hughes, DC Comics, 2008
After an arc in which Selina was replaced as Catwoman by her friend Holly, had a baby, and gave up the baby to keep her safe, she returned to the prowl.

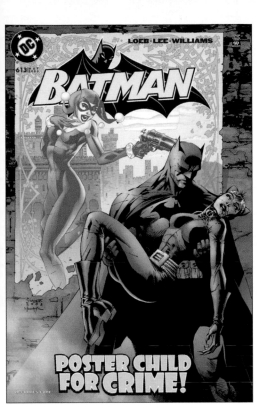

**TOP LEFT:** *Batman* #613, cover by
Jim Lee and Scott Williams, DC Comics,
2003
Outside of her own series, Catwoman
romanced Batman and learned his secret
identity in "Hush" but was ultimately
spurned because of Batman's mistrust.

**TOP RIGHT:** *Detective Comics* #850,
cover by Dustin Nguyen, DC Comics,
2009
The return of Hush didn't go so well for
Catwoman either; she had her heart
removed by the villain and was sidelined
for the bulk of the story.

**BOTTOM RIGHT:** *Gotham City Sirens*
#1, variant cover by J. G. Jones, DC
Comics, 2009
After her solo series ended, Catwoman
teamed up with her villainous pals Harley
Quinn and Poison Ivy for a new book.

**Poster image, Halle Berry in *Catwoman*, Warner Bros., 2004**
Many attempts at making a spin-off film for Michelle Pfeiffer's Catwoman ultimately led to Halle Berry playing a completely different character a decade later in this widely panned box office disaster.

**Anne Hathaway as Catwoman, *The Dark Knight Rises*, Warner Bros., 2012**
Catwoman returned to big screen when Hathaway played Selina Kyle in the final installment of director Christopher Nolan's Dark Knight trilogy. IMAGE COURTESY OF PHOTOFEST (PHOTOFESTNYC.COM)

**Leaked image of Catwoman from the *Batman: Arkham City* video game, Warner Bros. Interactive, 2011** | Catwoman had a lot of skin on display when she debuted in the popular *Arkham* video game franchise, and her appearances were laden with sexist, derogatory language.

**Publicity photo of Camren Bicondova as Selina Kyle, *Gotham,* Fox, 2014**
Bicondova plays a clever street urchin Selina who befriends a young Bruce Wayne in *Gotham*, a television series prequel to the Batman universe.

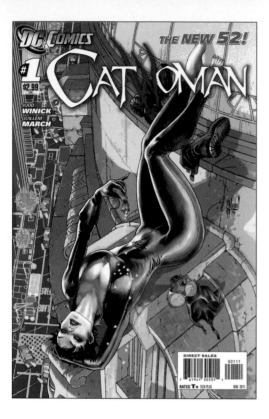

**TOP LEFT:** *Catwoman* #1, cover by Guillem March, DC Comics, 2011
DC rebooted their entire line again in 2011, and early interviews regarding the new *Catwoman* series promised sexiness above all else.

**TOP RIGHT:** *Catwoman* #0, cover by Guillem March, DC Comics, 2012
The "sexiness" continued a year later in ludicrous fashion, contorting Catwoman in an attempt to showcase all of her curves simultaneously. The cover was roundly mocked and eventually replaced.

**BOTTOM LEFT:** *Catwoman* #35, cover by Jae Lee, DC Comics, 2014
Selina Kyle left Catwoman behind to take over as head of a Gotham mob family in this bold new direction for the series.

the situation. Her breasts in particular were regularly front and center, seemingly not at all subject to gravity as they sat on her chest like weightless balloons no matter how Catwoman was positioned, even when hanging upside down. Balent also worked in a lot of skin, despite her being covered head to toe. Catwoman's costume often ended up torn and tattered because of fights and explosions, thus exposing her flesh underneath. With Selina Kyle, Balent rarely covered much of anything. At home, Selina wore skimpy lingerie and small, tight clothes, and she spent an inordinate amount of time in the shower. While undercover, her guises involved tiny maid outfits and leopard-print bikinis. Even in professional environments, Selina aimed for sexiness above all else; when she became a CEO in Manhattan, her blazer was cut almost to her navel and her skirt barely covered her behind.

Catwoman wasn't the only sexy character in the book. Almost every woman she encountered was similarly depicted. This led to scenes like a brawl in a castle in the Alps in which Selina, dressed in only a wet T-shirt, fought in a bathtub with two buxom gals in tight lederhosen. In another arc, the cybernetic armor of Cyber-Cat was as formfitting as Catwoman's own costume, and the story introduced another busty feline character named She-Cat, who wore a low-cut costume with fishnet patches on her rear. Balent continued this style in special issues as well. In one, Catwoman teamed up with Vampirella, a character whose costume consisted of two narrow strips of fabric that ran across her chest and merged into a tiny bikini bottom. In another, Catwoman was the hero of Gotham City in a gender-swapped Elseworlds tale in which she played the Batman role: a leather corset emphasized Catwoman's chest, a female Two-Face wore a bra that was white lace on one side and black leather studded with metal spikes on the other, and the book's Alfred was the vivacious Brooks, whose maid outfit was so short that her underwear was regularly visible.

In short, Balent's art was over the top. However, he wasn't an outlier. In the early 1990s, this style of art became popular in superhero comics, with artists enhancing the figures of their characters in a sort of hyperexaggerated realism. Men became muscled behemoths while women became curvaceous yet wasp waisted.* No one was immune, not even Wonder Woman; in 1994, Mike Deodato Jr. took over the art duties on her series and turned the Amazon's feminist utopia into a land of barely clad supermodels. The art in superhero books became so brazenly sexy that there were rumors that some artists, Balent included, were tracing pornography and simply adding a mask and a skimpy costume. As one of the most prolific artists of this era, Balent has become a poster boy for its excesses.

This style of art catered to a certain audience, primarily male. Balent was beloved by many *Catwoman* readers and constantly praised in the book's letter columns. Jay McIntyre declared, "Jim Balent is one of the best artists in DC's stable," and Dale Mayer wrote, "The art is worth looking at over and over. Seems that every new thing Jim Balent does tops all of his past work." Jeffrey Bridge was even more effusive: "Jim Balent is, in my opinion, talent on loan from the supreme one who rules the universe!"

A closer look at *Catwoman*'s letter column offers an indication of who was actually reading the book. The chart below shows the percentage of letters written by men over the course of Balent's tenure,

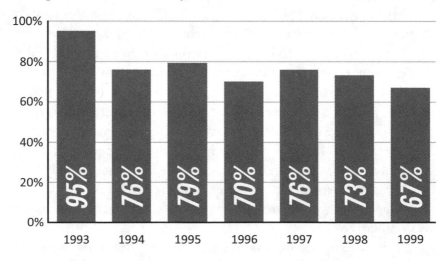

---

* This trend was so pronounced that it prompted some creators to head sharply in the other direction; *Sandman* writer Neil Gaiman later revealed that his work at the time was influenced by a desire "to write comics that women would read and that didn't have characters that looked like they had two watermelons strapped to their chest."

and they constituted a clear majority.* The male audience was somewhat low relative to the rest of the Batman line; men accounted for an average of 88 percent of the letters in *Batman*'s letter column in the same span, compared to 74 percent in *Catwoman*. A series with a female lead may have brought in more female readers, but the editors of *Catwoman* also appeared to be actively trying to include women in the column. Early in the book's run, a woman wrote in and noted that a previous letter column hadn't included any letters written by women, to which assistant editor Jordan B. Gorfinkel replied, "I would print letters from women if only they would write in!" A few issues later, Gorfinkel ran a column of letters written solely by women, and from then on the vast majority of columns featured at least one letter from a female reader. Nonetheless, men remained a strong majority despite this focus and the book's female lead, and their effusive letters suggested that Balent's art was the biggest draw.

The few detractors who made the *Catwoman* letter column followed a similar pattern that captured the book's major contradiction: they enjoyed the writing, and the art to a certain extent, but were put off by the sensationalized depiction of Catwoman. Shelby C. Pankratz wrote in, "This new series is off to a fine start," and complimented both the writing and the art, but she added, "My one complaint is that Catwoman's chest looks completely out of proportion. For a person who relies on balance and agility like she does, you'd think those huge protrusions would interfere tremendously." In another letter, Andrea enthused, "You're proving that a female super-hero can make a great and non-boring comic," but bluntly inquired, "I have to ask—why is Catwoman so busty?"

In response to Andrea's question, assistant editor Jordan B. Gorfinkel printed a letter from Mark Lucas, who had written in to defend Balent's art. Lucas acknowledged that "while Selina Kyle has been a part of comics for fifty years, the current depiction of her is the most endowed of the lot," but argued in favor of her sexy portrayal. He contended, "Jim has a certain flair for flowing lines and rounded curves," and explained:

---

* It should be noted that the lowest showing, 67 percent in 1999, was an odd year. The letter column disappeared from the book for several months, then returned to a lower page count. There were only nine letters printed in four issues in 1999.

As comics is a visual medium, artists need to present images graphically and utilize exaggeration of familiar images to achieve mass appeal. By their very nature, then, comics have the potential to use sexist-appearing figures. And they do! Comics use sex to sell their books like any other outlet in our culture. Shirtless men with abnormal biceps are standard fare.

Lucas's argument that both male and female comic book characters were idealized and exaggerated was a common one, and today continues to be a go-to response against those who criticize the sexualized depiction of female characters. It is, however, a false equivalency. While it is true that both men and women are drawn unrealistically in superhero comics, this is done for different reasons. In the 1990s in particular, superhero comics were a genre drawn, edited, and read primarily by men. Male heroes were drawn with exaggerated muscles in a reinforcement of male strength, as a sort of wish fulfillment for the male creators and readers. Meanwhile, female heroes were given exaggerated curves that objectified them and emphasized their sexual appeal. Basically, men were drawn to be strong and women were drawn to be hot, and those are not equal idealizations.

A few issues later, another letter explained a problem at the core of Balent's hypersexualized Catwoman. Laura McLellan was a fan of the writing in *Catwoman* but wrote:

> I know you're sick of hearing this, but please reconsider your stand on how Selina's body is drawn. Girls are surrounded by unrealistic images of women every day, and by filling comic books with women whose bodies are consistently out of proportion, you are simply encouraging more women to have poor self-images and unrealistic ideas about how they should look.

This portion of her letter didn't receive any editorial response.

By 2000 the art in superhero comics was beginning to change, especially in the Batman line. The homogeneity of the 1990s was replaced by an array of different styles with influences ranging from realism to cartoons to manga, and a new generation of artists began

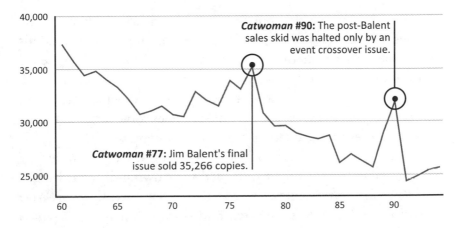

to take over the industry. Six years after he helped launch *Catwoman*, Balent was let go from the book; his last issue was *Catwoman #77* in February 2000. Balent was replaced with Staz Johnson and Wayne Faucher, who drew most of the rest of the series.

The change went over poorly with *Catwoman* readers. Despite creative shifts elsewhere in the industry, Balent had developed a significant fan base, and sales dropped noticeably when he left the series. The chart above shows the sales for *Catwoman* before and after Balent's departure. While Balent's last few issues benefited from a sales bump due to a crossover with the "No Man's Land" event, Balent's finale was the bestselling issue in well over a year. Even before "No Man's Land" began, sales on *Catwoman* had evened out at just over thirty thousand copies a month. The book wasn't a bestseller, but it had steadied at a decent level. *Catwoman*'s sales dropped to less than thirty thousand copies a month just two issues after Balent's departure, and only broke the thirty thousand barrier once more after that owing to a tie-in with yet another event, "Officer Down." By the end of the series' run, *Catwoman* had fallen to the twenty-five thousand range and was canceled and then relaunched soon after.

## Tarot: Witch of the Black Rose

By all accounts, Jim Balent is one of the nicest people in the comics business, and he genuinely disagrees when critics call his art sexist. Many artists handle such critiques poorly, blustering about free speech or hurling insults, but Balent is more serene. He earnestly believes that his art is an empowering celebration of women, and his next project after *Catwoman* explored this in detail. His new series doubled down on the sexuality that permeated his *Catwoman* run while simultaneously presenting a vocal message about female power and body acceptance. This later work provides some insight into the artistic choices that defined an era of Catwoman.

Soon after he left *Catwoman*, Balent and his wife, known by her pen name Holly Golightly, formed their own independent publisher, BroadSword Comics. The company's flagship title was *Tarot: Witch of the Black Rose*, written and drawn by Balent, in which "the young voluptuous warrior witch, Tarot battles for harmony against the forces of prejudice and darkness." The book premiered in March 2000 and has shipped bimonthly ever since for over one hundred issues.

The series had a lot in common with *Catwoman*. Balent didn't change his approach to the artwork, and later said of his transition to the new series, "The style of *Catwoman* sort of, especially in those early issues, you know, translated over to *Tarot*." The book also had a buxom female protagonist, and while she didn't have any feline features, the supporting cast did. Tarot had a friend named Boo Cat who was a brunette werecat, and the 3 Little Kittens, a team of action heroines in cat-themed costumes, were occasional guest stars.

While the book was far more blatant about presenting the characters in a sexual manner than *Catwoman* ever was, there was a line initially. Tarot's costume was considerably skimpier than Catwoman's, but while Tarot often found herself in an even further state of undress, the book avoided full frontal nudity by strategically covering just enough of her. Tarot's sister, Raven Hex, wore little more than a thong and a pair of metal spikes that covered her nipples, but her private areas were nonetheless concealed.* This line soon disappeared. Within a couple of years the women in *Tarot* were naked, in full detail, for nearly all of every issue. The book became a sex

---

* In the series' third issue, Raven Hex used the spikes to gouge out the eyes of a man who was ogling her, declaring, "If **all** you could see of me are my **breasts**, then you don't even **deserve** to see those!!!" It was a bizarre scene, to be sure, but not even in the ballpark of the weirdest things that happened in *Tarot*.

romp, with the characters constantly engaged in liaisons of a variety of configurations. Tarot's battles against the forces of darkness were little more than a pretense for her to lose her clothes due to an errant sword cut or a magical spell.

Left to his own devices without the constraints of a corporate owned publisher, Balent created a series that made his *Catwoman* run look chastely reserved in comparison. A review on the website *Comics Alliance* called *Tarot* "a book that's little more than a supernatural porn," but Balent believes that there's more to the series than that and explains, "I envision the books to first 'entertain' and then, second, to 'educate'. The theme of 'acceptance' and 'understanding' comes up a lot in the stories. Accepting people for who they are is very important." This partly refers to the book's Wiccan themes; Golightly is a self-described witch, and she and Balent pride themselves on accurately presenting Wiccan beliefs and practices in a positive manner.*

Their focus on acceptance also extends to body acceptance. When asked about how he portrays his female characters, Balent answers:

> I am still amazed to see that it is acceptable to show someone getting their teeth knocked out, shot in the head, or gored in a comic but it is unacceptable to show a large breasted woman . . . or a nude woman taking a bath. Talk about warped messages! The danger of saying her breasts are too big is that . . . there are some people out there that have those proportions. So if someone says, 'They are too big!' [. . .] then you deem everyone who doesn't fit your measurement 'unacceptable'. And you make them a social outcast. You make them feel like something is wrong with them, you tear down their self confidence. And that's just horrible!

To Balent, his sexualized art is about portraying women who are comfortable with their bodies and encouraging that in others, no matter their body type. Golightly sees the art as a counter to "a very

---

* Balent and Golightly also claim a Wiccan rationale for Tarot's constant nudity: she casts her spells skyclad, i.e. nude, a regular practice in some Wiccan circles.

unhealthy way of looking at the human body in our nation where it's fine to mangle it, and to kill it [yet] you can't show a positive, lovely, nude person [. . .] eating a cupcake nude, or doing anything positive and happy."

Tarot espoused Balent's beliefs in *Tarot: Witch of the Black Rose* #43 when she told a fellow witch who was insecure about her body, "The magick of you is that you are unique [. . .] It doesn't matter what size you are, if your breasts are larger or smaller, or if you are thinner or fluffier. All that matters is that you use the body you have." It was one of several scenes over the course of the book's run to present such a message, and the body positivity resonated with many *Tarot* fans. The back matter of *Tarot* is full of female readers who send in pictures and letters, the fans who come to see Balent at comic book conventions are evenly split along gender lines, and BroadSword's official Twitter account has 30 percent female followers. The series has a surprisingly large female readership who identify with Tarot and see her as a positive role model, particularly because of how she's drawn.

Balent's work on *Catwoman* garnered a similar response. He recalls, "I received a lot of positive mail from women of every breast size, but especially from larger size breast women, who have thanked me for showing a strong female character who has a voluptuous body and is smart. I received these letters for my work on *Catwoman* and for my work on *Tarot*. I'm very proud of each and every one of them." Clearly, Balent's art has resonated with some readers in an empowering way.

At the same time, Balent's work didn't always reflect his empowering message. When Tarot explained "the magick of you" to her fellow witch, the art was a full page of Tarot pressing her bare breasts together while staring out seductively at the reader in a pose better suited to a pornographic magazine than an uplifting lesson about body positivity. The rumors that Balent and other artists traced pornography existed because that's precisely what the art looked like. Balent's work fixated on both of his leads, and their various female associates, in a sexualized manner that wholly embodied the male gaze.* Despite his claims about empowerment, his art was indistinguishable from that of artists who intentionally reveled in objectification.

While Balent only drew *Catwoman*, he wrote *Tarot* as well as drawing it, and his treatment of his characters further undermined his message. The women in *Tarot* have been raped or sexually assaulted on multiple occasions, often at length and in detail. Sometimes this was done for suspense, to build to a triumphant scene of Tarot escaping her captors. Other times it was supposed to be comedic, with unwanted sexual activity played as a joke. Whatever the case, these scenes were always drawn in a manner meant to arouse the reader. Balent's casual use of these sexist tropes implies a certain degree of obliviousness, both in terms of how they might be read and how they undermine his supposed larger aim for the series.

There is an earnestness, perhaps even a naïveté, to Balent's discussions of *Catwoman* and *Tarot* that suggests he approaches his work with an aim to be empowering, not exploitative. His intention is to send a positive message for women with his books, but his own fetishes and underexamined male perspective muddies the end product. While he had the best of intentions during his *Catwoman* run, the degree to which his attempt to inspire women was successful is debatable. Some *Catwoman* readers strongly identified with his artistic intent, while others were more critical and saw only sexist objectification. Ultimately, Catwoman fans remain very much split on whether this era was a triumph or a travesty for the character.

---

* Moreover, the full frontal nudity in *Tarot* is reserved just for the women; there are far more Vicki Vales than Peter Parkers.

# 9

# *A Novel Perspective*

*I*n 2000 *Catwoman* editor Matt Idelson was looking for a new direction for the book. He'd taken over the series shortly before Jim Balent's departure, but continuing the sexy action angle without Balent's art went over poorly with fans. After eight years, *Catwoman* was in need of a makeover, so Idelson reached out to *Batman* writer Ed Brubaker for his thoughts on the character.

Brubaker was new to the superhero game, and he'd taken over *Batman* less than a year earlier. He was part of an emerging generation of comic book writers who came up through smaller, independent publishers before moving to superheroes, and he wrote and sometimes drew his own comics and graphic novels throughout the 1990s, including a couple of books at Vertigo, DC's mature readers imprint. Much of his work had a noir sensibility, which made him a good match for Batman and the world of Gotham City.

When Idelson asked Brubaker for his opinion on the current *Catwoman* book, Brubaker told him that while he thought she was a great character, he felt that the series itself wasn't very good and "kind of insulting to women readers." He was a fan of "Year One" and told Idelson, "What you should do is figure out a way to get her back to those East End roots, but then add that classiness of the high-society thief to it," essentially suggesting that he combine the grittiness of Frank Miller's Gotham with the elegance of Jeph Loeb and Tim Sale's *Batman: The Long Halloween*. Idelson liked Brubaker's approach and asked if he wanted to write the series. Brubaker was intrigued and said he'd take the job with two conditions: that he could get a new artist for the book and that they could give Catwoman a new costume. Idelson agreed to both terms.

Brubaker's top choice for artist was Darwyn Cooke, who had just finished work on his graphic novel *Batman: Ego*. It was Cooke's first comic book work in some time; he worked in animation as a storyboard artist and director for most of the 1990s, including stints on *Batman: The Animated Series* and *Batman Beyond*. Brubaker loved his stylish, cartoonish artwork, which he likened to a combination of iconic comic book artists Alex Toth and Jack Kirby, but Cooke was hard at work on what would become the Eisner Award–winning *DC: The New Frontier*.* When Brubaker told Cooke that he could redesign Catwoman, he couldn't resist and agreed to draw a four-issue arc for Brubaker.

Cooke put Catwoman in an all-black catsuit that was sleek and practical for a thief. It zipped up the middle, had her whip as a belt, and was drawn like actual fabric rather than a second skin. The suit also had a cowl with small cat ears and cat-eyed goggles. For Selina, Cooke gave her a short brunette haircut and described her as "sexy [and] strong, not sleazy." He wanted her look to be simple and elegant and cited Ava Gardner, Grace Kelly, and Audrey Hepburn as inspirations for Selina's appearance and style. Cooke aimed for classic beauty and drew her with realistic proportions in both of her identities.

When Cooke sent in the artwork for what was supposed to be *Catwoman* #95, Idelson and the rest of the editorial team in the Batman offices were blown away. They felt that the new take on Catwoman deserved a bigger debut, so they decided to push the story back six months and relaunch the series entirely. Idelson also proposed that Brubaker and Cooke create a four-part story to lead

---

* The Eisner Awards are the Academy Awards of the comic book world, the industry's highest honors.

into the new series that would run as a backup in *Detective Comics*. *Catwoman* ended in July 2001 with what appeared to be the death of Catwoman, and their backup story began the next month with Slam Bradley investigating whether she was really dead.

Slam Bradley was a Dick Tracy rip-off when he debuted in *Detective Comics* #1 in 1937, a private detective created by Jerry Siegel and Joe Shuster a year before the duo hit it big with Superman. His stories ran regularly until 1949, but he remained largely forgotten until Brubaker and Cooke brought him back. Gotham City's corrupt mayor had a grudge against Catwoman and hired Slam to make sure she was dead. After Slam investigated her and learned that she was Selina Kyle, Selina showed up in his office. He'd come to respect her, in both of her identities, and told her that he'd decided to drop the case. The mayor's goons beat Slam soundly for doing so, but he didn't care; he was smitten.

Idelson's backup story and relaunch gambit paid off well for DC. When *Catwoman* #94 ended the first series, it sold 25,774 copies. Brubaker and Cooke's new *Catwoman* #1 premiered in January 2002 with 49,413 copies sold, an increase of nearly double. The relaunch was the start of a three-year run that would go down as the most critically and commercially successful era in the history of Catwoman comic books.

## Brubaker's Three Dozen and One

Ed Brubaker's *Catwoman* was the opposite of her previous series in every possible way. Instead of brief, self-contained arcs, each story line built to the next one, and everything was connected, allowing Brubaker to explore Catwoman and the gray area in which she resided in depth. While there was still action and fun, the long-form nature of Brubaker's storytelling let Catwoman and the book's side characters evolve and grow.

Permanent side characters were a big change as well. Catwoman's main sidekick was Holly Robinson, Selina's young friend from "Year One." Now grown up, she and Selina reconnected and teamed up; Holly had been a junkie but kicked the habit, and she used her street connections to get information on criminals for Selina.* The pair moved back in together, and soon Holly was dating Karon, a pink-haired woman who worked at the local delicatessen.

Slam Bradley also became a regular in the book. He was another good resource for Selina, and they teamed up often to take down criminals. Their relationship was complicated; Slam was clearly in love with Selina, and that both clouded his judgment and added an awkwardness to their relationship. He also clashed with Batman, who was now a frequent guest star in the series. Batman and Catwoman's sporadic flirtations piqued jealousy in the older detective, leading to further tensions.

Brubaker was able to give Catwoman a regular supporting cast by establishing a firm setting. Rather than globe-trotting heists, Selina returned to her East End apartment from "Year One" in the book's first issue and soon became the neighborhood's protector; criminals worked in her domain at their own peril. Selina's relocation made her a fixture of Gotham City, linking her to the larger Bat-family and allowing for more natural tie-ins to crossovers and events. Catwoman's methods were harsher than Batman's, but she was cautiously welcomed by Batman and his associates as one of Gotham's guardians.

Owing to its gritty "Year One" influence and Brubaker's noir sensibility, the new *Catwoman* was fairly dark. Brubaker and Cooke's debut issue opened with the murder of a prostitute, and Catwoman was soon on the case. When the police found a second murdered prostitute, Catwoman watched in disgust as the cops rifled through her purse to steal her cash. Knowing that the police didn't care about catching her killer, Catwoman decided to nab him herself and avenge the women's death, declaring, "I will speak for them. Because no one else will."

Protecting the East End wasn't a simple, black-and-white exercise for Catwoman. When Batman told her, "I believe that deep down,

---

* Neither Brubaker nor Idelson remembered that Holly had been killed off in Catwoman's *Action Comics* feature in 1988, and weren't informed of this until they were several issues into the new series. Brubaker later explained Holly's "resurrection" in *Catwoman Secret Files and Origins*, chalking it up to DC's mid-1990s continuity-tweaking event "Zero Hour" in a tongue-in-cheek story titled "Why Holly Isn't Dead."

you're a really **good** person," he asked her if she felt that way about herself. She responded, "Yeah, sometimes I **do** . . . but I think it's just a lot more **complicated** than that." Catwoman wanted to do good, but she was practical about it. The guilt and past pains that motivated her to help people didn't stop her from continuing to cross lines. In an early issue, Selina told Holly that she'd stashed enough money away over the years to fund her new life, but smiled slyly when she added, "And if that runs out . . . well, I can always get **more**, can't I?" When she confronted the man who'd been killing prostitutes and learned that cruel experiments had turned him into a shape-shifter and he couldn't control himself, she initially offered to get him help. He fought her instead, and then all bets were off. Not knowing how it would affect him, Catwoman stabbed him in the neck with a Taser and then chopped his head off. When the disembodied head weakly asked, "What've you **done**?" she nonchalantly replied, "Y'know, I'm not really **sure**."

Things only got darker from there. For the first year and a half of *Catwoman*, every good beat was followed by a terrible turn.* It began with Holly, who was happily employed as Catwoman's eyes and ears on the streets of the East End, witnessing the murder of an undercover cop and then being framed for the crime. Once Catwoman got that situation sorted, she began a new project, using $28 million she got from stealing some diamonds to finance a community center. She was also cheered by the return of two faces from her past, her friend Sylvia from her younger days as a street thief and her sister, Maggie, now out of the convent and married to a man named Simon.

All of this went south in spectacular fashion. Soon after the community center opened, it was blown up by minions of Black Mask, a crime lord and the previous owner of the diamonds stolen by Catwoman. Sylvia was revealed to be in league with Black Mask, running a gang of street youths to keep tabs on Catwoman and stop her when necessary. Maggie and Simon got kidnapped and tortured

---

* Cooke drew the first four issues before returning to his other projects, and was followed by penciller Brad Rader, working with an assortment of inkers, and then Cameron Stewart, primarily inking his own pencils.

by Black Mask in a disturbing series of events culminating in the villain forcing Maggie to eat Simon's eyes. In all the chaos after the explosion and the kidnappings, Slam got hit by a car and Holly was assaulted by Sylvia's gang. In the end, Catwoman stopped Black Mask, but the damage was massive. Simon died from the constant torture, a distraught Maggie ended up in an asylum, and Holly went into shock after she killed Sylvia to save Selina.

It was a brutal series of issues, but all part of Brubaker's long-term plan. The Black Mask story line was followed by "No Easy Way Down," an innovative three-issue arc illustrated by Javier Pulido that explored the fallout. It was introspective and subdued, lacking the flash and action that usually characterized superhero comic books. Brubaker explained, "It's about surviving terrible things, and how guilty you can feel, and what you do to go on anyway. It's pretty rough stuff, emotionally, it's an almost all character arc, really." He'd later go on to call it "one of my favorite things I've ever written."

The story picked up six weeks later. Holly was still in shock and wasn't talking to Selina, while Selina and Slam were dating. But Selina was also drinking a lot and both sides of the couple had qualms about the timing of their relationship. They soon broke up, and Catwoman ended up hitting rock bottom when Batman caught her drunk stealing at the Gotham Museum. She then turned things around and decided, "I'm so tired of hating myself." She reached out to Holly and helped her work through her grief, knowing that together they could figure out how to deal with their traumas and move forward.

Exploring the emotional cost of being a hero in a real, prolonged way was a rarity in superhero comics in the early 2000s. Not that superhero comics are in any way realistic; Brubaker's *Catwoman* began with her battling a shape-shifter, after all. But even within the fantastical parameters of a superhero world, there was tragedy and failure and death, and the repercussions of that were rarely examined apart from a cursory panel or two of a hero staring grimly into the distance before moving on to the next adventure. A three-issue contemplative arc was a bold choice by Brubaker, but a fitting one. Catwoman was a character in transition, moving into a heroic role after a life of crime, and such a big change warranted Brubaker's delving into the ramifications therein. It also fit Brubaker's style; his *Catwoman* was more a novel than disparate stories, which freed him from the usual superhero conventions.

Brubaker stayed on *Catwoman* for another eighteen issues after "No Easy Way Down," and things changed for the titular hero. There were still villains to fight, but the darkness that overwhelmed Catwoman in the series' earlier issues never returned. She was more confident and settled into her role, moving forward while remedying the past. Selina and Holly got out of Gotham with a road trip to find Holly's long-lost brother, and Holly trained with the superhero Wildcat to learn how to fight. When they returned home, Catwoman took over Sylvia's street gang and turned the kids into her informants, and then began clearing criminals out of the East End with a vengeance.

*Catwoman* was a critically acclaimed title, and Brubaker was nominated for best writer at the Eisner Awards multiple times during his tenure on the book, but the book's biggest honor came from outside the comic book industry. In 2004 *Catwoman* won a GLAAD Media Award for Outstanding Comic Book from the Gay & Lesbian Alliance Against Defamation for the book's depiction of Holly and Karon's relationship. The couple were rarely at the forefront of the comic, and intentionally so. Brubaker made them a constant, normal presence, and he later recalled, "I was very conscious of wanting their appearances in the book to not be an After-School Special."

There was never any drama for Holly and Karon to overcome, no homophobic foes to oppose or clichéd attempts at moralizing. They were just there, together and supporting each other; after Holly killed Sylvia, it was Karon who took care of her while Selina went off the rails, and the narration of Holly and Selina's road trip consisted of Holly's letters to Karon. Depictions of gay and lesbian characters weren't yet common at the time, in comics or elsewhere. When Brubaker wrote a scene in which Holly and Karon kissed for the first time in the book, he was worried that DC would cut it, but they didn't. After the book won the GLAAD Award, Brubaker responded, "It's great to see a depiction of a normal, loving couple who just happen to both be women getting recognition."

While DC's editors were supportive of a lesbian couple in *Catwoman*, they nixed Brubaker's idea for his next arc. Brubaker planned a story line in which Selina died, everyone learned afterward that she was pregnant but not the identity of the father, and Holly took over as Catwoman.* It didn't sit well with the brass at DC, and they told him to go in a different direction. Brubaker had been laying the groundwork for this story for years and was disheartened when he wasn't allowed to tell it, so he decided to move on from the book.

His final issue was *Catwoman* #37 in January 2005, with a story fittingly titled "Character Driven." The book's previous arc had been part of the Batman line's "War Games" event, a gang war that left Catwoman feeling drained and wondering if her efforts in the East End were worthwhile. Then Holly threw her a surprise birthday party, and Catwoman realized that her work had brought her a family for the first time in a long time and how much that meant to her. It was an apt conclusion to her larger character arc moving from loner thief to part of a heroic team.

Brubaker wasn't done with Catwoman, though. He also cowrote *Gotham Central*, a series that focused on the cops who worked in the Gotham City Police Department's Major Crimes Unit, tracking down supervillains. Catwoman guest-starred in the book a month after Brubaker left her regular series; she was the chief suspect after a televangelist was found murdered. She refused to be brought in for questioning and instead caught the murderer herself, tracking him down and scaring him into giving himself up to the cops.

The *Gotham Central* arc was some of Brubaker's last work at DC Comics. He soon moved to Marvel where he had an iconic run on *Captain America*, bringing back Cap's long-dead sidekick Bucky Barnes; the story line later became the basis for the 2014 blockbuster film *Captain America: The Winter Soldier*.† Brubaker also finally won the Eisner Award for Best Writer during his time at Marvel after years of nominations, nabbing three of them over four years.

---

* Selina would have come back at some point, of course. No one stays dead in comic books.
† Brubaker cameoed in the film as one of the workers in the lab where the Winter Soldier was kept.

## Den Mother

*Catwoman* entered an odd limbo after Brubaker left, running through three different writers in six months before the fourth, Will Pfeifer, landed the job for good. Another big change rocked the book less than a year into Pfeifer's tenure: DC was in the middle of *Infinite Crisis*, a massive event that tore through its universe and affected every series, though Catwoman was on the periphery of most of the action. Nonetheless, the higher-ups decided that in the wake of the drama of *Infinite Crisis*, all of their superhero series would jump ahead a year in storytelling time, including *Catwoman*. The "One Year Later" initiative launched in May 2006, and introduced big changes to Selina's world.

Before the jump, Catwoman was fighting Black Mask, who had returned during the "War Games" event. When Black Mask captured and tortured Slam Bradley, carving a message for Catwoman into his chest, she decided to end things for good. In the final issue before the time jump, Catwoman shot Black Mask in the head at point-blank range, killing him.

*Catwoman* #53 picked up the story twelve months later, and began with Selina in the hospital, screaming in pain. It wasn't due to injury, though; she was having a baby, a little girl she named Helena. The book then turned to Catwoman fighting a street gang, but Holly was under the mask instead of Selina. The dramatic twists were all pillaged straight from the Ed Brubaker proposal editorial had rejected less than two years before. The only difference was that Selina was still alive; everything else, including the mystery of the baby's father, remained.

The mystery was solved months later in an issue that unveiled what happened during the gap year. After killing Black Mask, Catwoman had teamed up with Slam's son, Sam Bradley, to dismantle what remained of Black Mask's criminal organization. They became close while doing so, resulting in Selina's pregnancy, but Sam then died while confronting a villain. Deciding to prioritize the safety of her child, she left both Catwoman and Selina Kyle behind and moved from the East End to downtown Gotham City, adopting the alias Irena Dubrovna, an homage to a character in the 1942 film *Cat People.*

The story line was a rare exploration of motherhood in super-hero comics, a genre far more known for fathers. Comic book writer Kelly Sue DeConnick put it best: "The Marvel universe is founded on daddy issues," and the DC universe has adapted to follow suit with its heroes' constantly revised origin stories. Most superheroes are orphans, but their fathers are usually key to their backstory. In a famous scene in "Year One," Bruce Wayne talked to a bust of his dead father, discussing his attempts at fighting crime, when a bat broke through the window and landed on the bust, prompting Bruce to say, "Yes, Father. I shall become a bat." Superman's Kryptonian father Jor-El is key to his history, creating the rocket that sent him to Earth and, in many stories, encoding the rocket with an AI of himself to teach his son about heroism and his heritage. The tragic loss of fathers is at the core of many origin stories; Hal Jordan witnessed his father crash to his death while piloting a fighter plane, leading him to become a pilot and later Green Lantern, while the death of Peter Parker's surrogate father, Uncle Ben, led him to accept the responsibility of his new powers and become Spider-Man.

All of these characters had mothers, and there are some tales of their love and support, but their fathers are the source of their heroic inspiration. Moreover, the fathers were more than just fathers; Thomas Wayne was a doctor, and Jor-El was a scientist. The mothers were often only mothers, limited to being homemakers and caretakers. This is partly due to timing; most of DC's characters were created between the 1930s and 1950s, when working mothers were rare. But subsequent decades of reboots and revised origins for heroes hasn't done much to flesh out their mothers.

There also haven't been very many top-tier female superheroes with children. Sue Storm (a.k.a. the Invisible Woman) is a notable exception. She and her husband, Reed Richards (a.k.a. Mr. Fantastic), have two kids, Franklin and Valeria. They've been passed off to someone else for large swaths of the Fantastic Four's history, though. It's only recently that they've become more of a regular presence in their comics, a development that has been paired with a lessening of Sue's superhero role, though not Reed's. Catwoman herself was a mother on Earth-Two during the Bronze Age, but only in flashbacks; Helena Wayne was an adult when she began to appear in comics.* Shortly after Selina had Helena in the Modern Age, Clark Kent and Lois Lane briefly adopted a Kryptonian child. Lois's appearances soon involved less time at the *Daily Planet*, as work was replaced by her taking on all the domestic, child-rearing duties while Superman still flew around fighting bad guys. Significantly, all three of these women were married when they had children.

A single mother balancing a baby and her own busy life was new ground for superhero comics. Pfeifer, along with artists David Lopez and Alvaro Lopez, dug into all of the complications this dynamic brought to Selina's world. She was committed to motherhood but hated being on the sidelines and was soon back in her costume, racing across rooftops for fun just two issues into the "One Year Later" run. Her fun quickly turned to fear; the villains Angle Man and Film Freak saw her and were able to figure out her address. When she returned home her babysitter was out cold and the villains were holding Helena. Selina beat them soundly while calming Helena in the process, and then brought in the magician Zatanna to wipe their memories of any knowledge of her home or Helena.

Selina's troubles were just beginning. Holly got arrested, so Selina had to break her out of jail, and, after Film Freak launched an offensive against Gotham, she also had to stop a rampaging gorilla and defuse a nuclear bomb. Looking for additional safety, she asked the villain Calculator to erase her and Holly's records, and in return she had to break into LexCorp and steal a bauble from Lex Luthor. This was followed by an onslaught of villains: Blitzkrieg, then Hammer and Sickle, then a vicious Amazon splinter group. Hammer and Sickle were particularly dangerous, taking out Karon when she was babysitting Helena, kidnapping the baby, and then almost killing Helena after Selina got her back.† Hammer got blasted out a window

---

* Most of the children of superheroes have been adults, often through time travel shenanigans, superpower-fueled hypergrowth, or a reveal of a long-ago liaison. Even Franklin's and Valeria's ages have fluctuated wildly over the years; Franklin is a mutant with the power to manipulate reality, which has led to sporadic time warps.

† Hammer and Sickle are Russian villains and, delightfully, their real names are Boris and Natasha.

while still holding Helena, and Selina had to leap out after him, nab Helena, and use her whip to stop their plummeting descent.

After one of the rogue Amazons went after Helena, Selina was at her breaking point. She kept dreaming about other villains taking Helena, and so she got Batman to help her fake the deaths of "Irena Dubrovna" and Helena, then gave her up for adoption. Bruce Wayne found her a good family after Selina insisted that she not know where Helena ended up. The decision was so painful for Selina that she asked Zatanna to wipe Helena from her mind before ultimately choosing to remember her daughter, however much it broke her heart.

The arc didn't go over very well with readers. In the early 2000s, the audience for superhero comics was still largely young men, and even Brubaker's critically acclaimed run didn't garner much in sales; by the time Brubaker left the book, *Catwoman* was way down the sales chart in 79th place.* When Pfeifer's Helena arc ended, *Catwoman* had fallen to 124th place. The readership just wasn't that interested in a nonsexualized Catwoman, much less her travails as a single mother.

Nonetheless, *Catwoman*'s two-year depiction of Selina as a single mother marked a shift in how mothers were portrayed. Motherhood had been a shallow, overshadowed institution in comics for decades, but Pfeifer wrote a story with a solid emotional core despite the fantastical circumstances. While mothers in the real world don't have to deal with things like Soviet-inspired supervillains, Selina's broader concerns were reflective of mothers everywhere. The arc helped to expand the scope of motherhood in superhero comics, pushing the boundaries of what could be done with female characters moving forward.

## Identities and Events

The relaunch of *Catwoman* brought about a substantial evolution of the character, moving her beyond her previous superficial, sexualized

---

* Tellingly, other titles near *Catwoman* on the charts included *Batgirl*, *Birds of Prey*, *Emma Frost*, *Mystique*, *She-Hulk*, and *Wonder Woman*. There was only one female-led book in the top fifty that month, *Ultimate Elektra* #4 in the forty-fourth spot.

depiction, and this evolution continued outside her main title. For decades Batman and Catwoman's relationship had been unbalanced; Batman knew everything about Catwoman, including her secret identity, but Catwoman didn't know anything about Batman beyond the cowl. This created a skewed power dynamic that gave Batman a significant degree of control, until the story line "Hush" launched with *Batman* #608 in December 2002.

"Hush" was a massive event for the Bat-line. Written by Jeph Loeb with Jim Lee on art, the superstar team packed the twelve-issue story with guest stars and action, and garnered huge sales. Most event comics start with high sales and then drift down the charts with each successive issue, but "Hush" started big and only grew from there; its final issue sold double the amount of its debut issue, clocking in at nearly a quarter of a million copies sold. And Catwoman was in the middle of it all.

She began as an adversary, stealing a briefcase full of ransom money from Batman and delivering it to Poison Ivy because she was under the frondescent fiend's mind control, but soon she became an ally. A new villain was conspiring with Batman's foes to destroy him, and Catwoman didn't appreciate being taken advantage of. She teamed up with Batman to fight back and battled alongside him against Killer Croc, Harley Quinn, the Joker, and even Superman. Working together rekindled their romance, and Batman revealed his secret identity to a very surprised Catwoman in *Batman* #615.

The romance didn't work out; Batman was worried that it was caused by Poison Ivy's spell and broke things off. But the status quo had changed dramatically. Knowing that Batman was Bruce Wayne made Catwoman a somewhat trusted member of Gotham's crime-fighting team. It also helped her revitalize the East End. The duo remained friendly, and Bruce provided a lot of money for Selina's various projects to help the community. Most significantly, it put Catwoman on an even footing with Batman for the first time in her comic book history. With all the cards on the table, Catwoman now had access to the leverage and control that Batman had always enjoyed.

Catwoman's strong depiction in her own series combined with the revelations in "Hush" to bring the character to the forefront of the DC universe, but this wasn't the best place for a female character to be in the early twenty-first century. DC had a penchant for big event stories, and for sacrificing female characters to make these events dramatic and memorable. The Elongated Man's wife, Sue Dibny, was killed in *Identity Crisis*, and the Atom's ex-wife, Jean Loring, was the book's villain. The new female Robin, Stephanie Brown, died in "War Games," Wonder Woman became a scapegoat during *Infinite Crisis*, and Lois Lane's sister, Lucy, died during the "New Krypton" event. While Catwoman was able to survive the event cycle, she took a few hits along the way.

One event undermined her heroic character arc. After Sue Dibny's death in *Identity Crisis*, the book revealed that Sue had been raped by the villain Dr. Light years before. The Justice League had then used Zatanna's magical powers to erase his memory of doing so and turned him into a less harmful foe. It was part of a pattern of mind wipes in which the League altered the behavior of villains. A tie-in story in *Catwoman* #50 revealed that Selina was one of these villains.

A flashback showed the 1990s-era Catwoman aboard the Justice League satellite, held down on a table with Zatanna telling her, "We're going to **help** you. Help you get on the **right** path." Using her magical backward-talking spell, Zatanna intoned, "Nrut, anileS . . . nrut morf **nialliv** ot **oreh**." This revelation shook up Catwoman in the present; two issues later, she killed Black Mask, partly as a reaction against her magical reprogramming. This tie-in undercut four years of character development, taking away Catwoman's agency and reducing her slow evolution to someone magically flipping a switch in her brain. The issue did cause a brief spike in sales, though, which is what event tie-ins were created to do, above all else.

Another event tie-in failed at this aim, and ended up dragging down *Catwoman*. *Salvation Run* was a 2007 event meant to lead into an even bigger event, *Final Crisis*, but no one seemed to care. A government task force decided to get rid of villains altogether, and transported Earth's worst criminals to a distant planet, where they fought with each other for seven issues. Despite a lot of hype and tie-ins with several other series, *Salvation Run* #1 premiered way down the charts in fifty-seventh place and the rest of the series fell from there.

Catwoman was one of the villains sent off-world, and her series tied in to the event for four issues. This was just three months after the end of the Helena arc, and Pfeifer had yet to establish a new direction for the series. The *Salvation Run* crossover was likely an attempt to boost sales for *Catwoman,* and initially it worked, with sales going up for the first issue of the tie-in. But *Salvation Run* was dead in the water, and it took *Catwoman* down with it. By the end of the four issues, sales for *Catwoman* were lower than before the arc began. Once Catwoman returned to Gotham, her book only lasted another four issues before it was canceled.

Even without her own series, events still plagued Catwoman. In 2008 the Bat-books were building up to "Batman R.I.P.," an event that momentarily killed Batman,* and Catwoman was simultaneously brought to the fore and sidelined in the *Detective Comics* prelude to the event, "Heart of Hush." The title was somewhat inaccurate, since Selina's heart was more central to the story: Hush attacked her and cut out her heart, leaving her connected to machines that kept her alive while Batman frantically searched for her missing organ. Hush later told Batman that he did it "because I wanted to hurt you in the **worst way** I could. I know what the gutter slut means to you." Eventually Batman got Selina's heart back, and she survived the ordeal and even teamed up with a few of her friends afterward to pillage the entirety of Hush's multimillion-dollar fortune. But this revenge only took up three pages after she'd been out of commission for three issues, a paltry catharsis to this blatant damsel in distress scenario.

The follow-up to "Batman R.I.P." didn't go well for Catwoman either. Various contenders fought for the right to take over Batman's mantle in "Battle for the Cowl" and one of them, former Robin Jason Todd, kicked Catwoman off a roof and left her splayed and unconscious on top of a now smashed-in car. However, "Battle of the Cowl" led to some new series, including another headlining gig for Catwoman alongside Harley Quinn and Poison Ivy in *Gotham City Sirens*.

---

\* Sort of. "Batman R.I.P." tied into *Final Crisis*, in which Batman was shot with an Omega Beam by the intergalactic villain Darkseid. He appeared dead, but he was actually displaced in time and eventually found his way back to the present day.

While the book seemed like a return to the fun of *Gotham Girls*, especially with *Batman: The Animated Series* writer Paul Dini at the helm, it was surprisingly dark and continued Catwoman's unpleasant run. The book began with Catwoman still reeling from her past injuries and the gals taking her in, but they did so only to use her to find out Batman's secret identity. They eventually made up, but new problems arose. Selina's sister, Maggie, returned and attacked her, then was possessed by a vengeful angelic force, and ultimately begged Selina to kill her. Meanwhile, Talia al Ghul came after Catwoman, upset that she knew Batman's identity, and blew up her house.

Things finally turned around for Catwoman in 2011. She took on a protégé, Kitrina Falcone, a young member of the Falcone crime family with a penchant for theft who worked with her as Catgirl. When Batman told her that it wasn't safe to have a child as a sidekick, she wasn't having any of it and pointed out his hypocrisy. After several unpleasant years, Catwoman was reestablishing herself and taking control of her life, just in time for the universe to end. A quarter of a century after *Crisis on Infinite Earths*, DC Comics was preparing to wipe the slate clean and relaunch its entire superhero line again.

Catwoman went out in defiant fashion, though. The final issue of *Gotham City Sirens* revealed that Catwoman had an arrangement with Batman; she'd been protecting Harley Quinn and Poison Ivy, watching them closely instead of Batman locking them up. When Batman had enough of this arrangement and wanted to take them in, Catwoman refused. Instead of turning them over, she declared, "I'm my **own** woman. I'm doing what I want to do," and helped them escape. Catwoman's last act in this universe was staring down an angry Batman as her friends got away.

# 10

# *Cinematic Catastrophe*

he ceremony for the twenty-fifth annual Golden Raspberry Awards was an illustrious affair. The awards—better known as the Razzies—were dedicated to "saluting the worst that Hollywood has to offer each year," and the show took place at the Ivar Theatre in Hollywood on February 26, 2005. Nominees from the past year's slate of films included Ben Affleck, Halle Berry, Vin Diesel, Colin Farrell, Angelina Jolie, Arnold Schwarzenegger, and Val Kilmer, though Halle Berry was the only one who showed up.

Berry was no stranger to award shows. Three years before, she'd been nominated for best actress at all of the major film awards for her role in *Monster's Ball* and won several of them, including an Academy Award. Her Oscar was especially noteworthy; Berry was the first woman of color to win the Academy Award for Best Actress in a Leading Role, and to this day remains the only such recipient.

Her follow-up ventures were not as successful. One of the first projects Berry boarded after her Oscar win was *Catwoman*, in which she portrayed a new take on the feline hero. The film was a critical and commercial flop, so much so that it ended up leading the twenty-fifth Razzies in nominations and was represented in nearly all the major categories. The only exceptions were categories for which *Catwoman* didn't meet the criteria; if it could be nominated, it was. Supporting actors Benjamin Bratt, Lambert Wilson, and Sharon Stone all received nods, and it was up for worst picture, worst director, and worst screenplay, along with a worst actress nomination for Berry.

*Catwoman* "won" in four of its seven categories, and Berry was on hand to accept her worst actress award. Actors usually wanted nothing to do with the Razzies; winning one was hardly an honor. But Berry was a good sport and delivered her acceptance speech with her Razzie in one hand and her Oscar in the other.

Berry came out on stage to a standing ovation and pretended to cry, mimicking her emotional Oscar speech. Noting that "you don't win a Razzie without a lot of help from a lot of people," she went through a list of thank-yous, most notably to Warner Bros. for "putting me in a piece of shit, god awful movie." She joked with her manager, bringing him out on stage to tell him, "If I get a chance to do another movie, maybe you should read the script. [. . .] Just counting the zeroes behind the one really isn't enough." She then teased her castmates, saying, "In order to give a really bad performance like I did, you need a lot of bad actors around you." Ultimately, Berry concluded with old advice from her mother: "If you could not be a good loser, then there's no way you can be a good winner."

*Catwoman* also won worst picture, and former Catwoman Julie Newmar was on hand to accept the award on the producers' behalf. The humorous chastening of the ceremony was a fitting wrap-up for *Catwoman*, which had been a comedy of errors from start to finish. A film that looked to be a surefire hit when it began development years earlier ultimately ended up as more than just a bad take on Catwoman; it was a failure so resounding that it set back female superheroes in film for over a decade.

## Development Hell

It all began in 1993, when Warner Bros. began planning a solo Catwoman film soon after *Batman Returns* debuted. Catwoman was the movie's breakout character, and the studio wanted to capitalize on her appeal. All the major players were interested in returning:

*Batman Returns* writer Dan Waters was hired to pen the script, Michelle Pfeiffer wanted to reprise her role, and Tim Burton was considering directing the film even though he'd parted ways with the main Batman film franchise. The pieces appeared to be in place, though it would take ten years and more than a dozen writers for the project to come to fruition.

The first step was Waters's script. It seems that Waters was emboldened by the positive response to his quirkily dark approach to writing *Batman Returns* and doubled down on it with *Catwoman*. The script was violent and action packed, filled with twisted humor and a cast of dysfunctional characters. Waters called it "definitely not a fun-for-the-whole-family script."

The story began months after the events of *Batman Returns*, with an amnesiac Selina Kyle who had no recollection of what transpired in Gotham City. She now lived with her mother in Oasisburg, a take on Las Vegas, and worked an unsatisfying job at a casino. Oasisburg was protected by a group of male superheroes called the Cult of Good, and through the machinations of an underdeveloped mysterious "old hag" character, Selina learned that the Cult were actually murderers and thieves who preyed on the city. After the Cult killed the old woman, Selina found a key on her body that led her to her Catwoman costume. The costume jogged her memory, and soon Catwoman was out on the town, chastising rough mothers and slapping around sexist frat boys.

Catwoman's primary conflict was with the Cult of Good. She faced off against them soon after she returned to her costume, besting them in what would have made quite a movie scene if it had ever been filmed. She caught a bullet in her teeth at one point, and she ended the fight by blowing up a statue honoring the Cult of Good. Inspired by Catwoman's stand against the aggressively masculine Cult, many of the women of Oasisburg made their own Catwoman outfits and took to the streets to get revenge on the men who had wronged them.

After a variety of twist and turns, as well as an odd romantic subplot in which Selina romanced the Cult's leader, Captain God, the Cult of Good turned on the city publicly and the Catwomen came together to stop them. Catwoman landed the final blow by using a bow and arrow to pin a tracking device to Captain God; a missile was following the tracker, and it blew him up in spectacular fashion. The script called for a shot in which Captain God "detonates in a vivid-as-PG-13-allows burst." The end of the Cult of Good led to a new, happier era for Oasisburg, and the script concluded with a poetic voice-over from Catwoman with lines like, "We stopped being lame and started being suave—it was really quite SIMPLE. Meanness and Smugness and Bossyness we popped like a PIMPLE."

The script was bizarre, to say the least. It also lacked the subtle feminist critique of patriarchy that ran through *Batman Returns*, trading that for a muddled, on-the-nose approach to gender politics. The villains were caricatures, especially Captain God; to start, his real name was Brock Leviathan.* In response to the rise of the Catwomen, he declared, "Men realize more than ever we have to go for the win. Whatever you said we were too much of, we have to become more of. Violent. Domineering. Uncaring. We're taking back lost ground!" Later in the script, he murdered a Cult of Good member when he learned that she was a woman disguised as a man.

Side characters continued in this misogynistic vein. A psychologist named Dr. Penelope Snuggle opined, "The pursuit of power turns women into monsters and very unhappy monsters at that. Women, stop trying to be Catwomen and start being women." After Catwoman returned, a bystander observed, "She's a disgusting, filthy beast—and probably a feminist."

The feminist side of the script was similarly on-the-nose with the legion of Catwomen, but it took a wonky turn. Originally the women were feminist anarchists, tearing down whatever angered them: wives attacked abusive husbands, women tore down billboards advertising breast implants, a gang broke up a beauty pageant, and some teen Catwomen soaped the cars of their leering male teachers. Then the women turned on each other and attacked their fellow Catwomen over things like costumes, life choices, and preferred targets. Before long, they dissolved into infighting and brawls. The Catwomen came

---

* Selina's other romantic option was a reporter named Lewis Lane. Throughout the film, she dated both Lane and Leviathan even though she was certain one of them was Captain God.

back together in the end, but the protracted quarreling made them look more crazed than righteously indignant.

Warner Bros. passed on the script. Waters delivered it on the same weekend that the Burton-less *Batman Forever* premiered, and his script was radically different from the new tone of the Batman film franchise. Directed by Joel Schumacher, *Batman Forever* was colorful and somewhat silly, ideal for action figures and other merchandise for young fans. It also earned more at the box office than its predecessor. Waters's dark, cynical follow-up to *Batman Returns* wasn't what the studio was looking for anymore. With development of *Catwoman* now at a standstill, Tim Burton moved on to other projects, which caused Michelle Pfeiffer to drop out as well. She wasn't interested in returning to Catwoman without Burton because "it was really his vision that made it so special," and Warner Bros. was left with nothing.

But the studio didn't give up on the project, despite new complications. There were likeness-rights issues in Pfeiffer's contract that prevented Warner Bros. from using Selina Kyle in the film unless Pfeiffer was playing her. With Pfeiffer out, the studio had to find a new alter ego for Catwoman, as well as a new lead actress. They landed the latter in 2001 when Ashley Judd boarded the film, and by then Warner Bros. had a new script on hand, written by Theresa Rebeck and Kate Kondell.

The lead character was Patience Price, a pet groomer who lived in a small town outside Gotham City. When she was a child, her mother invented a microchip that revolutionized dishwashers, but her boss killed her to steal the invention for himself, and her death was ruled a suicide. Years later, the boss was a wealthy man who ran the town. When Patience found evidence that he'd killed her mother, he had Patience killed as well, but cats brought her back to life and gave her cat powers. She began to fight back against the boss as Catwoman, and the script described her as "Robin Hood with PMS." She also romanced Bill Lone, the only police detective who believed Patience's claims about her mother's murder; Owen Wilson was rumored to be up for the role. In the end, Catwoman defeated the boss in a battle set at a zoo.

The script was far removed from previous takes on Catwoman and was torched when it leaked. One reviewer said that it was "lame, derivative, and a tremendous letdown" and snarked, "All that's missing from this new *Catwoman*, besides originality, are brains and soul." Another website opined that it felt more like *Scooby-Doo* than a superhero movie. The studio hired John Rogers to revise the draft, and when he read it for the first time he thought that they'd pulled a prank on the new guy and wondered where the real script was.

Rogers wanted to return Catwoman to her "cool thief" roots, but the studio had other ideas. To Rogers, it seemed that the producers "had no coherent attitude towards this character" except for one hang-up: they were adamant that the script explain how she got her cat powers. Rogers tried to explain that Burton just made them up, and that cat powers weren't a part of any other version of Catwoman. In fact, Burton had tried to make his Catwoman ambiguous; she might have had powers, but she may have just been tough and lucky. The producers weren't swayed. Cat powers were their priority.

Rogers gave them what they wanted with a mythological backstory of cats resurrecting women who have been wronged throughout history, dating back to the goddess Bast in ancient Egypt. Patience was just one in a long line of Catwomen that also included Selina Kyle. It was the only idea in his script that made it into the final film. In his draft, Patience was a veterinary scientist murdered by her boss and then resurrected. She set about investigating why she was murdered, and Roger described the script as "daytime Patience uses her brain to put together the clues that night time Catwoman goes out and gets by kicking ass and being awesome." Eventually the two sides of her personality were integrated and she got her revenge on her boss.

While very little from Rogers's script survived, it was the draft that sold Halle Berry on the movie in 2003. Ashley Judd had left the film after two years of slow development, moving on to another feline project, a revival of "Cat on a Hot Tin Roof" on Broadway, and Warner Bros. quickly brought in Berry.* They'd also hired French director Pitof, a special effects specialist whose 2001 film *Vidocq* was a moderate success. The team was coming together, but the studio

---

* They offered the part to Nicole Kidman first, but she turned it down.

remained unsure of the script. Writing duo John D. Brancato and Michael Ferris came in to do yet another pass.

Their script followed the same formula of Patience being killed by an industrialist, becoming Catwoman, and exacting revenge while stopping the industrialist's wrongdoing. This time, Patience was an accountant at a cosmetics company; the producers believed that "female superheroes must have a female oriented storyline," and so Rogers's scientist angle was replaced with beauty products. Patience discovered that the company was also manufacturing chemical weapons, but the new twist was that the industrialist's wife was behind everything, from Patience's death to the weapons sales. She even murdered her husband and framed Catwoman for the crime. Catwoman bested her in the end, of course; in stereotypical fashion, the villain was undone by her own vanity, killed while fixing her face as her building collapsed around her.

This script became the basis for the film, though the producers weren't very confident in it. Just a few months before filming was about to begin, they hired Ed Solomon to write a new script that reports described as a "tear-down-and-build-again-from-the-ground-up" draft. Ultimately, Warner Bros. decided to go with what they already had. After a complicated arbitration process, the Writer's Guild of America officially credited four different writers for *Catwoman*, though many more had worked on a variety of scripts over the years.* The studio sent the shooting script to everyone involved in the arbitration, and John Rogers later recalled that he didn't think it was very good but that he figured, "Well, how bad could it get in like the four next months before it starts shooting? [. . .] I did not anticipate really the warp speed, the almost Doppler effect of horrible that occurred in the interim."

---

* Arbitration decides which writers had the biggest contributions to the script and thus receive on-screen credits and residual payments. Reportedly, at least ten to fifteen and upwards of twenty different writers were involved in arbitration for *Catwoman*. In the end, Rebeck, Brancato, and Ferris received "story" credits, while Brancato, Ferris, and Rogers got "screenplay" credits.

## The *Catwoman* Calamity

While the shooting script for *Catwoman* was far removed from the original concept of the film, it was, at worst, bland. It lacked the quirks and charm of Burton's original take on the character and the plot was fairly formulaic; it wasn't going to be a masterpiece, but there wasn't anything particularly disastrous about it, either. Then, between shooting the film and substantial reshoots after early test screenings went poorly, things took a turn. The end result resembled the shooting script in structure, but myriad small changes combined to turn the film into an unintentional farce.

The film's opening credits sequence was an attempt at a dramatic beginning with a lengthy montage of Catwomen throughout history. When the podcast *How Did This Get Made?* reviewed *Catwoman*, comedian Paul Scheer remarked, "I knew we were in trouble just from the beginning with like the faux Enya music over like the Ken Burns documentary on cats."* A voice-over from Halle Berry explained, "It all started on the day that I died," because "the day that I died was also the day I started to live."

Her character, renamed Patience Phillips, was now a graphic designer at a cosmetics company, and her only companions were her cat and her quippy officemates, one a flamboyant gay stereotype and the other a man-crazy gal who didn't notice that she got a headache every time she used the company's new beauty cream, Beau-line, even when those headaches landed her in the hospital. Berry shuffled through the early scenes of the film in drab, oversized clothes, trying to project a nervous discomfort, with limited success; someone who'd been regularly named one of the most beautiful women in the world playing a dull wallflower was a hard sell.

Patience soon met Tom Lone, a police officer played by Benjamin Bratt, when he saved her after she climbed out her window to rescue a trapped cat, and the two struck up a romance. Meanwhile, the company's owners George and Laurel Hedare, portrayed by Lambert Wilson and Sharon Stone, were at odds over George replacing Laurel

---

* Jason Mantzoukas then chimed in, "I knew we were in trouble when the director had one name."

with a new model as the face of the company. They were also covering up the dangerous effects of Beau-line, as demonstrated by Patience's coworker. When Patience stumbled across a discussion of the cream's harmful potential while delivering new artwork late one night, she was killed and then subsequently resurrected by a group of cats.

The transition from mild-mannered Patience to fierce Catwoman unfolded awkwardly. Patience found herself intermittently feisty; after her meek apology to her boss was dismissed, her anger surged and she replied, "OK, then let me try the remix: I'm sorry for every second I wasted working for an untalented, unethical egomaniac like you." She was shocked at her own outburst, which was just the start of a split-personality narrative. Soon she broke up a loud party across the alley that kept her awake, cut off her hair, and robbed a jewelry store, recoiling in surprise when she regained her senses after each escapade. An address attached to the collar of one of the cats that saved Patience led her to Ophelia Powers, an expert on these feline resurrections and the abilities they brought, but Patience spent most of their first meeting distracted by a ball of catnip.

Eventually, Patience learned to embrace her new powers and personality and became Catwoman, donning a costume to mark her transition. The costume consisted of a black cowl with catlike ears, a top that was little more than a black leather brassiere, shredded black leather pants, long black leather gloves with claws, and open-toed stilettos. It didn't leave much to the imagination. The first image of Halle Berry in the costume premiered in *Time* magazine in September 2003, and it did not go over well. The nerd culture website *Ain't It Cool News* reported on the costume with a post headlined, "Wanna see a pretty ridiculous photo of Halle Berry in the Catwoman outfit?" Another site, *Comic Book Movie*, lamented, "Oh no, Halle! Say it isn't so!" before stating, "As you can see, the costume is awful." While the studio thought that she looked sexy and cool, the costume was uniformly dismissed as trashy; when a producer asked writer John Rogers what he thought of the outfit, he responded, "Well, she looks like a Quebecois stripper."

Along with the costume, Patience embraced her feline nature. Some of this was played for comedy; her apartment was littered with empty cans of tuna, and she scarfed down sashimi at an alarming rate while on a date with Tom at a Japanese restaurant. But the bigger feline component was Berry's physicality as Catwoman. She was wholly dedicated to the role and later revealed, "I watched hours and hours of videotape, you know, *National Geographic*, anything I could get my hands on with cats and lions and tigers." Unlike the tense and nervous Patience, Berry's Catwoman was lithe and smooth. She moved fluidly through her scenes, stalking her prey and then pouncing on them with sharp fury.

Berry captured the movement of Catwoman well but, like most aspects of the film, it was overplayed. Her constant physical flair combined with sassily delivered, clunky dialogue to give the film a campy feel. And Berry wasn't the only one chewing the scenery. Sharon Stone was particularly evocative, even though she didn't have much to work with. The signature line in her final battle with Catwoman came when Stone's Laurel was about to deliver the coup de grâce and snarled, "Game over," to which Catwoman replied, "Guess what? It's overtime!"*

The poor dialogue wasn't helped by the direction. Even the simplest scene was shot from at least a dozen different angles, all of which were cycled through rapidly; Pitof bounced between close-ups and long shots seemingly at random, changing angles each time, all while tossing in occasional shots of cats, a top-down look, or an unnecessary swooping shot. This gave the film a frenetic, almost spastic feel that made it difficult to watch. In one scene, Catwoman threw a foe out a door, and the simple action of his descent was shown from seven different angles in just two seconds.

Pitof's special effects work wasn't strong, either, despite his background in the field. One ill-conceived scene had a cat-powered Patience face off against Tom Lone in a one-on-one basketball game. The transitions from the actors to their more athletic stand-ins to CGI were obvious, even through the blur of Pitof's constant cuts. The CGI transitions were weak in general, especially with Catwoman; the moves that went beyond human stunt capabilities were obviously

---

* Laurel was able to hold her own with the superpowered Catwoman because her excessive use of Beau-line had made her skin as hard as marble.

animated, and poorly so. This was partly due to a time crunch caused by the substantial reshoots near the film's release, but regardless of the reason, the end result was a film that often looked shoddily made.

Although *Catwoman* aimed for an empowering message as Patience learned to stand up for herself and fight back as Catwoman, the execution was lacking on all fronts. The film's final scene tried to bring everything together with Berry's dramatic reading of her "Dear John" letter to Tom. She explained that while he'd helped her learn what was special about herself, she was going off on her own to embrace her new nature. The voice-over was full of hollow platitudes, and concluded: "You see, sometimes I'm good. Ooh, I'm very good. But sometimes I'm bad. But only as bad as I wanna be. Freedom is power. To live a life untamed and unafraid is the gift that I've been given, and so my journey begins." This was followed by Catwoman seductively strutting across the top of a building toward a glowing moon, with her swaying rear end as the focal point of the shot; it was one of the longest sustained shots in the film.

*Catwoman* premiered on July 23, 2004, and came in third at the box office behind *The Bourne Supremacy* and *I, Robot*, barely besting *Spider-Man 2* to take the third spot even though the web-slinger had already been in theaters for four weeks. The film ultimately grossed $40 million domestically and $42 million internationally, for a combined total far short of its $100 million production budget. On top of the poor audience response, critics hated *Catwoman*, too. Roger Ebert remarked, "What a letdown," and called the film "tired and boring" before suggesting that Pitof "was probably issued with two names at birth and would be wise to use the other one on his next project." The *A. V. Club* called *Catwoman* "essentially an excuse to pose Berry in ever-skimpier outfits"; *Variety* snarked that it "plays like a Lifetime movie on estrogen overdose, barely held together by a script that should have been tossed out with the kitty litter." The headline for *Time* magazine's review simply read, "Me-Ouch!"

## White Male Superhero Domination

*Catwoman* is unique among superhero films as the only movie in the booming genre thus far with a lead character who is both a woman and a person of color. Unfortunately, the disastrous response to the film may be why it remains unique, even more than a decade after its release. Rather than chalking up *Catwoman*'s failure to its quality, studio executives seem to have put the blame on the casting and steered strongly in the opposite direction with superhero films ever since.

Halle Berry's casting in *Catwoman* was a clear nod to Eartha Kitt, who broke new ground when she took on the role back in 1967. The film went even further than the old *Batman* show; Berry was African American and her costar, Benjamin Bratt, was Hispanic. Producer Edward L. McDonnell said of the film, "It's produced by people of color and stars people of multiple color. You don't make any distinction and I think that's something you have never seen before in a movie." Berry was particularly proud of this fact, and in interviews before the film's release she noted, "More films with people of color in leading roles will be made if people go out and support this film." As it turned out, the reverse of her statement was true as well.

While casting people of color in the two leads roles was a progressive choice, *Catwoman* didn't play into the heritage of either character in any significant way. In fact, it's been criticized by some for this lack of connection. Historian Deborah Elizabeth Whaley contends:

> Lone and Phillips are racially ambiguous characters that show no ties to their ethnic ancestry; they bear no signs of ethnicity or culture to mark them in terms of race. A twenty-first century Black Catwoman could not break new ground or carve out meaningful gender, racial, and sexual spaces while remaining squarely situated in a 1960s approach of inclusion by way of non-threatening, colorblind representation. In this sense, Berry's racial difference in the film made little difference at all, and was less radical than that of her 1967 predecessor.

The ethnicity of the main characters didn't define *Catwoman* at all, but it clearly carried weight with studio executives.

There hasn't been a superhero film with a person of color in the lead role since 2004; *Blade: Trinity* came out in the same year as *Catwoman*, closing the franchise. Since then the superhero film market has exploded, with white leads in every one of them. People of color have played supporting characters and villains, but have yet to headline a film. Warner Bros.' *Suicide Squad* in 2016 was the first superhero ensemble in which white actors did not make up the majority of the main cast.* A person of color isn't scheduled to be the title character of a movie until Marvel's *Black Panther* in 2018, though Luke Cage did star in his own Netflix television series in 2016.

*Catwoman* isn't solely to blame, of course. Most superheroes were created between the 1930s and 1960s, a period not known for diverse representation. Moreover, certain sections of the superhero fan community are notorious for their overreactions to race-swapped casting; the news that Michael B. Jordan would be portraying the traditionally white Johnny Storm in the 2015 reboot of the *Fantastic Four* was met with appalling levels of vitriol across the Internet. It should also be pointed out that superhero movies are not unique in their paleness. Across virtually all genres, the North American film industry is vastly underrepresentative in its casting, particularly with lead roles. But while the failure of *Catwoman* may not be the only explanation for this dearth of superhero diversity, it's certainly a contributing factor.

The film has played a far larger role in the lack of female leads in superhero cinema, as evidenced by a leaked email from a major studio executive. A 2014 hack of Sony revealed correspondence between Marvel CEO Ike Perlmutter and Sony CEO Michael Lynton in which Perlmutter cited the poor performances of several female-led movies in an attempt to prove that such films were not viable. He said of *Catwoman*, "Catwoman was one of the most important female characters within the Batman franchise. This film was a disaster." Perlmutter also mentioned 2005's *Elektra*, which underperformed

---

* And just barely so; six of the eleven main cast members were people of color: Adewale Akinnuoye-Agbaje, Adam Beach, Viola Davis, Karen Fukuhara, Jay Hernandez, and Will Smith.

but did manage to bring in more than its budget, and *Supergirl*, which was released thirty years earlier and was hardly a relevant comparison; *Catwoman* was the only real fiasco in the bunch.

It can hardly be a coincidence that Marvel Studios has yet to release a film with a female lead. There have been fifteen films released thus far in the Marvel Cinematic Universe, all of them headlined by men apart from *Avengers* and *Guardians of the Galaxy* films in which the male heroes outnumbered the female heroes by a considerable margin. *Ant-Man and the Wasp* is in development for 2018; it would be the twentieth Marvel Studios film and the first with a female character in the title, though she has to share it with a male hero. Marvel is also developing a *Captain Marvel* film that would be its first solo movie starring a woman. Its release date has already been pushed back twice, and it's currently scheduled for 2019.

Other studios lack Perlmutter's smoking gun, but their output has been similar. At 20th Century Fox, the X-Men franchise has either been ensemble casts or male led, as have the rest of the studio's superhero properties. Warner Bros. put out solely male-led superhero films after *Catwoman* until *Suicide Squad* in 2016, and Wonder Woman just debuted her first solo movie in June 2017. The failure of *Catwoman* managed to hold back women in superhero films for more than a decade.*

In the meantime, male-led franchises have failed with no ill effects. After the Batman franchise petered out in the late 1990s, Warner Bros. rebooted it with *Batman Begins* in 2005, and another new Batman debuted in 2016 in *Batman v Superman: Dawn of Justice*. The last two entries in the Superman franchise bombed in the 1980s, and the reboot *Superman Returns* was a disappointment in 2006, yet they tried Superman again with *Man of Steel* in 2013. There have been three Spider-Mans, two different versions of the Fantastic Four, and three Hulks. All the while, *Wonder Woman* floundered in development for twenty years before it eventually came together,

---

* Things went slightly better for female leads on the small screen, though it still took some time. In 2015 *Agent Carter* debuted on ABC, *Jessica Jones* premiered on Netflix, and *Supergirl* took to the skies on CBS; they were the first superhero shows headlined by women in over a decade.

and Black Widow has been a standout supporting character in the Marvel Cinematic Universe but has yet to headline her own movie.

The clear lesson studios should take from the failure of *Catwoman* is the importance of a solid script and a good director, not that an entire gender isn't suitable for a genre. The superhero boom has been massive across the board; the audience for the majority of these blockbusters has been at least 40 percent women, and yet none of these films have a female lead. Executives citing *Catwoman* as evidence for why female-led movies won't work is an obvious nonsensical cover for their own sexism; if it wasn't *Catwoman*, it would be something else. But this scapegoating is the legacy of *Catwoman*, one that the superhero film industry is finally starting to move beyond.

# 11

## Sidekick Tales

*T*he poor performance of the *Catwoman* movie may have set back women in superhero films for over a decade, but there was no blowback for Batman. As *Catwoman* bombed in the summer of 2004, shooting was well underway on *Batman Begins*, a new take on the Caped Crusader from acclaimed director Christopher Nolan. Warner Bros. had let the property lie fallow since Joel Schumacher's second Batman film, *Batman and Robin*, had a disappointing run in 1997; plans for a fifth film in the franchise were scrapped, and the studio eventually decided to move forward with a full reboot. It was a wise decision. *Batman Begins* was a critical and commercial hit in 2005, and its 2008 sequel, *The Dark Knight*, broke the North American opening weekend box office record and went on to earn over $1 billion worldwide.

The success of the new franchise also cemented Batman as Warner Bros.' primary superhero property across all media in the 2000s. The studio attempted to develop several other superhero films, with little to no success. *Superman Returns* didn't perform well enough to garner a sequel, nor did *Green Lantern* a few years later. A Wonder Woman film languished in development hell, and a Justice League movie with famed director George Miller at the helm fell apart just before shooting was due to begin. Lesser known properties like

*Constantine*, *Jonah Hex*, and *The Losers* also failed to make much of a splash. Meanwhile, Marvel was dominating cinemas with 20th Century Fox's X-Men franchise, Sony's Spider-Man movies, and its own Marvel Studios' Avengers line.

Marvel's cinematic popularity resulted in the company besting Warner Bros. elsewhere, including toys, games, and other merchandise; Marvel became so successful that Disney bought the company in a multibillion-dollar deal in 2009. The only real answer Warner Bros. had to the rising prominence of Iron Man, Spider-Man, and Wolverine was its hit Batman franchise, and so he became the key player in all of its noncinematic endeavors. From cartoons to television to licensing for video games and toys, different versions of Batman were everywhere. Even when something went moderately well, like the studio's 2013 Superman film reboot *The Man of Steel*, Warner Bros. brought in a new Batman for the sequel just to shore things up.

This preponderance of Batman led to roles for all of Gotham City's costumed citizens, including Catwoman. While Patience Phillips was never heard from again, Selina Kyle returned across a variety of media, though she was rarely in the spotlight. Batman was the undisputed star and Catwoman primarily played a supporting part. So many different takes on the character led to a mixed bag in which some aspects of her past incarnations, both heroic and problematic, came back and new elements were added to her depiction. The end result was a more prominent role for Catwoman, but one that pigeonholed her in a sidekick narrative that often emphasized her sexuality over her skill set.

## Film and Television

The most widely seen version of Catwoman thus far in the twenty-first century was in Christopher Nolan's *The Dark Knight Rises*, which closed out his Batman trilogy in 2012. Unlike Tim Burton and Joel Schumacher, who brought an over-the-top, cartoonish approach to Batman and Gotham City, Nolan aimed for realism above all else. Rather than building a stylized world around Batman, he saw his Dark Knight as "an extraordinary character against the background of an ordinary world." Nolan's films were still superhero movies, requiring a certain degree of suspension of disbelief, but they were grounded. Christian Bale's Batman costume was basically light armor, and all of his gadgets and vehicles were things that conceivably could exist. Instead of creating a gothic and ornate city, they shot in Chicago and changed very little. Even the villains were fairly practical, with little in the way of outlandish outfits or plots; the Joker was the only one with real visual flair, but he lacked anything in the way of zany accoutrements, and his plans largely revolved around just blowing things up.

A woman in a cat costume didn't fit well with Christopher Nolan's vision of Gotham, and when his brother and cowriter Jonathan suggested introducing Catwoman in the third film, he wasn't sold on the idea. Jonathan felt that she was important to the Bat-mythos, and told his brother, "You've gotta have her, because she has a delicious greyness to her that helps define who Batman is. She keeps wavering on this line of, 'Is she a good guy or a bad guy?' Well, she's kind of neither. And that's why, to me, that relationship and that character only enhances the universe—and the Batman character." The director eventually came around, and he and his brother reimagined her as "a bit of a con-woman, something of a grifter. A hard-edged kind of criminal." In the end, the name Catwoman didn't appear in the film at all. She was Selina Kyle throughout the movie, though a few newspapers referred to her as "the Cat" while recounting her exploits, in a nod to her Golden Age origins.

After exploring Bruce Wayne's journey from young orphan to Batman in *Batman Begins* and having him save the city from the Joker and Two-Face in *The Dark Knight*, Nolan's final installment picked up eight years later. With the villains defeated, Gotham was largely crime free so Batman retired, but the arrival of the crusading Bane promising a reckoning for Gotham brought Batman back to save the city once again.* Catwoman found herself caught in the

---

* Nolan's Bane, as played by Tom Hardy, bore little resemblance to the luchador-inspired behemoth who took over Gotham City in the comics' 1990s *Knightfall* event, apart from the requisite breaking of Batman's back.

middle of their war, torn between her self-interest and her better nature.

For the role of Catwoman, Nolan auditioned several actresses including Gemma Arterton, Jessica Biel, Anne Hathaway, Keira Knightley, Blake Lively, Kate Mara, and Charlotte Riley. The auditions were cloaked in secrecy due to the film's high profile; Hathaway actually thought that she was auditioning for the role of Harley Quinn. After the initial auditions, Biel, Hathaway, and Mara all did screen tests for the part, and Nolan ultimately went with Hathaway.

Anne Jacqueline Hathaway was born in Brooklyn, New York, and raised in New Jersey, where she acted in school plays and sang in choruses before attending the American Academy of Dramatic Arts. After her breakthrough performance in *The Princess Diaries* in 2001, Hathaway bounced through a variety of period pieces, romantic comedies, and dramas in the years that followed, including her Oscar-nominated role in *Rachel Getting Married* in 2008.* *The Dark Knight Rises* was her most physical role by far, and her training started ten months before filming even began. Hathaway threw herself into the preparation, working five days a week on straight exercise and stunt training, as well as dance to aid the fluidity of her movement. She later admitted, "I always thought I had worked hard in the gym and it turns out that what I thought was hard, in Catwoman's world, is actually light to moderate. I've had to ratchet everything up."

Hathaway's physical work in the film was particularly impressive given that she had to perform the bulk of her stunts in three-inch stiletto heels. Her costume borrowed from Darwyn Cooke's Catwoman redesign, a tight black catsuit with gloves and boots, though Cooke had insisted that his Catwoman wear flats. Instead of a cowl, Hathaway's long brunette hair hung behind her, and she wore a pair of goggles that, when pushed up on her head, resembled cat ears.

Selina Kyle appeared early in *The Dark Knight Rises*, infiltrating a party at Wayne Manor by posing as a waitress in order to gain access to the treasures housed within. When Bruce Wayne caught

---

* Hathaway later won an Academy Award for Best Supporting Actress in 2012 for her role in *Les Misérables*.

her wearing pearls pilfered from his supposedly uncrackable safe, Selina snarked, "Oops. Nobody told me it was uncrackable." She then knocked him down, escaped out a window, and charmed her way into a departing town car. The pearls weren't her primary target; she was after Bruce's fingerprints, aiming to trade them with a nefarious buyer for a "clean slate" computer program that would wipe her criminal record and erase her identity.

The film hinted at a "Year One" inspired past for Selina, continuing the trilogy's adaptation of the story after *Batman Begins* drew heavily from the Frank Miller work. Selina lived in an apartment with a younger woman played by Juno Temple who, though named Jen, closely resembled Holly Robinson. She also told Bruce, "I started out doing what I had to do. Once you've done what you had to, they'll never let you do what you want to," perhaps a reference to time as a prostitute. Few details were forthcoming, and Selina was soon swept up in the movie's main plot.

Selina's pursuit of the "clean slate" got her into trouble with the wrong people, and she betrayed Batman to Bane in order to save her own life, even though Batman had helped her earlier in the film. She tried to leave Gotham before Bane's revolution began but was arrested, then was freed when Bane took over the city and released everyone from prison. After Bane cut off the city from the rest of the world, Selina protected her neighborhood and soon grew tired of Bane's thuggish reign.

When Batman returned, she joined his resistance after he promised her the "clean slate." He also gave her his Bat-Bike so that she could use its firepower to open up an escape tunnel for civilians to flee the city. Selina said that she'd open the tunnel and then leave, fearing the detonation of Bane's nuclear weapon, but Batman told her, "There's more to you than that." She disagreed, replying, "Sorry to keep letting you down," and told Batman that he should leave with her. In the end, she did stay, saving Batman from Bane and helping him track down the bomb before he flew it out of Gotham to save the city.

*The Dark Knight Rises* was a hit across the board, with over $1 billion in worldwide box office and positive reviews from critics.

While reviewers often differed on the merits of various plot points and cast members, one constant throughout the reviews was praise for Hathaway's portrayal of Selina Kyle. The *Washington Post* called her "the sensational secret weapon of this production" and the *A.V. Club* hailed her as "the most dynamic character in the *Dark Knight Rises*." *Vulture* simply stated, "It's Anne Hathaway's movie." Critics appreciated the lightness that her sass and style brought to the film, with CNN writing that her "slinky, light-fingered, high-kicking thief is the film's best idea of fun," and *Rolling Stone* lauding her for "bringing welcome humor to a movie about to be enveloped in darkness."

Several critics noted how different Hathaway's portrayal was from past versions of the character, particularly Michelle Pfeiffer's iconic outing. Both women were independent and mercurial, but Hathaway was more grounded, a calculating thief rather than a stylized supervillain. However, Pfeiffer's Selina retained her independence through to the end of *Batman Returns* while Hathaway's Selina took an odd turn in the final moments of *The Dark Knight Rises* that reduced her to a prize for Bruce Wayne and continued a problematic trend in Nolan's franchise.

Both *Batman Begins* and *The Dark Knight* were male-centric affairs, with only one female actor in a lead role in each film. Katie Holmes played Bruce's childhood friend and love interest Rachel Dawes in the first movie; she was an original character, created to add a romantic subplot. Maggie Gyllenhaal took over the role in the franchise's second installment, in which she dated Harvey Dent before the Joker murdered her, leading to the film's dramatic final act. Although the character was an accomplished lawyer, she served as little more than a damsel in distress and romantic interest, as well as fuel for Batman's perpetual angst.

*The Dark Knight Rises* boasted two female leads, but they were again relegated to romantic roles. Marion Cotillard's Miranda Tate slept with Bruce before the film revealed that she was actually Talia al Ghul, and she later died, too. Selina escaped romantic hijinks for most of the movie; she flirted with Bruce and Batman, but she was very much her own woman with her own priorities and stayed firmly unattached. Meanwhile, Bruce's romantic failings became a major plot point when Alfred expressed his disappointment at Bruce returning to the cowl rather than pursuing love and a family. The butler described his idyllic dream to one day come across a happily coupled Bruce in an Italian café, and this conversation led to the two men parting ways.

As the film drew to a close, Selina's romantic feelings for Batman began to show. When she told him to leave Gotham with her, there was a certain degree of longing behind her words, and she kissed Batman passionately before he flew the nuclear bomb out of Gotham and to his certain doom. But he miraculously survived, and the movie closed with Alfred at an Italian café, spying Bruce and Selina together. She had become the fulfillment of Alfred's romantic wish for Bruce.

Slotting all of a film franchise's lead women into various romantic roles was a rather narrow approach to female characters, and one that was especially ill suited to Selina. *The Dark Knight Rises* spent two hours giving Selina her own story alongside the film's other narratives, including that of Joseph Gordon-Levitt's Detective John Blake. Both Selina and Blake were connected to Batman but separate from him, sometimes working with him and sometimes doing their own thing. In the end, Batman left Blake the keys to the Batcave, and the film's conclusion hinted at the start of the young man's new heroic journey. Meanwhile, Selina didn't get her own ending; she was Batman's reward, and the culmination of his and Alfred's narrative in a happily-ever-after that the franchise had built toward for Bruce, but not for her. Ultimately, both this final scene and the franchise's poor record with female characters undermined what was an otherwise strong portrayal of Catwoman.

A new take on Catwoman debuted just two years later with Fox's *Gotham*, a television series set in the fabled city in an era before Batman. The lead character was Jim Gordon, here a young detective rather than the grizzled commissioner familiar to most fans. *Gotham*'s aim was to slowly build the iconic characters of Batman lore; regulars included Edward Nygma as a police forensic scientist who later becomes the Riddler, and Oswald Cobblepot as a mafia lackey who later becomes the Penguin. Bruce Wayne was a main character as well, a teenager who met Gordon when the murder of Thomas and Martha Wayne was the first case in the series' pilot.

The only other witness to the murder was a young Selina Kyle, a street urchin who watched in shock from a fire escape in the alley where the Waynes were killed. She was played by Camren Bicondova, who was known more for her dancing than her acting before she was cast in *Gotham*; when she was twelve years old, Bicondova and her all-girl dance group 8 Flavahz came in second place on *America's Best Dance Crew*, and she had danced in a variety of films and music videos. The teenager wasn't particularly familiar with Catwoman when she auditioned for the role and relied on the character description of "street thief, pick pocket, orphan, tough when cornered" to develop her take on Selina. She also put her dance training to use to incorporate catlike movements, just as Julie Newmar had done fifty years before.* Bicondova's portrayal of Selina, known as Cat to her friends, soon became a fan favorite, a bright spot in the relentless bleakness of the series. Showrunner Bruno Heller was so impressed with her performance that he ended up using her more than he'd anticipated, and she was nominated for a Saturn Award for Best Performance by a Younger Actor in a Television Series for her work on *Gotham*'s first season.†

The show's pilot opened with Selina, dressed in a leather jacket, hoodie, and goggles as she ran across the city's rooftops. She then pickpocketed her way through a crowd, nabbing a wallet full of cash for herself and a carton of milk for her cat, before she saw the murder of the Waynes. Over the next few episodes, Selina used her eye witness testimony to curry favor with Jim Gordon. After she was rounded up to be sent to a children's home upstate, she told him that she knew who killed the Waynes. She was lying; the killer was masked and facing away from her, but she traded this promise of information for her freedom and then used a pen to escape her handcuffs and flee Gordon's custody.

---

\* Newmar is a big fan of Bicondova, calling her performance "purrfection" and expressing admiration for the serenity and believability she brings to the role.

† The Saturn Awards are presented annually by the Academy of Science Fiction, Fantasy and Horror Films; Bicondova lost to Maisie Williams, who plays Arya Stark on *Game of Thrones*.

After another theft brought Selina back to Gordon's attention, he sent her to stay at Wayne Manor with Bruce and Alfred. She and Bruce slowly developed a friendship that was cemented when gunmen attacked Wayne Manor and the duo fled to the city, where Selina fought off goons and used her street connections to keep them safe. The street urchin and the orphaned millionaire were an odd pair but a cute one, and their adventure ended with a kiss. While their relationship was strained when Bruce learned that Selina had lied about knowing who killed his parents, she remained his protector as the series progressed.

Bruce would one day become Batman, but as a young teenager he was generally useless in the ways of combat, stealth, and theft. His investigation of his parents' deaths frequently put him in danger, and Selina was always there to get him out of it, partly because he couldn't and partly because she cared about him and wanted to keep him from going down a dark path. When Alfred was nearly killed by someone trying to derail the investigation, Selina helped Bruce track down the perpetrator. Bruce was about to push him out a window after he threatened to have the two of them murdered when Selina, noticing that Bruce was conflicted, stepped in and did the deed herself, killing the man. It was a line that she was comfortable crossing but that she knew would have haunted Bruce.*

The start of *Gotham*'s second season found Selina on the outs with everyone at Wayne Manor. Alfred was appalled that she'd killed someone, telling her that Bruce would be better off without her in his life before threatening her and declaring, "Do yourself a favor, treacle, and jog on." Bruce was romancing Silver St. Cloud, who Selina thought was bad news, and Bruce sided with Silver over Selina. So Selina began her own story, reconnecting with her friend, Bridget, whom she knew from her first years on the streets. Bridget's brothers had forced her into a life of crime, and Selina helped her escape after she killed a police officer. She tried to get her out of the city, telling her, "You remind me of me, if I was a doofus." Bridget ultimately took a dark turn, becoming the pyromaniac villain Firebug

---

* Selina also helped Bruce break into an office at Wayne Enterprises. They attended a gala together in fancy dress, and Selina nabbed the executive's key and made a copy while Bruce kept him distracted. The scene was rather adorable.

and killing her brothers, but Selina still tried to help her and worked with Gordon to track her down safely before she was killed when her suit malfunctioned.

Selina's suspicions about Silver also proved true, and Bruce reached out to her for help. She broke into Silver's apartment, finding documents proving that she was the tool of the villain Theo Galavan, and assisted Bruce in a fake kidnapping to get Silver to admit all she knew. After Bruce was nabbed by Galavan in the show's fall finale, Selina led a team that included Gordon, Alfred, and the Penguin into his hideout through a secret entrance, and fought alongside the grown men as they battled Galavan's associates to save Bruce.

She continued to help her friends in the second half of the season, protecting Bruce and letting him stay with her when he left Wayne Manor to try to better understand criminals by living on the streets. Selina stitched him up after he got assaulted by a drug dealer, and put up with his Robin Hood tendencies despite her frustration at him giving away half of their stolen loot. After Bruce returned to his mansion, Selina broke into Arkham Asylum when she learned that Bridget wasn't dead and had been experimented on by the fiendish Hugo Strange. Despite finding a mind-controlled Bridget who didn't remember her and attacked her, Selina stayed with her, tried to help her regain her memory, and ultimately freed her from the asylum. She also saved Bruce and Jim Gordon in the process; they'd run afoul of Strange as well, and Selina broke them out, allowing them to save the city from a potentially devastating nuclear bomb.

In a world of villains and morally compromised heroes, Selina was arguably the most steadfast character in *Gotham*. Gordon was often motivated by anger instead of justice and made rash decisions that compromised his badge, while Alfred was more goon than English gentleman. Even Bruce was all over the map, torn between revenge and being the good man his parents raised him to be. Meanwhile, Selina was constant. She had complete disdain for the police and authority of any kind and would commit crimes and kill if she had to, but above all else she was loyal to her friends. Her time on the streets had given her an internal strength and her own code that, while nontraditional, was nonetheless consistent and always in service of those closest to her.

She was also multifaceted. Selina was a supporting character in Bruce's story, but she had her own adventures as well, and her relationship with Bruce had several aspects. While there was the typical romantic angle, she was also his protector, his partner, and his friend. She didn't fit easily into any one box. Bicondova played Selina with nuance, imbuing her with a nonchalance that belied her true compassion. It was a layered take on the character, and a stark contrast to Catwoman's portrayal in other Batman media in the 2010s.

## Games and Toys

Catwoman is no stranger to video games. She's appeared in several over the years, including movie tie-ins for both *Batman Returns* and *Catwoman* across several platforms, and in 1999 she starred in her own Gameboy Color adventure. She wore the tight purple costume of the Jim Balent era on the game's cover, though within the game she was a decidedly less curvaceous boxy mass of pixels. The game's story centered on Catwoman stealing an artifact for Talia al Ghul and then keeping it for herself, resulting in several levels of battling Talia's minions. The game play was limited and finicky, and archaically basic; one review warned, "This game should not be part of your Game Boy Color utility belt," and "There's no reason left to check out this kitty's catbox. All you'll find is poop."

For decades, Batman video games were notoriously bad, so much so that they became a running joke among gamers, with reviewers often expecting the games to be poorly made and still ending up disappointed. This all changed with *Batman: Arkham Asylum* in 2009. Created by Rocksteady Studios and Eidos Interactive and written by *Batman: The Animated Series* scribe Paul Dini, the game had Batman fighting through scores of Gotham's most iconic villains after the Joker took over Arkham Asylum and released all of its inmates. *Batman: Arkham Asylum* was a smash on every level; it sold eight million copies, won several awards, and is now regarded as one of the best video games of all time.

Catwoman wasn't in the game, apart from a brief appearance of clawed gloves and cat-eyed goggles in one of the rooms of the asylum, but she was a major part of the 2011 sequel, *Batman: Arkham City*. The sequel was an even bigger hit than its predecessor, selling eleven million copies and winning game of the year from many award shows and publications. Dini returned to write the game, in which part of Gotham City was cordoned off and turned into a super prison, forcing Batman to fight through even more villains to nab the mastermind behind it all, Hugo Strange.

While Batman was the primary protagonist of *Batman: Arkham City*, Catwoman was a playable character within the game, starring in her own story line that occasionally intersected with Batman's. It all began when she broke into a safe in Two-Face's headquarters to get back some loot that he'd taken from her, which led to them sparring throughout the game. Two-Face captured her early on and put her on trial while she hung over a vat of acid, but she freed herself and escaped after Batman showed up. Catwoman then teamed up with Poison Ivy to break into Strange's vault and went after Two-Face again after he ransacked her apartment and rigged it to explode when she returned home. She cornered Two-Face and took him out, and finally ended her story line by tracking down his goons to collect the rest of her pilfered loot.

The video game industry is notorious for its lack of playable female characters, so including Catwoman in *Batman: Arkham City* in such a big way was a bold move by Rock Steady. She got to fight her way through several different levels and settings and also had her own unique set of upgradeable weapons and accessories, including a whip and a bolo. Another side portion of the game was special Riddler challenges, some of which could only be completed by Catwoman. The developers ensured that the game play was different for Catwoman as well, making a clear contrast between the lithe cat burglar and the bulky crime fighter. *Kotaku* reviewer Kirk Hamilton wrote, "The best thing about playing Catwoman is setting her sprinting, leaping, and swinging about the open map. [. . .] Once I got the hang of it, I found that there is a crazed quality to her that Batman lacks, and it's really fun."

Unfortunately, despite the care put into the mechanics of Cat-woman, the game's writing and design choices troubled many play-ers. Throughout the game, the legions of nondescript goons that Batman and Catwoman faced made comments to add some color to the proceedings, muttering as they stood idly while the protagonists stalked them or shouting out when they were attacked. While Bat-man was occasionally called a "freak," Catwoman was almost exclu-sively referred to as a "bitch," and with great vitriol. The gendered insult was spat out over and over, with lines like "Bitch deserves it" and "I'll make you meow, bitch." Two-Face continued the offen-sive rhetoric, telling his goons, "I want you guys to blow that bitch apart!" and "Find her and skin that cat-bitch!" The name-calling was relentless—and offputting for many players, male and female. Alex Cranz of *FemPop* noted, "It's not like 90% of misogynistic things occurring in video games and comics where women take note and men tell them to shut the hell up. The use of the word 'bitch' is so overt and the voice acting so malicious sounding that guys are stop-ping and wondering what the hell is going on."

The disconcerting dialogue was paired with a very sexualized depiction of the character. Catwoman wore the now-standard black costume with a cowl and goggles, but the sex appeal was upped con-siderably. When she first appeared and disturbed a group of goons, voice actor Grey DeLisle purred in a sultry tone, "Sorry to disappoint you, boys. It's just little old me." Catwoman then sashayed toward them, her costume skintight on her shapely figure and her zipper pulled midway down her torso, exposing a considerable amount of cleavage.* The costume had been tweaked from Darwyn Cooke's original design: rather than a bodysuit that connected to the cowl, the suit and cowl were separated, thus allowing the suit to unzip and open outward, baring her chest. This continued to be her standard look throughout the game. While Catwoman had always been a sexy character, this design turned her into a sex object.

---

* The graphics quality of video games is extremely high these days, far more comparable to modern CGI than the pixel figures of years past. This depiction of Catwoman was both realistic and detailed.

Most of the game's female characters were similarly clad. Harley Quinn traded her usual full-body clown outfit for tight slacks and a skimpy vest that emphasized her cleavage. Poison Ivy was also on display, wearing a wide-open straitjacket barely held together with a clasp across her bust and no pants at all; instead, she was adorned in a small pair of leafy briefs.*

Catwoman's playable levels gave her more of a presence in *Batman: Arkham City* than the other women, and several of her cut scenes further emphasized her sexualized depiction. When Two-Face put her on trial, she was hung upside down over a vat of acid yet her cleavage remained perfectly intact, somehow defying gravity despite the wisps of fabric that held her breasts in place. She also hinted at offering sexual favors for her release, seductively saying, "I'm sorry I've been a bad kitty. Untie me and I'll make it up to you." The developers even worked sensuality into Catwoman's fight scenes; one of her signature takedown moves was to jump on an unsuspecting goon, straddling him and kissing him passionately before knocking him out.

DC Comics put out tie-in comic book series for the game that continued this take on Catwoman. A prequel miniseries written by Paul Dini with art by Carlos D'Anda put Catwoman in the same outfit, with D'Anda's cartoonishly stylized art adding further emphasis to her chest area. The debut issue of the follow-up series *Batman: Arkham Unhinged* began with Selina in a tight dress, then in her underwear, then in her low-cut costume with a series of panels that focused on her body for several pages, including a close-up shot of her torso, before finally showing her face. Her zipper had slid down from its position in the game as well, slipping perilously close to her navel. She did zip up her costume for occasional scenes over the course of the series' run, though, something that never happened in the video game.[†]

---

* It should be noted that Oracle, a.k.a. former Batgirl Barbara Gordon, was fully clothed; the skimpy new looks were just for the female villains.

[†] Amusingly, Catwoman was zipped up at the end of the first issue when she was knocked out and kidnapped by Batman, and when she woke up in the Batmobile at the start of the following issue, her costume was unzipped again, a clear editorial oversight that reflected poorly on Batman's reputation as a gentleman.

*Batman: Arkham City* was followed by *Batman: Arkham Origins* in 2013, which didn't involve Catwoman apart from a brief appearance in a tie-in game for handheld consoles like the Nintendo 3DS and Playstation Vita. She returned for the franchise's final outing, *Batman: Arkham Knight*, in 2015, and was a playable character again, though in a minimal role. The game had Batman working to stop a citywide attack by the Scarecrow, who was working with the mysterious new villain, Arkham Knight. Meanwhile, Catwoman spent most of the game as a prisoner of the Riddler.

The Riddler captured Catwoman early on, and when Batman showed up to save her she'd been equipped with an explosive collar that would detonate if she left the Riddler's hideout. Batman then had to run off and complete tasks to collect nine keys to unlock the collar and free her while she stayed behind. Catwoman was playable only in occasional, brief battles with the Riddler's robots, in which the player had the option to flip between Batman and Catwoman during the brawl. The game did do away with the gendered insults that permeated her last appearance, but the revealing costume remained, in even more detail due to the improved graphics of new gaming consoles. When Batman finally collected enough keys to free Catwoman, her response was, "How should we celebrate? I know a couple of poor, defenseless museums. But then again, I also know a couple of hotels."

Catwoman got a fun moment later in the game after she arrived to help Batman out of a jam as he captured the Riddler, and they had the following exchange:

CATWOMAN: "Thanks, Selina, for the daring, last-minute rescue. It was very heroic."
BATMAN: It was under control.
CATWOMAN: Sure it was. Now be a good damsel and bestow a kiss on your gallant hero.

It was an amusing reversal of the game's typical tropes. Catwoman also got her own extra downloadable level a few months after the game's release that finally put her in the spotlight again.

Titled "Catwoman's Revenge," the level had Catwoman return to the Riddler's hideout, fight through his goons and robots, and hack into his computer to steal his multimillion-dollar fortune. But ultimately, the enduring legacy of the *Arkham* franchise has been Catwoman's objectified appearance, and she's displayed a substantial amount of flesh in a variety of forms since its debut.

An animated short film included on the 2011 direct-to-DVD release of Warner Bros. Animation's *Batman: Year One* adaptation focused on Catwoman, voiced by Eliza Dushku, and specifically her cleavage. After saving a cat wearing a jeweled necklace from the villainous diamond smuggler Rough Cut, Catwoman infiltrated the Kitty Corner, a local strip club where Rough Cut was known to repose. The scene began with a lengthy strip routine by a blonde dancer that pushed the boundaries of the DVD's PG-13 rating. She was followed by Catwoman, who took the stage in costume and worked the pole for a full minute, unzipping her costume nearly to her crotch so as to entrance Rough Cut and his goons. She then brought out her whip and, after momentarily using it as a prop in her strip tease, took out the goons. Only after the fighting was done did she rezip her costume.

This focus on showing Catwoman's skin has continued with the myriad statues and toys that feature the character—usually with considerable cleavage, though some designs have been more creative in their means of objectification. Of the thirty-two different Catwoman statues and toys currently featured on a popular entertainment memorabilia site, thirteen show a fair amount of skin in a manner meant to titillate, six of the thirteen statues and seven of the nineteen toys and actions figures. On DC Comics' own official online shop, nearly half of the Catwoman statues and toys have her displayed in such a manner. Moreover, the vast majority of items that have her covered up do so because they are associated with a particular, fully clad version of the character, usually from the 1966 *Batman* television show or *Batman: The Animated Series*.

Of the toys and statues featuring a version of Darwyn Cooke's modern Catwoman design, it's an even split between cleavage and covered up. It's an odd turn of events for a costume that was a corrective reaction to a sexualized take on the character, designed to be practical above all else. The massive popularity of the *Batman: Arkham* video games overwrote the costume's original intent in the comic books, changing the public perception of Catwoman from stylish thief to sex kitten. Then, in 2011, the new look and its lascivious implications made its way into the world of comics when DC launched a brand-new *Catwoman* series.

# 12

# Perusing the New 52

In 2011 DC decided to reboot its entire comic book line again. *Crisis on Infinite Earths* was a quarter century past, and the universe's current continuity had grown so long and unwieldy that it was becoming inaccessible for new fans. DC wanted another fresh start, so they sent the Flash running through the past in *Flashpoint*, an event series in which the speedster's time travel shenanigans drastically altered the DC universe. In trying to fix the universe, the Flash ended up creating a new one that was similar to but not exactly like the original; everyone was younger and had slightly different costumes, and, most important, no cumbersome backstories. DC debuted fifty-two new series in September 2011, all with fresh #1 issues, and *Catwoman* was one of the new titles.

Much like with *Crisis on Infinite Earths*, DC's relaunch of the Bat-books was a little bit fuzzy. Characters like Superman and Wonder Woman got complete reboots; not one speck of their past continuity remained. This was largely because their books weren't selling well before the New 52 relaunch, and so DC's editors figured that there wasn't much worth saving there. But the Bat-books were enjoying a fairly successful run with a lot of fan favorite characters, and DC didn't want to scrap everything they'd built. Thus, the continuity of the Bat-books wasn't rebooted so much as condensed and simplified to carry over a lot of the popular elements into the new universe.

Except for Catwoman. Despite having become a key player in the Bat-books in recent years, Catwoman's history was completely wiped. When *Catwoman* #1 debuted, the series had a whole new cast of characters with no connection to her past adventures. Holly and Slam were gone, replaced by a revolving door of new associates. As the series went on, it became clear that Selina's entire familial history was changed as well. Her sister no longer existed, and her Hispanic heritage was overwritten. Everything was erased, including "Year One," which didn't fit within the new universe's condensed Bat-history and was discarded.

Catwoman was stripped down to her bare bones. She was still a thief, but the details of her life were a blank slate. The only holdover from the old universe was her romantic connection with Batman, and that was significantly altered by a return to the old status quo: Batman knew that Selina Kyle was Catwoman, but Catwoman no longer knew that Bruce Wayne was Batman, restoring their previous skewed power dynamic.

Her costume was tweaked as well, in a familiar way. While Catwoman kept the black bodysuit, she now sported a separate cowl, just like in the *Batman: Arkham* games. With all of her other history erased, her depiction in the wildly popular *Batman: Arkham* universe became the primary influence on how Catwoman was portrayed in the early days of the New 52 universe, with predictable results.

## Sexy, Sexy Times

*Catwoman* was relaunched by two industry veterans. Writer Judd Winick was an award-winning indie comics creator before he moved to DC Comics, where he spent the 2000s penning runs for several well-known characters, including Green Lantern, Green Arrow, and Batman. The art was by Guillem March, who was familiar with Catwoman from his time drawing *Gotham City Sirens*. March was a rising star at DC who'd drawn several books and many covers since joining DC two years earlier, and he'd had steady work in the European comics industry before landing with the American publisher.

DC's New 52 line was meant to reintroduce the publisher's characters to their fan base as well as potential new fans intrigued by the fresh start. The first issues were a way to encapsulate who the characters were, defining their key attributes and how the publisher viewed them as well as how they'd be portrayed moving forward. In an interview before the first issue was released, Winick discussed his approach to the character and declared, "It's a very sexy title! [. . .] This is a tough, sexy, violent, somewhat over-the-top book, which is everything Catwoman should be." He continued to focus on Catwoman's sexiness throughout the interview and told readers, "Think sexy. Think feline, with the whip, the costume. You know? She has a tremendous amount of sex appeal, and none of us want to shy away from that." Winick also discussed his interest in a low-tech, old-school approach to her heists, but even while mentioning Catwoman's other attributes he returned to her sex appeal, "But also think intelligent. That's part of why she's sexy."

The book's aim was clear, and when *Catwoman* #1 hit stores in September 2011, more than Catwoman's thieving skills were on display. The cover showed Catwoman reclining atop a tall building, head tilted back, hand in her hair, her mouth slightly open. Her zipper was pulled down to show off her sizable cleavage as the costume strained to contain her bust. It was a cover designed for one thing, especially with Catwoman pouring a bag of small, sparkly diamonds over her chest and down her body; discarding a valuable haul in such a manner was hardly a showcase for her intelligence.

The issue's opening pages delivered the goods promised by the cover. Selina was hastily leaving her apartment as skull-masked villains broke down her door, trying to put on her costume while collecting her cats. The first page's four panels all focused on her torso, particularly her lacy red bra as she raced, half-clothed, through the room.* Her face wasn't shown until the third page when, still half-

---

* The opening was very similar to the first few pages of *Batman: Arkham Unhinged* #1, though that was likely unintentional. *Catwoman* #1 came out just a few weeks before *Batman: Arkham Unhinged*'s first digital issue premiered, and the books were developed by completely separate editorial departments. Nonetheless, it speaks to the publisher's larger approach to Catwoman that such similarly exploitative scenes were crafted at the same time in such different branches of the company.

clothed, she burst out of a window in a splash page that caught her midbackflip. She didn't get her costume on and zipped up until the issue's fourth page.

Catwoman didn't stay clothed for long. She went undercover as a bartender in a hotel suite filled with Russian mobsters and prostitutes, swapping her costume for a tight, sleeveless blouse and a red wig. After recognizing a criminal from her past who had murdered one of her friends, she cornered the man in the bathroom, capturing his attention by opening her shirt wide to display a new lacy bra, this one purple. She then beat him soundly while again half-clothed, slamming his head against the countertop and scratching him repeatedly.

The debut outing ended with a visit from Batman, and a four-page sex scene. Catwoman undid his utility belt while he unzipped her costume as they kissed and grappled across the room. *Catwoman* #1 closed with another splash page, this one an awkwardly staged coupling in which Catwoman straddled Batman, his pants pulled down and her full-body costume zipped open as they copulated with their masks still on.

The reviews for the issue were poor. Greg McElhatton of the website *Comic Book Resources* gave the book one star and wrote, "This doesn't feel like a superhero (or supervillain, or antihero) comic. This feels like a soft core skin flick." Erik Norris's review on *IGN* was titled, "Selina Kyle clearly doesn't like wearing clothes," and he gave the book a rating of "Awful." In a scathing back-and-forth at the *A.V. Club*, Oliver Sava called the issue "a bunch of gratuitous images surrounded by cliché narration about risk and painfully stupid dialogue," while Keith Phipps stated, "I hate this book from the cover down. [. . .] It's about squeezing a lot of lurid sex and violence into the barest outline of a plot."

Overt objectification was a theme with several female characters throughout the New 52. The debut issue of *Red Hood and the Outlaws* had a beach scene in which Starfire sported a teensy bikini in several pinup poses across a two-page spread; she then propositioned one of her teammates. While crime fighting, Starfire wore a costume that covered next to nothing. *Voodoo* #1 opened in a strip club, with the titular character stripping throughout the issue before performing a private show for a patron, shape-shifting into a clawed alien, and killing him at the end of the book. Just like *Catwoman*, both of these books were written and drawn by men.\*

DC's treatment of women inspired a flurry of commentary and think pieces, perhaps none more pointed than *Comics Alliance* editor Laura Hudson's response to the argument that the characters were powerful, sexually liberated women.† Hudson wrote that she "would very much like to see confident ladies who enjoy sex and are having a fun sexy time" but that "this is not about these women wanting things; it's about men wanting to see them do things, and that takes something that really should be empowering — the idea that women can own their sexuality — and transforms it into yet another male fantasy." She then pointed out, "Female characters are only insatiable, barely-dressed aliens and strippers because someone decided to make them that way. It isn't a fact. It isn't an inviolable reality, especially in a comic book universe that has just been rebooted."

In the wake of these reactions, DC quietly decided to tone down *Catwoman*. Years later March revealed that the book's third issue was supposed to end with Catwoman showing up at Wayne Manor and stripping naked in front of a security camera to get Bruce Wayne's attention. A full-page spread showed Catwoman stark naked, smiling coyly, with small panels of Bruce and Alfred's reactions inserted to cover part of her breasts and her nether regions; the next page had a large panel with Selina nude on Bruce's big screen, her nipples obscured by Bruce and Alfred's strategically placed heads. The fourth issue would have opened with Selina still naked and Bruce bringing a blanket to cover her, which she never put on over the course of the next four pages.

Editorial decided to go in a different direction, and the already drawn and colored pages were scrapped. When he later showed the

---

\* The New 52 line faced a great deal of criticism when it was first announced due to its lack of female creators. Of the 160 creator credits across the titles, 3 were women, or 1.9 percent.

† Hudson began the piece with a discussion of the opening pages of *Catwoman* #1, which led her to ask, "Can't you show us the playful or confident look in her eye as she puts on her sexy costume? Because without that it's impossible to connect with the character on any other level than a boner, and I'm afraid I don't have one of those."

pages on his website, March noted, "I guess it all have [sic] to do with the sexy depiction of Selina in these original pages," though that wasn't the sole motivation. Winick's plan was to reveal that Catwoman knew Bruce Wayne was Batman, thus the visit, and this was kiboshed as well. Winick ended up writing completely new pages for March to draw to replace the discarded work, taking the story in a different direction that let Catwoman stay clothed.

The series remained relatively low key for some time. Catwoman's décolletage was still a regular feature, and there were occasional moments of sexy shenanigans; she broke into a mansion via the grate of its swimming pool while clad in her mask and a paw-print bikini in *Catwoman* #8, and covered up a fight in her apartment by screaming like she was having sex a few issues later. But by and large, the book shifted its focus and stayed under the radar for the remainder of its first year.

Only for that first year, however. When DC announced prequel #0 issues for September 2012 to celebrate the New 52's first anniversary, Guillem March's cover for the book put *Catwoman* back in the news again. The covers for the #0 issues were uniform in design, with each book's titular character bursting through a faded black-and-white reprint of the title's #1 issue cover. March's *Catwoman* cover had her launching toward the viewer, one clawed hand extended while her other limbs were bizarrely positioned, their connection to her torso poorly defined. Catwoman's body was contorted so as to allow a clear view of both her rear end and her bust; her breasts jutted out in front of her, with the costume unzipped, of course, while her rear swung up behind her. The pose was awkward as well as physically impossible.

This kind of contortion is common in the comic book world, so much so that fans have coined a term for the phenomenon: the brokeback pose. In a brokeback pose, a female character is drawn in a manner that showcases both her breasts and her behind simultaneously, twisting her in a way that would surely snap her spine in the real world. As the audience for comic books has shifted in the new century and female readers and creators have grown in prominence, the brokeback pose has been increasingly derided as objectifying nonsense. It is often ridiculed and parodied, most famously with the Hawkeye Initiative, which began when comic book creator Noelle Stevenson suggested that artists replace hypersexualized drawings of female characters with the male superhero Hawkeye in the same pose. Scads of fan art followed.

The same thing happened to March. The cover was roundly mocked once the art was revealed, and parodies soon followed. Kate Beaton of *Hark! A Vagrant* drew Catwoman with a sharply curved spine, her breasts pointing outward while her rear end pointed straight up; Beaton also added some dialogue: "It's OK if you're titillated, Batman. I'm **meant** to be a sexy character." Artist Catie Donnelly drew a series of scenes in which Catwoman was stuck in her cover pose. In one, Catwoman was delicately perched across two chairs at the chiropractor's office, unable to move and asking a fellow patient to hand her a copy of *Vogue*. In another, Catwoman had fallen over and was trapped upside down as Batman and Robin looked on in concern; when Batman asked, "Hey bro, you need a hand?" Catwoman just replied, "Let's fuck." Former *Catwoman* artist Cameron Stewart drew a side view of the cover, shortening her torso and replacing her legs with one thick appendage that had a foot protruding from her bottom and an arm coming out of the back of her head. Artist Josh Rodgers just went with the basics, redrawing the cover as a mass of breasts and butt cheeks with a face in the middle and cat ears on top.

Hilarity ensued as the art was shared across social media and posted on several of the major comic book news sites. When *Catwoman* #0 hit stores a couple of months later, March had redrawn the cover. She was in a similar pose, but her torso was extended, her costume was zipped up, and all of her limbs connected to her body properly. It was still slightly in the brokeback vein, but far less contorted than March's original piece.

No one at DC Comics seemed to learn anything from the multiple outcries over these exploitative depictions of Catwoman, as evidenced by the launch of *Justice League of America* in April 2013. The book was a counter to the flagship *Justice League* title; fearing the power of the independent Justice League, the government agency

A.R.G.U.S. assembled a team to challenge the league, and brought in Catwoman as its counter to Batman.* Artist David Finch's first issue was a bit over the top, showing Catwoman unzipped yet again, with the zipper pulled down even farther than March usually placed it, enough to reveal that she wasn't wearing a bra. The second issue went even further. At the team's first official meeting, Catwoman's zipper was down to her navel and the sides of her costume were pulled wide open to expose most of her chest and stomach. Writer Geoff Johns's dialogue called attention to her attire, with Catwoman telling fellow hero Vibe, "My eyes are up here, sweetheart."

The response to Catwoman's depiction in *Justice League of America* was minimal. After *Catwoman*'s first year, DC appeared to have alienated fans to such a degree that they could no longer be bothered to care. Catwoman was killed two issues later, though her death was soon revealed to be a fake-out involving a shape-shifter. She remained on the team for the next year but with a minimal role, and she eventually quit after the upheaval of DC's *Forever Evil* event.†

## The Ups and Downs of Comic Book Sales

The axiom that sex sells did not prove true with *Catwoman*. Apart from the gratuitous depiction of Catwoman, the rest of the book's content was surprisingly dark. Selina's close friend Lola was brutally killed early in the run, sending Selina into a downward spiral fueled by a death wish. The action in the series was violent and graphic, the villains were vicious, and the new supporting cast was an untrustworthy group prone to secrets and betrayal. Winick tried to inject some levity in the series, but that only served to make the dark moments more jarring. Readers didn't connect well with the

---

* A.R.G.U.S. stands for Advanced Research Group Uniting Super-humans. It's the poor man's version of Marvel's S.H.I.E.L.D., quite frankly.

† The event involved evil doppelgängers from a different universe capturing the Justice League and taking over the world. It was a whole big thing. Catwoman helped Batman save Dick Grayson, and all the thanks she got was Batman telling her to go straight and that he couldn't be with her.

book and sales dropped at a steady clip, from a high of 57,216 for *Catwoman* #2 to a low of 34,117 for *Catwoman* #12, Winick and March's final issue. They moved on to other projects, and *Catwoman* went in a new direction.

Winick was replaced with Ann Nocenti, a writer best known for her work at Marvel, including a long run on *Daredevil* in the 1980s. She focused on film and journalistic work through the 1990s but later came back to comics; she was already writing *Green Arrow* when she took over *Catwoman* and soon launched a *Katana* title as well. Nocenti was originally joined by two Spanish artists, penciller Rafa Sandoval and inker Jordi Tarragona, both veterans of superhero comics. Later in the run, Nocenti teamed with American artist Patrick Olliffe, an artist with more than two decades of experience drawing superheroes for both DC and Marvel.*

The new creative team took *Catwoman* in several different directions. First, they tied into her role in *Justice League of America* with an arc that involved A.R.G.U.S.'s Black Room, a secret area that contained mystical artifacts. Catwoman was briefly possessed by a magical force and ended up fighting a demon for a few issues. The next arc sent Catwoman underground as she explored the secret cities buried beneath Gotham City and tried to broker a peace deal between the citizens of Charneltown and the Warhogs. After that, Catwoman was a valiant crime fighter in a bright, utopian Gotham before she realized that she was trapped in a mass delusion. Finally, Catwoman returned to her roots by joining a competition to decide who was the greatest thief in the world.

It was all a bit weird and scattered, and the readership's mass exodus continued. The first issue of Nocenti's debut arc began with 35,020 copies sold, and by the end of the run two years later the series hit a low of 18,945. DC's threshold for considering the cancellation of a series was about 20,000 copies sold per issue, and by this point several of the original New 52 series had already been canceled

---

* While Sandoval, Tarragona, and Olliffe were the primary artists on *Catwoman*, they were occasionally joined by other pencillers and inkers when production got behind schedule. Tom Nguyen inked much of Olliffe's work, but there were several other inkers working with him during the run.

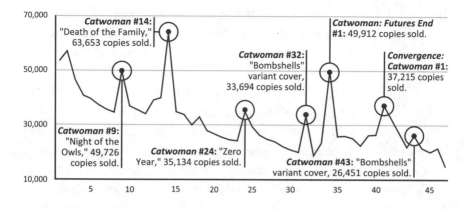

and replaced by new books, but *Catwoman* continued. The series was uniquely positioned; while sales were declining in the long term, the book was occasionally buoyed by crossovers with major events in *Batman* and the rest of the DC universe.

The chart above shows the sales figures for *Catwoman* for the first several years of the New 52 era. The book started off high, as did the bulk of DC's new line; the debut of the New 52 was a behemoth that catapulted DC to its highest sales in years. *Catwoman* did relatively well initially, opening as the twenty-fourth bestselling title of the fifty-two new books, high enough to put it in the top half of the line. The book improved in its second month, as did the bulk of the New 52 titles, but then the numbers began to fall.

The only respite from the decline was *Catwoman* #9, which was marketed as a tie-in to *Batman*'s popular "Night of the Owls" story line. *Batman* was the runaway hit of the New 52 line, remaining at or near the top of the charts for years after the novelty of the relaunch wore off elsewhere. Wanting to capitalize on the book's early success, the Batman line's editorial team quickly devised crossover stories for the other books under their purview, and it paid off well. *Catwoman*'s sales increased 43 percent from the previous issue, and the sales bump lingered; it took another three issues for *Catwoman* to drift back down to its pre-crossover sales level.

More crossovers soon followed. A tie-in with *Batman*'s second arc, "Death of the Family," rocketed *Catwoman* to its highest sales yet, though the next event a year later proved less fruitful, perhaps due to waning interest in the series' primary story line. While a year later "Zero Year" provided a 45 percent sales jump from the previous issue, sales were so low to begin with that the jump didn't amount to much.*

Line-wide events kept *Catwoman* afloat as well. DC's regular celebrations of the anniversary of the New 52's launch typically bumped up sales slightly each September, none more so than DC's "Futures End" event in September 2014. The issues were set five years in the future, and featured lenticular covers that shifted images as the reader moved the book. Fans and retailers were intrigued, and sales skyrocketed for the month, including a big gain for *Catwoman*. The book received another boost when DC launched its two-month "Convergence" event in 2015, a series of forty miniseries that replaced its regular books while the publisher moved from New York to Los Angeles. *Convergence: Catwoman* was set in the 1990s, purple-suited era of Catwoman, and sold much better than her usual adventures.

DC also benefited from variant covers. A comic book's primary cover featured artwork connected to the story contained in the book, while a comic with a variant cover had the same story inside but featured an alternate cover with different art, usually unconnected to the interior. Variant covers were printed in lesser quantities, making them collector's items. DC began running themed variant covers on select titles in its superhero line each month starting in January 2014; for example, in October 2014 they did monster-themed variants for Halloween, and in December 2014 Darwyn Cooke drew all of DC's characters in panoramic covers. The covers provided a slight sales bump to the books that bore them, because retailers tended to order extra copies of the variant covers in addition to their standard order for each book.

Of all the monthly themes, DC's "Bombshells" variants were particularly impactful on *Catwoman*'s sales. The theme first appeared in June 2014, and featured DC's female heroes and villains in 1940s garb, posed in a classic pinup style. The covers were cute and flirty

---

* Even with the boost, the numbers for *Catwoman*'s "Zero Year" crossover were lower than the issue *before* the book's crossover with "Night of the Owls" two years earlier.

instead of racy, and sold like hotcakes. Ant Lucia's cover for *Catwoman* #32 featured a faux pulp magazine with a "breathtaking Gotham City heist thriller" titled "Crack of the Whip!" that starred Catwoman, pictured in a black dress and sunglasses while holding a diamond. Sales improved a whopping 67 percent from the previous issue on the strength of the cover alone.* The "Bombshells" soon expanded into prints, statues, and other merchandise, as well as their own comic book, and DC brought back the theme a year later, though the sales bump wasn't nearly as big for *Catwoman*.†

There is a theme of diminishing returns across all of these promotions. The first "Bombshells" variant outsold the second. The "Death of the Family" crossover outsold the later "Zero Year" crossover. DC's earlier "Futures End" event outsold "Convergence." Such is the nature of gimmick-based sales; they work for a while, but eventually lose their impact. Many industry analysts are concerned about the superhero market's current reliance on variant covers, events, and relaunches. They appeal to die-hard fans but alienate new readers and create a business that depends on flash more than substance.

Readers buying books because of covers, be they variants or adorned with logos for events, instead of what's inside leads to an artificial bubble that will inevitably burst. Such a crisis rocked the comic book industry in the early 1990s, when variant covers exploded because fans were buying them in bulk in hopes that they'd be worth a fortune some day. But a comic book needs to be rare to be valuable, and thousands of fans buying the same variant covers simply created a glut in which the comics were worth less than their cover price. Thus, the variant cover market bubble burst, and sales dropped dramatically, throwing the industry into chaos. Marvel even had to

---

* Some of DC's variant covers were listed as 1:25, meaning that for every twenty-five copies of an issue a retailer ordered, one would have the variant cover, but the "Bombshells" line was open order, so retailers could order as many copies of the variant cover as they wanted. They certainly went to town with *Catwoman*.

† Catwoman is a side character in the *DC Comics Bombshells* comic book series, written by Marguerite Bennett with art by a range of artists, including Mirka Andolfo and Laura Braga. The book is set in an alternate universe World War II in which female superheroes fight the war, and Catwoman is Contessa Selina Digatti, a European aristocrat who aids the Allied forces.

declare bankruptcy, though they continued publishing a diminished line of books while going through the bankruptcy process.

*Catwoman* in the early 2010s was a prime example of this artificial bubble. The sales for the regular issues show that readers weren't particularly interested in the book's contents over its first three years. From the initial highs to the final lows over this span, sales for non-event issues of *Catwoman* tumbled 67 percent, down to a rate where it was almost not worth publishing. But the events and variant covers kept the book afloat. When a snazzy cover or crossover could boost sales so dramatically, not a lot of care had to be put into the book's contents.

After three years, DC attempted another tried-and-true sales gimmick with *Catwoman*, the revamp, but this time they focused on the inside instead of the outside. A new creative and editorial team took the series in a radical direction that made *Catwoman* creatively and culturally relevant for the first time in the New 52 era, and finally stopped the sales skid.

## Selina Kyle, Mob Boss

*Catwoman* wasn't the only DC series mired in perpetually dark and violent story lines. The entire New 52 line had a grim and gritty vibe, and the Bat-books under group editor Mike Marts were particularly bleak. Tragic arcs were followed by even more tragic arcs, relationships were constantly strained, and the Bat-family endured years of perpetual suffering. The heroes were not allowed to be happy, to such a degree that when J. H. Williams III and W. Haden Blackman had Batwoman propose to her girlfriend, Maggie Sawyer, editorial nixed their plans for the couple to get married even though they'd pitched it long before and had been building to it for some time; Williams and Blackman ended up quitting *Batwoman* over the change.

Marts left DC for Marvel two and a half years after the relaunch, and Mark Doyle took over as group editor of the Bat-books. Doyle was a veteran editor at Vertigo, DC's mature readers line, where he developed a varied array of titles ranging from the horror western *American Vampire* to the quirky *Sweet Tooth* to science fiction like

FBP: *Federal Bureau of Physics*, *Trillium*, and *The Wake*. He brought a similar approach to the Batman line, replacing the dark homogeneity of the Marts era with a broad spectrum of tones and styles. *Batgirl* lightened up, got a new costume, and moved to Burnside, Gotham's hipster district. The new *Gotham Academy* followed a group of young students having fun adventures at the city's prestigious, eerie boarding school. Dick Grayson left Nightwing behind to become a secret agent for Spyral, a covert UN agency, in *Grayson*. Doyle's motto was, "A Batman book for every fan, for every genre."

For *Catwoman*, Doyle turned to Genevieve Valentine, an award-winning novelist known for her fantasy and science fiction writing. Valentine had never written a comic book before, but she'd been a Catwoman fan since she was a kid and was keen to explore "the moral gray area she lives in that's just big enough for her to reinvent herself as necessary and small enough that she's often bumping up against its edges." Valentine was paired with artist Garry Brown, a relative newcomer to comics who'd made a big splash in a short amount of time with work at several of the industry's major publishers.* Their *Catwoman* thrust Selina into the world of Gotham's organized crime families in the middle of a mafia war.

Doyle prefaced the series' new direction in the pages of *Batman Eternal*, a weekly ensemble series that starred most of Gotham's heroes. The book revealed that Selina was the daughter of Rex "the Lion" Calabrese, a crime boss who ruled Gotham's underworld before he was deposed and imprisoned when Selina was a young girl. She did her best to ignore her mafia heritage, but when conflict between Gotham's crime families began to tear the city apart, Rex told her that the only way for peace was to unify the mafia under the Calabreses, with Selina as the head of the family. Selina refused initially, but after seeing her young friend Jade killed in the cross fire, she agreed to assume the mantle.

The story picked up in *Catwoman* #35 in October 2014. Valentine and Brown changed not just the tone of the series but the entire

---

* The last few issues of the run were drawn by David Messina after Brown moved on to other projects. Messina was an Italian artist with a variety of European and American credits, best known for his work on IDW's *Star Trek* line.

genre. Doyle called *Catwoman* "the most Vertigo-esque" series in the new Batman line. This was no longer a superhero book; it was a crime thriller. The bright colors were gone, no one had superpowers, and there were no bombastic fight scenes. Across the arc's debut issue, there was roughly a third of a page of combat action. The rest was tense discussion and posturing as Selina negotiated her way through the complex maze of Gotham's crime families. Brown's art aimed for a neo-noir feel that he described as "lots of shimmering cities and harsh light." It was a book full of shadows and subtle looks.

Selina walked a fine line as the new head of the Calabrese family. She wanted to change Gotham for the better by bringing stability to its underworld and cleaning up the city, but she was beholden to the old ways of the mafia. Her first initiatives involved selling caches of guns to get them out of Gotham and slyly sabotaging a shipment of heroin by allowing her cousin Nick to tip off the police. However, when the other families found out that Nick had gone to the police, Selina had to deal with the betrayal in the expected manner, and she had him killed. While she wasn't a typical mob boss, her hands weren't clean, either.

She had to eliminate Nick to retain the respect of the other, male-led families, a running theme throughout the story. The crime bosses had trouble accepting a woman in a position of power, and even Ward, her own consigliere, questioned her at every turn. Selina also found herself at odds with Black Mask, returned as a rival mob boss, and Batman, who didn't approve of her new role. The new *Catwoman* was an examination of powerful women in traditionally male spaces, and the innumerable difficulties therein.

Valentine underlined this theme by prominently featuring a quote from a famous historical woman in each issue that was relevant to the story at hand. As Selina took over her family in the first issue and reflected on entrenching herself within the unsavory methods of the mafia, Valentine quoted a letter from Queen Elizabeth I of England in which she was "provoked for our defence to use such means as otherwise of ourselves we did never allow or like." Queen Elizabeth was a favorite throughout the run, as was Lucrezia Borgia, the Italian Renaissance power player. They were joined by Caterina

Sforza, a fifteenth-century Italian countess and regent; Egyptian queen Cleopatra; Eleanor of Aquitaine, a French queen in the Middle Ages; and Empress Pulcheria, the fifth century ruler of the Eastern Roman Empire.*

This assortment of powerful women was reflected in the book's cast. Selina was aided by her cousin Antonia, who had extensive knowledge of the Calabreses' business and their dealings with the other families of Gotham but had never been given a prominent role because she was a woman. After Selina took over the family, Antonia became her second in command and had her full trust, often representing the Calabreses and negotiating in her stead.

Eiko Hasigawa, the heir to the Gotham branch of the Yakuza, also had a large part in the book. She and Selina were initially at odds; Eiko's father was reluctant to join the Calabrese-led alliance and soon allied himself with Black Mask. Eiko disagreed with her father's actions and took up the mantle of Catwoman to covertly oppose him. This brought her to Selina's attention, and eventually they teamed up to fight against Black Mask's faction.

Selina's relationship with Eiko led to the arc's most newsworthy moment. In *Catwoman* #39, after Selina barely escaped an assassination attempt from the Hasigawas' alliance, Eiko donned her Catwoman gear and visited Selina's penthouse apartment to warn her that the faction was planning to go to war against the Calabreses. Eiko lamented, "I can't help you after this—my father will be watching me," and told Selina, "Be careful. **Please.**" Selina then moved in close to Eiko and kissed her. Eiko asked, "Was that for me, or the **suit?**" Selina wasn't sure, but she thought to herself, "If we survive this, might be nice to find out."

The issue established Selina as canonically bisexual, a move that Valentine said "wasn't a revelation so much as a confirmation." The kiss was more than a onetime event to end an issue on a shocking note; it added a new dimension to Selina's sexuality that would be

---

* One issue featured Chinese poet Li Bai's "Song of Changgan," a poem about a merchant's wife. Valentine had wanted to quote famed Chinese pirate Ching Shih, but she left no writings behind, so Valentine used this poem from the Tang dynasty. While Li Bai was a man, the poem focused on the woman's love, devotion, and fortitude.

a part of the character moving forward. News of the kiss made the rounds beyond the usual comics and entertainment avenues, garnering coverage in most major newspapers as well as high-profile outlets like *Vanity Fair*, CNN, and the BBC. The coverage was generally positive, and the change was met with no real outrage apart from the occasional Internet commenter.*

Establishing Catwoman as bisexual and allowing Valentine to definitively state that her bisexuality was canon was a bold, progressive move for DC comics relative to its chief rivals. Later in the year, Marvel released *Angela: Queen of Hel*, a new series with a female lead who was clearly in a romantic relationship with another female character. Marvel editor-in-chief Axel Alonso was asked in his weekly softball question column, "Is it accurate to say that Angela is the first gay or bisexual lead character in the All-New, All-Different Marvel era?" and he cagily replied, "That's a question for readers to ponder and answer for themselves. We're not looking to put labels on the character or the series." Alonso's response was widely derided, particularly because just a few weeks earlier he was asked whether Hercules, a character who had previously been bisexual, would be bisexual in his new series and Alonso definitively stated that he would be straight. Meanwhile, Catwoman was queer and DC launched a new series starring Midnighter, a gay character written by a bisexual writer, Steve Orlando. Writers Amanda Conner and Jimmy Palmiotti also confirmed that longtime pals Harley Quinn and Poison Ivy were girlfriends in their ongoing *Harley Quinn* series. DC's LGBTQ+ representation wasn't perfect, as evidenced by the mishandling of Batwoman and Maggie Sawyer's engagement, but the publisher was making strides toward better representation.

However, Catwoman's new romance didn't last for long. At its core, this mob story of war and betrayal could only ever be a tragedy. The gang war became increasingly complicated as battle lines were drawn. The Calabreses had to partner with the Penguin while Black Mask grew suspicious of the Hasigawas after seeing Eiko in

---

* Internet comment highlights included, "Boy oh boy. Normalizing perversion. Are comics for kids where this is even a question to be asked, let alone discussed???" and "Leftys have to defile everything."

her Catwoman garb. He ultimately turned on the Hasigawas and murdered Eiko's father. Selina and the Penguin took down Black Mask and made peace in Gotham, but it wasn't enough for Eiko. She was the new head of the Hasigawa family, and wanted vengeance as well as the end of Gotham's crime families. She threw a party for the families that remained and killed them all, save for the Calabreses, who hadn't been invited. Selina arrived too late to stop the bloodshed, and their last meeting was a brawl; in the end, Selina let Eiko escape rather than face the police, but their relationship was over. Afterward, Selina left Gotham. She'd already stepped down as head of the Calabreses and put Antonia in charge of the family, and now she was on to her next adventure.

The end of the story was also the end of Valentine and Messina's run on *Catwoman*. DC returned the character to her traditional thieving ways, with writer Frank Tieri and artist Inaki Miranda at the helm. It was a surprising change; after three years of steadily falling sales, the new *Catwoman* had garnered strong reviews and sales had leveled out relatively well. The run started out with sales of 25,970 and ended at 21,661, a fall of only 17 percent. Winick and March's run lost 40 percent of its beginning sales, and Nocenti's run plummeted 46 percent. But the comic book industry is a business that perpetually craves a return to the status quo, and so the old Catwoman came back.

The move didn't pay off. Tieri and Miranda took over the book with *Catwoman* #47, a fine, conventional caper tale that found Catwoman in New York City on a job that went sideways in a mysterious way. Usually, a new creative team means a bump in sales as retailers increase their orders, anticipating that customers will be curious to try at least the first issue of the new direction, but the book got no such bump. *Catwoman* #47 sold only 15,038 copies, a whopping 31 percent decrease from the final issue of the mob era and a troublingly low number for the continuation of the series. Sales continued to fall from there and the book was canceled soon after the new arc began, drawing to a close with *Catwoman* #52. DC Comics recently relaunched its superhero line yet again, debuting a variety of new #1 issues as part of its "Rebirth" initiative. It was a relaunch, not a reboot, so the continuity carried on, but for the first time in more than two decades, Catwoman wasn't headlining a comic book series.* While she'll inevitably be back, for now she remains benched, yet again.

---

* Catwoman recently resurfaced in *Batman* #9. She was in Arkham Asylum, immobilized in a straitjacket and a Hannibal Lecter–style mask, awaiting death by lethal injection for 237 counts of murder. But Batman needed her for a special mission and busted her out.

# Conclusion

*A* "nine lives" motif has followed Catwoman throughout her existence. In the Golden Age, Catwoman tricked her goons into thinking she actually had nine lives with a series of clever ruses. In *Batman Returns*, Catwoman tauntingly counted down her remaining lives as Max Shreck shot her before she eventually killed him. Selina Kyle began her recent run as a mob boss by taking in her new surroundings and musing, "Not bad, as ninth lives go." It's become a bit of a cliché, used often by many, but it's apt. Few comic book characters have been reborn as often as Catwoman.

Generally speaking, comic book characters who have been around as long as Catwoman have survived because they've become iconic, and imagery is key to that. Batman always wears a cape and a pointy-eared cowl along with a bat on his chest, no matter the incarnation. Wonder Woman always has a tiara, a lasso, and bullet-deflecting bracelets to go with her star-spangled outfit. These key elements get seared into the public consciousness to such a degree that many superheroes can be identified with even the most minimalist artwork.

Other iconic characters have a consistent aim. Superman is the big blue boy scout, always there to help someone in need. Lois Lane is a tenacious reporter, forever chasing down a front-page scoop.

Their behavior is so cemented that readers and viewers immediately pick up on the slightest change; if Superman is being a jerk to someone in need, they know that something's gone down and there are malevolent forces at play.

Catwoman has no such constants. Her appearance has varied wildly over the years: her hair has differed in cut and hue, she's worn an assortment of costumes that cover every color in the rainbow, and even her ethnicity has changed. Her look has usually maintained a feline theme, but she's not the only cat-based character in comics. Catwoman is not defined by any specific style or imagery.

Nor by any specific role, apart from a penchant for thievery. Sometimes she's a villain, sometimes she's a hero, and most of the time she occupies a very gray area between the two from which she can pivot to either end of the spectrum without warning. In her comics, Catwoman has been a burglar, a romantic interest, a murderer, a vigilante, a dominatrix, a mob boss, and more. Her appearances in other media have been similarly contradictory; on television, she's been a campy villain and a teen street urchin. In movies, she's been a vengeful lazarus in a gothic fairy tale, the ridiculous heroine of an unintentional farce, and a con artist in a city gone mad. Forget nine lives; that's not nearly enough.

Despite her myriad incarnations, Catwoman has achieved iconic status. She is inarguably the best-known female villain in comics and has a broader fan base than the vast majority of female heroes. Each distinct era of Catwoman comes with its own following who ardently love that version of the character, and therein lies the key to her longevity. Catwoman has been many things to many fans, accumulating a fan base that spans generations and different types of media. There is a quality to the character that transcends and unites her across her disparate lives, regardless of her outfit or her aim, a confident defiance that's been present ever since her first appearance when Batman unmasked her and she brazenly replied, "Well, what's the matter? Haven't you ever seen a pretty girl **before**?"

Catwoman has never particularly cared about what's expected of her. She's done her own thing her own way for her own reasons, no matter the circumstances. This made her a villain in the Golden

Age, a pariah in the Silver Age, and a morally mercurial figure ever since. This defiance has also imbued the character with a strength that supersedes her momentary circumstances, even when DC puts her on the shelf or male creators turn her into a sex object.

Throughout her history, Catwoman's faced the best and worst that the superhero industry has to offer. She's been a marquee star and blatantly objectified, sometimes at the same time. But her over-arching narrative isn't one of survival or perseverance, of having to overcome these rough moments. It's one of reinvention, of following every benching or fetishized depiction with a new incarnation that forgets the past and blazes on with the fierce independence that's characterized her over the decades. There's always another life just around the corner, with heroes to outwit and treasures to steal.

# *Acknowledgments*

So many fantastic people have been helpful in putting *The Many Lives of Catwoman* together, as well as supportive of *Investigating Lois Lane*, over the past year. In particular, I'd like to thank Adrienne Barbeau, Gwenda Bond, Maria Burchill, Lauren Burke, Kelly Sue DeConnick, Heather Hogan, John D. Iles, Cal Johnston from Strange Adventures (the best comic book shop in the world), Rich Johnston at *Bleeding Cool*, Anne Elizabeth Moore, Hope Nicholson, Marc Tyler Nobleman, Jacque Nodell, everyone at Photofest (especially Todd, and Mark who dug out some great images for me), Caitlin Rosberg, Katie Schenkel, Genevieve Valentine, and everyone at the Tantallon Public Library.

It's also great to be back with Chicago Review Press for our third book together. Everyone there is wonderful to work with, and I very much appreciate all of the effort they put into my bizarre history books. My thanks to my editor Yuval Taylor for getting behind my ideas and making them better, Devon Freeny for making the book read well, Jon Hahn for making it look nice, Mary Kravenas for getting the word out, and Olivia Aguilar for all of the press. Also, thanks to everyone at IPG for their distribution prowess.

Before anyone else sees any chapters, Michelle Hegarty of Modified Editing digs into them and straightens them out. Her insights made this book much better, and I learn so much from her every time we work together.

My agent, Dawn Frederick of Red Sofa Literary, is just the best. Seriously, ask anybody. She embraces my ideas, helps me refine them, and gets them out there into the world with tireless zeal.

Finally, big thanks to my parents, who are endlessly supportive and also the kind of people who buy their son a set of vintage *Batman Returns* Catwoman paper dolls for Christmas. They're swell folks. Thanks as well to my sister, Katie, and my new brother-in-law, Tom, for being great travel buddies on book events. My family in general is a wonderful bunch.

# Source Notes

## Introduction

"It's too bad she has to be a crook" . . . *Batman* #3 (Fall 1940).

## 1. Perjured Origins

When she first debuted in . . . *Batman* #1 (Spring 1940).
pretending to be an old woman . . . Ibid.
society gal throwing legendary soirees . . . *Batman* #10 (April–May 1942).
She donned a mask in her third . . . *Batman* #3 (Fall 1940).

## The Men Behind Catwoman

The creation of Catwoman, and the Batman mythos more broadly, is laden with lies and misinformation that mostly stem from Bob Kane. Kane had a part in creating this world, but Bill Finger's massive contribution was largely unknown until recent years. Through his research and his book *Bill the Boy Wonder: The Secret Co-creator of Batman*, Marc Tyler Nobleman has brought Finger the credit he deserves, and this section owes a great debt to his work. Insights into Kane and the early years of the comic book industry were aided by a variety of interviews, primary sources, and the intriguing research cited below.

Kane's tombstone even reads . . . "Bob Kane," Find a Grave, August 12, 2000, www.findagrave.com/cgi-bin/fg.cgi?page=gr&GRid=11708.

"who has written most of the classic . . ." Julius Schwartz, "Batman's Hot-Line," *Detective Comics* #327 (May 1964).

Finger appeared at New York Comicon . . . Michael Eury and Michael Kronenberg, *The Batcave Companion* (Raleigh, NC: TwoMorrows, 2009), 52.

an article by Jerry Bails . . . Jerry Bails, "If the Truth Be Known, or 'A Finger in Every Plot!,'" *CAPA-alpha* 12 (September 1965).

He sent a lengthy response to *Batmania* . . . Bob Kane, "An Open Letter to All 'Batmanians' Everywhere," *Batmania Annual* #1 (April 1967).

But instead of going home . . . Jim Steranko, *The Steranko History of Comics*, vol. 1 (Reading, PA: Supergraphics, 1970), 44.

The two had met at a cocktail party . . . Dwight Zimmerman, "Interview with Fred Finger," in *Alter Ego: The Comic Book Artist Collection* (Raleigh, NC: TwoMorrows, 2001), 141.

FN They also grew up in the same neighborhood . . . Ibid., 129.

Kane had been working for Eisner & Iger . . . Charles Brownstein, *Eisner/Miller* (Milwaukee: Dark Horse, 2005), 289.

He had red tights, blond hair . . . Marc Tyler Nobleman, *Bill the Boy Wonder: The Secret Co-creator of Batman* (Watertown, MA: Charlesbridge, 2012).

the first six-page script . . . The story debuted in *Detective Comics* #27 (May 1939).

Kane's father had asked around for some legal advice . . . Arie Kaplan, *From Krakow to Krypton: Jews and Comic Books* (Philadelphia: Jewish Publication Society, 2008), 54.

FN When Finger first brought up a sidekick . . . Gary Groth, "Jerry Robinson: Been There, Done That," *Comics Journal*, February 5, 2011, www.tcj.com/jerry-robinson-been-there-done-that/2/.

a blatant copy of a panel . . . Arlen Schumer, "The Bat-Man Cover Story," *Alter Ego* 2, no. 5 (Summer 1999): 4–5.

including a litany of images copied . . . Robby Reed, "The Haunting of Robert Kane, Part 3!" *Dial B for Blog*, www.dialbforblog.com/archives/391/.

One of his first ghost artists . . . Groth, "Jerry Robinson: Been There, Done That."

FN Kane drew so little that he didn't . . . Eury and Kronenberg, *Batcave Companion*, 90.

"Look, you're very successful now . . ." Brownstein, *Eisner/Miller*, 135.

editor Jack Schiff told him to stop . . . Jack Schiff and Gene Reed, "Reminiscences of a Comic Book Editor," in *The Comic Book Price Guide*, vol. 13, ed. Robert M. Overstreet, (1982), 68.

"We continued with the charade . . ." Julius Schwartz and Brian M. Thomsen, *Man of Two Worlds* (New York: HarperCollins, 2000), 118.

Kane came in and claimed that he was underage . . . Glen Weldon, *The Caped Crusade: Batman and the Rise of Nerd Culture* (New York: Simon & Schuster, 2016), 65.

Kane's lawyer threatened legal action . . . Brownstein, *Eisner/Miller*, 233.

"Bob was the luckiest man in the world . . ." Ibid., 135.

"He was a very good visual writer . . ." Mark Cotta Vaz, *Tales of the Dark Knight: Batman's First Fifty Years, 1939–1989* (New York: Ballantine, 1989), 30.

He was a perfectionist . . . Ibid.

"My father had a very weak spine" . . . Zimmerman, "Interview with Fred Finger," 145.

He was fired briefly in the 1960s . . . Alan J. Porter, "The Dubious Origins of the Batman," in *Batman Unauthorized: Vigilantes, Jokers, and Heroes in Gotham City*, ed. Dennis O'Neil and Leah Wilson (Dallas: BenBella Books, 2008), 92–93.

"Bob Kane is certainly not a copyist . . ." "Meet the Artist!" *Batman* #1 (Spring 1940).

"good old elbow grease" . . . Bob Kane, "Batman's Hot-Line," *Detective Comics* #328 (June 1964).

Leonardo da Vinci's flying machine . . . Bob Kane with Tom Andrae, *Batman & Me* (Forestville: Eclipse, 1989), 35.

"I must admit that Bill never . . ." Ibid., 44.

"She burned up the screen . . ." Ibid., 107.

FN Hedy Lamarr and her "feline beauty" . . . Michael Uslan, introduction to *Catwoman: Nine Lives of a Feline Fatale*, by Bill Finger et al. (New York: DC Comics, 2014).

FN Anne Hathaway studied Lamarr . . . Geoff Boucher, "*Dark Knight Rises* Star Anne Hathaway: 'Gotham City Is Full of Grace,'" Hero Complex, *Los Angeles Times*, December 29, 2011, http://herocomplex.latimes.com/movies/dark-knight-rises-star-anne-hathaway-gotham-city-is-full-of-grace/.

claimed that Marilyn Monroe inspired . . . Kane, *Batman & Me*, 127.

FN Kane claimed that Monroe had . . . J. Randy Taraborrelli, *The Secret Life of Marilyn Monroe* (New York: Grand Central Publishing 2009), 139.

Lew Schwartz drew the bulk of the story . . . *Batman* #49 (October–November 1949).

FN Bob Kane's cousin Ruth Steel . . . Eric Obenzinger, "Ruth Steel Interview (Age 96)—May 22, 2011," YouTube, May 27, 2011, www.youtube.com/watch?v=0HfIuUKpTPU.

"We knew we needed a female nemesis . . ." Kane, *Batman & Me*, 107.

"male readers would appreciate a sensual . . ." Ibid.

"Cats are cool, detached . . ." Ibid., 108.

FN "You always need to keep women . . ." Ibid.

Jerry Robinson said that Catwoman was wholly . . . Jim Amash, "Building 'Batman'—and Other True Legends of the Golden Age," *Alter Ego*, no. 39 (August 2004): 11–12.

Thomas Andrae, the cowriter of . . . Marc Tyler Nobleman, "Interview with Co-author of Bob Kane's Autobiography," *Noblemania*, March 30, 2014, http://noblemania.blogspot.ca/2014/03/interview-with-co-author-of-bob -kanes.html

"*National Geographic* had a great issue . . ." Steranko, *Steranko History*, 48.

## The Cat Debuts

Early Catwoman stories are accessible via a variety of Batman collections from DC, including thorough chronological reprints in their pricey hardcover Archives line, the cheaper softcover Chronicles line, and a new line of large Golden Age Omnibuses. Select Catwoman stories are also reprinted in *Catwoman: Nine Lives of a Feline Fatale* and *Catwoman: A Celebration of 75 Years*. Some issues are also available digitally on ComiXology, and that library is always growing.

the book began with Robin going . . . *Batman* #1 (Spring 1940); this issue is the source of all the quotes for the next several paragraphs as well.

women appeared in just . . . Stats tabulated by author, available by request. Contact information is available at https://thanley.wordpress.com.

"Thomas Wayne, his wife, and son" . . . *Detective Comics* #33 (November 1939).

FN "Martha Wayne's weak heart stopped . . ." *Batman* #47 (June–July 1948).

Bruce had a fiancée named Julie Madison . . . First appeared in *Detective Comics* #31 (September 1939).

"I understand! It's all right" . . . *Detective Comics* #49 (March 1941).

Bruce dated Linda Page . . . First appeared in *Batman* #5 (Spring 1941).

"Well, Linda . . . gotta go now" . . . *Detective Comics* #54 (August 1941).

On a later date at a carnival . . . *Detective Comics* #69 (November 1942).

"Say—mustn't forget I've got . . ." *Batman* #1 (Spring 1940).

She returned as the Cat-Woman . . . *Batman* #2 (Summer 1940).

The Cat-Woman was back in the following . . . *Batman* #3 (Fall 1940).

She pretended to be Marguerite Tone . . . *Batman* #10 (April–May 1942).

## Feline Fatale

These temptresses became key players . . . Jane Billinghurst, *Temptress: From the Original Bad Girls to Women on Top* (New York: Douglas & McIntyre, 2012), 115.

there was often a tragic element . . . Elisabeth Bronfen, "Femme Fatale—
   Negotiations of Tragic Desire," in *Rethinking Tragedy*, ed. Rita Felski
   (Baltimore: Johns Hopkins University Press, 2008), 290.
wanton sexuality and manipulation . . . Billinghurst, *Temptress*, 119.
"It does give us one of the few periods . . ." Janey Place, "Women in Film
   Noir," in *Women in Film Noir*, ed. E. Ann Kaplan (London: British Film
   Institute, 1998), 47.
"is not a subject of feminism . . ." Mary Ann Doane, *Femmes Fatales: Femi-
   nism, Film Theory, Psychoanalysis* (New York: Routledge, 1991), 2–3.
he was going to escape and she was going . . . Billinghurst, *Temptress*, 122.
A femme fatale named Queenie . . . *Batman* #5 (Spring 1941).


## 2. A Conspicuous Pause

Many parent and teacher groups took issue . . . Bart Beaty, *Fredric Wertham
   and the Critique of Mass Culture* (Jackson: University Press of Mississippi, 2005), 106.
Some critics even got up in arms about . . . Bradford Wright, *Comic Book
   Nation: The Transformation of Youth Culture in America* (Baltimore:
   Johns Hopkins University Press, 2001), 27.
"inadvertently" flipped them off a roof . . . *Detective Comics* #28 (June 1939).
or snapped their necks . . . *Detective Comics* #30 (August 1939).
"A deep respect for our obligation . . ." "A Message to Our Readers: Introduc-
   ing the Editorial Advisory Board," *Detective Comics* #56 (October 1941).
Josette Frank had her name removed . . . Les Daniels, *Wonder Woman: The
   Complete History* (San Francisco: Chronicle Books, 2000), 72.

### Capturing Catwoman

DC's Batman Archives, Chronicles, and Golden Age Omnibuses remain the
best source for Catwoman stories from this era, though they end around the
late 1940s. Digital coverage on ComiXology is currently spotty after the early
1940s, though a few of Catwoman's later Golden Age stories have been collected in special edition Catwoman books.

She posed as a beautician . . . *Batman* #15 (February–March 1943).
"I sort of wish the Batman were driving . . ." *Batman* #3 (Fall 1940).
"How brave and strong he is!" . . . *Batman* #10 (April–May 1942).
"Batman wasn't hurt was he? I only meant . . ." *Detective Comics* #122 (April
   1947).
she tried to make time with Batman . . . *Batman* #39 (February–March 1947).
Catwoman posed as a fashion magazine editor . . . *Batman* #47 (June–July 1948).

He showed genuine concern for . . . *Batman* #15 (February–March 1943).

he and Robin helped couples . . . See *Detective Comics* #108 (February 1946), *Detective Comics* #117 (November 1946), *Detective Comics* #131 (January 1948), *Detective Comics* #154 (December 1949).

"Well, kitten, I've just hung a bell . . ." *Batman* #42 (August–September 1947).

"A little spanking will do the trick . . ." *Batman* #22 (April–May 1944).

FN "Let us be discreet and withdraw . . ." Ibid.

The earliest incarnation of the outfit . . . *Batman* #35 (June–July 1946).

The now-iconic version of the costume . . . *Detective Comics* #122 (April 1947).

Catwoman drove around in her Kitty Car . . . *Detective Comics* #122 (April 1947).

Catwoman drove back to the Catacombs . . . *Batman* #35 (June–July 1946).

The story began with Catwoman blackmailing . . . *Detective Comics* #122 (April 1947).

she hypnotized her jailer and broke . . . *Batman* #35 (June–July 1946).

she arranged for her gang to send . . . *Batman* #42 (August–September 1947).

she just made a run for it . . . *Batman* #45 (February–March 1948).

her goons no longer trusted her . . . *Batman* #35 (June–July 1946).

After she was left out of a book . . . *Batman* #45 (February–March 1948).

FN "Your exploits are so terrific that . . ." Ibid.

she came up with clever, literary crimes . . . *Batman* #42 (August–September 1947).

## Pet Shop Gal

The early 1950s aren't particularly well collected by DC generally, and the Batman line is no exception. Some Catwoman stories from this era are reprinted in *Catwoman: Nine Lives of a Feline Fatale* and *Catwoman: A Celebration of 75 Years*, but most are tricky to get hold of.

"the most cleverest, most dangerous . . ." *Batman* #62 (December–January 1951).

"Fasten your safety belts! If we . . ." Ibid.

"He came here to remind me of another life . . ." *Batman* #65 (June–July 1951).

Batman's doubts continued . . . *Batman* #69 (February–March 1952).

"She's been reformed since Batman nipped . . ." *Detective Comics* #203 (January 1954).

She was back a few months later . . . *Batman* #84 (June 1954).

In September 1954 Catwoman appeared . . . *Detective Comics* #211 (September 1954).

## Into Thin Air

For information on Dr. Fredric Wertham, Bart Beaty's *Fredric Wertham and the Critique of Mass Culture* is invaluable, as is Carol Tilley's "Seducing the Innocent: Fredric Wertham and the Falsifications That Helped Condemn Comics." For the juvenile delinquency crisis generally, David Hadju's *The Ten-Cent Plague: The Great Comic-Book Scare and How It Changed America* and Amy Kiste Nyberg's *Seal of Approval: The History of the Comics Code* are both fantastic.

**Wertham also opened a low-cost mental** . . . Beaty, *Fredric Wertham*, 89–90.

**Wertham testified about the harmful effects** . . . Ibid., 85.

**his research on the damaging psychological** . . . Ibid., 95.

**Wertham wanted comic books to be rated** . . . Fredric Wertham, *Seduction of the Innocent* (New York: Rinehart & Company, 1954), 334.

**Newsstands and spinner racks were full** . . . "Horror on the Newsstands," *Time* (September 27, 1954), www.time.com/time/magazine/article /0.9171,820350,00.html.

**"Only someone ignorant of the fundamentals . . ."** Wertham, *Seduction of the Innocent*, 189–190.

**"He is buoyant with energy . . ."** Ibid., 191.

**"The Batman type of story may stimulate . . ."** Ibid.

**In her recent evaluation of Wertham's archives** . . . Carol L. Tilley, "Seducing the Innocent: Fredric Wertham and the Falsifications That Helped Condemn Comics," *Information & Culture* 47, no. 4 (2012): 383–413.

**Wertham appeared before a Senate subcommittee** . . . Dr. Fredric Wertham, "Testimony of Dr. Fredric Wertham, Psychiatrist, Director, Lafargue Clinic, New York, N.Y.," April 21, 1954, available at www.thecomicbooks .com/wertham.html.

**"within the bounds of good taste"** . . . William S. Gaines, "Testimony of William S. Gaines, Publisher, Entertaining Comics Group, New York, N.Y.," April 21, 1954, available at www.thecomicbooks.com/gaines.html.

**"In these stories there are practically . . ."** Wertham, *Seduction of the Innocent*, 191.

**labeling Superman a Nazi** . . . Ibid., 34.

**Wonder Woman a lesbian** . . . Ibid., 192.

**DC and several other publishers banded together** . . . Wright, *Comic Book Nation*, 172.

**Nearly every publisher who didn't submit** . . . Amy Kiste Nyberg, *Seal of Approval: The History of the Comics Code* (Jackson: University Press of Mississippi, 1998), 124–125.

He was well respected by the writers . . . Eury and Kronenberg, *Batcave Companion*, 8; and Schiff and Reed, "Reminiscences," 66.

Schiff preferred action-packed supervillain . . . Schiff and Reed, "Reminiscences," 67.

When Schiff resisted, Mort Weisinger strong-armed . . . Eury and Kronenberg, *Batcave Companion*, 7–8.

a bully who was generally reviled . . . Ken Quattro, "Woolfolk on Weisinger," *Comics Detective* blog, April 16, 2012, http://thecomicsdetective .blogspot.com/2012/04/woolfolk-on-weisinger.html.

Schiff introduced Batwoman . . . First appeared in *Detective Comics* #233 (April 1956).

Several stories involved romantic encounters . . . See *Batman* #119 (October 1959), *Batman* #122 (March 1959).

imagined the two married . . . See *Batman* #131 (April 1960), *Batman* #145 (February 1962), *Batman* #154 (March 1963).

Robin got a potential girlfriend as well . . . First appeared in *Batman* #139 (April 1961).

"Greetings from the Batman Family" . . . *Batman Annual* #2 (Winter 1961).

not even mentioned except for . . . *Detective Comics* #311 (January 1963).

Cat-Man battled Batman atop a giant . . . *Detective Comics* #311 (January 1963).

including her mash-up of Poe's . . . *Detective Comics* #318 (August 1963).

He proved he had nine lives . . . *Detective Comics* #325 (March 1964).

Kathy Kane even donned a new feline costume . . . *Detective Comics* #318 (August 1963).

including Poison Ivy . . . First appeared in *Batman* #181 (June 1966).

Schwartz killed off Batman's butler . . . *Detective Comics* #328 (June 1964).

He later recalled that he did so because . . . Schwartz, *Man of Two Worlds*, 119–120.

# 3. Same Cat Time, Same Cat Channel

She was the "Special Guest Villainess" . . . "The Purr-fect Crime," *Batman* (TV), season 1, episode 19, directed by James Sheldon (Warner Bros., 1966).

Very few people inside ABC believed that . . . Joel Eisner, *The Official Batman Batbook: The Revised Edition* (Bloomington: AuthorHouse, 2008), 12.

He read up on old Batman comics . . . Weldon, *Caped Crusade*, 80.

he wanted to play everything as square . . . Eisner, *Official Batman Batbook*, 11.

FN West's costar Burt Ward believed that . . . Burt Ward, *Boy Wonder: My Life in Tights* (Los Angeles: Logical Figments, 1995), 69.

The actors rarely had more than two takes . . . Eisner, *Official Batman Batbook*, 236.

They even cut corners on stunts . . . Ward, *Boy Wonder*, 10, 16.

The hastily produced pilot went over poorly . . . Eisner, *Official Batman Batbook*, 11.

## Julie Newmar: Season 1

The entire *Batman* series is now available on DVD. For decades, *Batman* could only be seen in syndication because rights issues and complications between Warner Bros. and 20th Century Fox prevented a home video release. Everything was solved in 2014, and now *Batman* is available in a variety of collections.

he had Suzanne Pleshette lined up . . . Eury and Kronenberg, *Batcave Companion*, 67.

Her younger brother was down . . . Eisner, *Official Batman Batbook*, 88.

Julie Newmar was born Julia Chalene Newmeyer . . . "Biography," Julie Newmar official website, http://julienewmar.com/biography/.

The only female villain to appear before Catwoman . . . "Zelda the Great" and "A Death Worse than Fate," *Batman* (TV), season 1, episodes 9–10, directed by Norman Foster (Warner Bros., 1966).

The story was based on an issue of *Detective Comics* . . . *Detective Comics* #346 (December 1965).

"should work in dames where possible" . . . Eisner, *Official Batman Batbook*, 60.

Her first two-part show was written . . . "The Purr-fect Crime" and "Better Luck Next Time," *Batman* (TV), season 1, episodes 19–20, directed by James Sheldon (Warner Bros., 1966).

The production of *Batman* was so slapdash . . . Julie Newmar, interviewed in "The Many Faces of Catwoman," on *Catwoman* (Warner Bros., 2005), DVD.

One key change she made was lowering . . . Adam West with Jeff Rovin, *Back to the Batcave* (New York: Berkley Books, 1994), 133.

"It seemed so natural to put on those . . ." Scotty Mars, "Interview with Catwoman Julie Newmar," YouTube, May 3, 2013, www.youtube.com/watch?v=96i9u-ynA4A.

"It was so wonderful being on that show . . ." Eisner, *Official Batman Batbook*, 158.

Catwoman's first episode began . . . "The Purr-fect Crime," *Batman* (TV).

When the story resumed the following evening . . . "Better Luck Next Time," *Batman* (TV).

## Lee Meriwether: *Batman: The Movie*

Plus, the bigger movie budget would allow . . . Eisner, *Official Batman Batbook*, 139.

some say that she was busy with another project . . . Bob Garcia, "Batman: Catwoman," *Cinefantastique* 26/27, no. 6/1 (February 1994): 19.

others that she had a back injury . . . Joel Eisner, "The Batscholar on Batman: The Movie," *To the Batpoles* (blog), October 4, 2011, http://tothebatpoles .blogspot.ca/2011/10/batscholar-on-batman-movie.html.

As a young girl, whenever Meriwether got . . . Meriwether in "The Many Faces of Catwoman."

"I curled myself up in the chair . . ." Ibid.

"one of the nicest experiences . . ." San Diego County News Channel, "Interview with Lee Meriwether," YouTube, July 28, 2011, www.youtube.com /watch?v=p4lijTeld3Q.

"I could not sit at all comfortably . . ." Ibid.

Romero had to escort her around the sets . . . Eisner, *Official Batman Batbook*, 138.

"Sexy, yes, but kittenish sexiness" . . . Meriwether in "The Many Faces of Catwoman."

"Today Gotham City, tomorrow the world" . . . *Batman: The Movie*, directed by Leslie H. Martinson (Warner Bros., 1966).

"United Underworld, feh! . . ." Ibid.

FN A name that Meriwether had to memorize . . . Eisner, "Batscholar on Batman: The Movie," *To the Batpoles*.

"I don't think you mean that, Batman . . ." *Batman: The Movie*.

## Julie Newmar: Season 2

teamed with the Sandman . . . "The Sandman Cometh" and "The Catwoman Goeth," *Batman* (TV), season 2, episodes 33–34, directed by George Waggner (Warner Bros., 1966).

also cameoed in one episode . . . "Ma Parker," *Batman* (TV), season 2, episode 10, directed by Oscar Rudolph (Warner Bros., 1966).

targeted cat's-eye opals . . . "Batman Displays His Knowledge," *Batman* (TV), season 2, episode 50, directed by Robert Sparr (Warner Bros., 1967).

priceless violins . . . "Hot off the Griddle" and "The Cat and the Fiddle," *Batman* (TV), season 2, episodes 3–4, directed by Don Weis (Warner Bros., 1966).

even the Gotham Mint . . . "Scat! Darn Catwoman," *Batman* (TV), season 2, episode 41, directed by Oscar Rudolph (Warner Bros., 1967).

She used a special device . . . "The Cat's Meow," *Batman* (TV), season 2, episode 29, directed by James B. Clark (Warner Bros., 1966).

a four-seat getaway rocket . . . "The Cat and the Fiddle," *Batman* (TV).

developed a drug that turned . . . "That Darn Catwoman" and "Scat! Darn Catwoman," *Batman* (TV), season 2, episodes 40–41, directed by Oscar Rudolph (Warner Bros., 1967).

Catwoman even had her own protégé . . . Ibid.

"The princess of plunder! The saints . . ." "Hot off the Griddle," *Batman* (TV).

"If we weren't on opposite sides . . ." Ibid.

"Batman, are you spoken for?" . . . "The Cat and the Fiddle," *Batman* (TV).

Marsha, Queen of Diamonds . . . "Marsha, Queen of Diamonds" and "Marsha's Scheme of Diamonds," *Batman* (TV), season 2, episodes 23–24, directed by James B. Clark (Warner Bros., 1966).

When the Dynamic Duo were faced with . . . "The Greatest Mother of Them All," *Batman* (TV), season 2, episode 9, directed by Oscar Rudolph (Warner Bros., 1966).

FN A later episode revealed that Catwoman's . . . "Catwoman Goes to College," *Batman* (TV), season 2, episode 49, directed by Robert Sparr (Warner Bros., 1967).

a surprised Catwoman exclaimed . . . "The Bat's Kow Tow," *Batman* (TV), season 2, episode 30, directed by James B. Clark (Warner Bros., 1966).

The couple shared a float . . . "Catwoman Goes to College," *Batman* (TV).

Catwoman offered to surrender after . . . "Scat! Darn Catwoman," *Batman* (TV).

"Then you can be mine forever, Batman . . ." "The Cat's Meow," *Batman* (TV).

"Oh, nobody loves me!" . . . "Catwoman Goes to College," *Batman* (TV).

"Your propinquity could make a man . . ." "Batman Displays His Knowledge," *Batman* (TV).

"There's no room for another man . . ." Ibid.

"I wasn't so fond of that mushy stuff . . ." Ronald L. Smith, *Sweethearts of '60s TV* (New York: St. Martin's Press, 1989), 124.

"a Western of truly stunning absurdity" . . . Vincent Canby, "The Screen: 'Mackenna's Gold' in Apache Country," *New York Times*, June 19, 1969, www.nytimes.com/movie/review?res=9A0CE4DE1639EF3BBC4152DFB 0668382679EDE.

FN Newmar holds two patents . . . Brian Cronin, "TV Legends Revealed: Catwoman's Invention Provided Cheeky Assist?" *Comic Book Resources*, June 26, 2013, www.cbr.com/tv-legends-revealed-catwomans -invention-provided-cheeky-assist/.

Newmar reprised her role . . . *Batman: Return of the Caped Crusaders*, directed by Rick Morales (Warner Bros., 2016).

but with a sequel already announced . . . Aaron Couch, "William Shatner to Voice Two-Face in 'Batman: Return of the Caped Crusaders' Sequel," *Hollywood Reporter*, October 6, 2016, www.hollywoodreporter.com /heat-vision/william-shatner-voice-two-face-936010.

## Eartha Kitt: Season 3

Batmania was fading fast . . . Les Daniels, *Batman: The Complete History* (San Francisco: Chronicle Books, 1999), 115.

"I was in dire need of comfort . . ." John L. Williams, *America's Mistress: The Life and Times of Eartha Kitt* (London: Quercus, 2014), 258.

"We felt it was a very provocative idea . . ." Eisner, *Official Batman Batbook*, 390.

"I didn't have to think about her . . ." Carlin Flora, "Eartha Kitt: She Growls, She Purrs," *Psychology Today*, September 1, 2006, www.psychologytoday .com/articles/200609/eartha-kitt-she-growls-she-purrs.

FN "I liked that she was my size . . ." Eisner, *Official Batman Batbook*, 390.

"Ridiculous! Nonsense! Foolish prattle! . . ." "Catwoman's Dressed to Kill," *Batman* (TV), season 3, episode 14, directed by Sam Strangis (Warner Bros., 1967).

Kitt's second story line was a rare two-part . . . "The Funny Feline Felonies" and "The Joke's on Catwoman," *Batman* (TV), season 3, episodes 16–17, directed by Oscar Rudolph (Warner Bros., 1967–1968).

"an ironic, signifying statement on whiteness . . ." Deborah Elizabeth Whaley, "Black Cat Got Your Tongue? Catwoman, Blackness, and the Alchemy of Postracialism," *Journal of Graphic Novels and Comics* 2, no. 1 (June 2011): 10.

"How could a feline feloness like you . . ." "Catwoman's Dressed to Kill," *Batman* (TV).

Bruce Wayne was entranced over the telephone . . . "The Wail of the Siren," *Batman* (TV), season 3, episode 3, directed by George Waggner (Warner Bros., 1967).

The first unscripted interracial kiss . . . *Movin' with Nancy*, directed by Jack Haley Jr. (NBC, 1967).

The first scripted interracial kiss . . . "Plato's Stepchildren," *Star Trek*, season 3, episode 10, directed by David Alexander (NBC, 1968).

the landmark *Guess Who's Coming to Dinner* . . . *Guess Who's Coming to Dinner*, directed by Stanley Kramer (Columbia, 1967).

Catwoman organized a sit-in . . . "Catwoman Goes to College," *Batman* (TV).

"woman power" advocate Nora Clavicle . . . "Nora Clavicle and the Ladies' Crime Club," *Batman* (TV), season 3, episode 19, directed by Oscar Rudolph (Warner Bros., 1968).

Catwoman was a tall brunette with white skin . . . "The Entrancing Dr. Cassandra," *Batman* (TV), season 3, episode 25, directed by Sam Strangis (Warner Bros., 1968).

There was a deal in place for NBC to pick up . . . Eisner, *Official Batman Batbook*, 445.

Kitt's was only in a couple . . . *Batman '66* #15 (October 2013) and *Batman '66* #63 (June 2015).

## 4. A Streak of Heartbreaks

"Holy cats! Who's this female fiend . . ." *Superman's Girl Friend Lois Lane* #70 (November 1966).

"The Catwoman. She's one of Batman's arch . . ." Ibid.

The next issue resolved everything quickly . . . *Superman's Girl Friend Lois Lane* #71 (January 1967).

### Trial and Error

Bronze Age comics aren't particularly well collected by DC Comics, especially in the comprehensive, chronological form like it's done with the Golden and Silver Age. Occasional famous runs have been reprinted, and Catwoman appears in a few of them, but broadly speaking it's a spotty era for collections. ComiXology has collected swaths of this era digitally, however.

quickly introduced Commissioner Gordon's daughter . . . *Detective Comics* #359 (January 1967).

The story began with her Kitty Car prowling . . . *Batman* #197 (December 1967).

"Now—give me your answer! . . ." Ibid.

"It's all over, Batman! You just lost . . ." *Batman* #210 (March 1969).

"We all have a common cause . . ." Ibid.

"in a nutshell, an unfortunate attempt" . . . Letter from Steve Berry, *Batman* #214 (August 1969).

he was angry that Catwoman wasn't . . . Letter from Scott Gibson, *Batman* #214 (August 1969).

Wonder Woman had been revamped entirely . . . The mod era began in *Wonder Woman* #178 (September–October 1968).

Diana was in Tibet searching for . . . *Wonder Woman* #201 (July–August 1971).

There they worked together to rescue Jonny . . . *Wonder Woman* #202 (September–October 1972).

she infiltrated a circus to try to steal . . . *Batman* #256 (May–June 1974).

began a spree of jewel thefts . . . *Batman* #266 (August 1975).

same costume along with a widow's veil . . . *Batman* #291 (September 1977).

The comic book market was shrinking . . . M. Keith Booker, *Comics Through Time: A History of Icons, Idols, and Ideas*, vol. 2, *1960–1980* (Santa Barbara, CA: Greenwood, 2014), 547.

She was referred to as Selena . . . *The Brave and the Bold* #131 (December 1976).

"NO! NO! NO! That is most definitely not . . ." Letter from Brian D. Scott, *The Brave and the Bold* #134 (May 1977).

## Sudsy Drama

"I am the Catwoman no longer!" . . . *Batman* #308 (February 1979).

FN It turned into a love square for a while . . . *Superman* #380 (February 1983).

Talia al Ghul entered his life . . . First appeared in *Detective Comics* #411 (May 1971).

They soon broke up because she couldn't bear . . . *Detective Comics* #476 (March–April 1978).

Bruce got one of his most trusted employees . . . *Batman* #308 (February 1979).

"I may not be the Catwoman any longer . . ." *Batman* #315 (September 1979).

Selina later forgave Bruce . . . *Batman* #317 (November 1979).

FN Somewhat ominously, one of their first outings . . . *Batman* #319 (January 1980).

her interest in Egyptian cat artifacts . . . *Batman* #322 (April 1980).

her appreciation of fine jewelry . . . *Batman* #319 (January 1980).

Selina began to complain of headaches . . . *Batman* #321 (March 1980).

diagnosed with an exotic disease . . . *Batman* #322 (April 1980).

She swore that she didn't do it . . . *Batman* #323 (May 1980).

he apologized to Selina and, in her Catwoman . . . Ibid.

"I'm wondering if seeing Batman with Talia . . ." *Batman* #332 (February 1981).

Selina was back after Bruce . . . *Detective Comics* #509 (December 1981).

"I've never been as happy as I am . . ." *Batman* #345 (March 1982).

story's cliff-hanger had Catwoman hanging . . . Ibid.

a wife who betrayed her politician husband . . . *Batman* #349 (July 1982).

Catwoman posed as a deceased stripper . . . *Batman* #350 (August 1982).

"Consider this call a warning. If you value your life . . ." *Batman* #354 (December 1982).

"I'm not playing games, Vale! . . ." *Detective Comics* #521 (December 1982).

Catwoman ran them off the road . . . *Batman* #355 (January 1983).

FN Catwoman's dialogue during the fight suggested . . . Ibid.

Initially, Catwoman was just back in town . . . *Batman* #389 (November 1985).

Catwoman was struck with a bolt of lightning . . . *Batman* #390 (December 1985).

"What are you trying to do, give me heart failure?" . . . Letter from Elvis Orten, *Batman* #394 (April 1986).

"I don't think I can face Gotham City . . ." Letter from Phetsey Calloway, *Batman* #394 (April 1986).

"If Catwoman dies, I'll drop my subscription . . ." Letter from Bob G. Prat, *Batman* #394 (April 1986).

almost losing her led Batman to end things . . . *Batman* #392 (February 1986).

The duo double dated with Black Canary . . . *Detective Comics* #559 (February 1986).

Batman thought that Catwoman was spending time . . . *Batman* #399 (September 1986).

Catwoman ended up breaking things off . . . Ibid.

the Joker used a machine to alter Catwoman's brain . . . *Detective Comics* #569 (December 1986).

### Another World

Earth-Two stories have been haphazardly collected in a variety of books over the years, while a lengthy run of the Huntress's adventures was reprinted in *Huntress: Dark Knight Daughter* in 2006; that book is currently out of print.

The Flash discovered the universe in 1961 . . . Earth-Two first appeared in *The Flash* #123 (September 1961).

the Huntress, a new Earth-Two character . . . First appeared in *DC Super-Star* #17 (December 1977).

"Batman was watching that night . . ." Ibid.

"I was thirty years old and I didn't want . . ." *The Brave and the Bold* #197 (April 1983).

becoming Gotham's police commissioner . . . *All-Star Comics* #68 (September–October 1977).

felt like she was gaining strength from her deceased . . . *Wonder Woman* #280 (June 1981).

"Helena Wayne carries on her father's mission . . ." *Wonder Woman* #273 (November 1980).

"I do so want to spend my life being just as good . . ." *Wonder Woman* #286 (December 1981).

"You will never be without me . . ." *Wonder Woman* #307 (September 1983).

"I can't go on thinking that someday . . . someday . . ." *Wonder Woman* #320 (October 1984).

"Those are my father's traits . . ." Ibid.

Catwoman was dutifully killed off . . . "Premiere," *Birds of Prey* (TV), season 1, episode 1, directed by Brian Robbins (Warner Bros., 2002); *Earth 2* #1 (July 2012).

## 5. Gone Astray

Batman found attempting to steal the tires . . . *Batman* #408 (June 1987).

FN they were given the opportunity to vote . . . *Batman* #427 (December 1988).

### Frank Miller

All of Frank Miller's 1980s work at DC and Marvel, from *Daredevil* to *The Dark Knight Returns* to *Batman: Year One*, have been collected and recollected in an assortment of different volumes, special editions, and formats. They are considered foundational texts of the Modern Era of superhero comics and are widely available. Catwoman's subsequent adventures have fallen by the wayside, however, though some are available on ComiXology.

when Miller's editor let him take over the writing . . . *Daredevil* #168 (January 1981).

"I have never read a Frank Miller book . . ." Susana Polo, "The Writer Who Made Me Love Comics Taught Me to Hate Them," *Polygon*, March 1, 2016, www.polygon.com/2016/3/1/11139828/the-dark-knight-returns.

Miller's most famous creation was Elektra . . . *Daredevil* #168 (January 1981).

she was killed by another villain . . . *Daredevil* #181 (April 1982).

"There's a hole in me. A great . . ." *Daredevil* #183 (June 1982).

she ended up committing suicide . . . *Daredevil* #220 (July 1985).

Miller brought her back as a drug addict . . . *Daredevil* #227 (February 1986).

Karen was out of the country . . . *Daredevil* #229 (April 1986).

FN she was killed off to cause more turmoil . . . *Daredevil* #5 (March 1999).

Miller returned to Elektra . . . Frank Miller and Lynn Varley, *Elektra Lives Again* (New York: Marvel, 1990).

"Selina, Bruce. I'm lonely" . . . *Batman: The Dark Knight* #1 (1986).

"You get the hell out of—" . . . *Batman: The Dark Knight* #3 (1986).

The Joker had left her hog-tied . . . Ibid.

she didn't appear again until one panel . . . *Batman: The Dark Knight* #4 (1986).

"Selina . . . don't stop now . . ." *Batman* #404 (February 1987).

"Damn it—nobody hurts Holly" . . . Ibid.

Selina also lent a hand . . . *Batman* #406 (April 1987).

"We're changing our line of work . . ." Ibid.

"I don't know, Selina—I mean . . ." Ibid.

three months had passed and Selina . . . *Batman* #407 (May 1987).

"I'll have to do something really nasty . . ." Ibid.

"The subtle, three issue build-up . . ." Letter from Kirk Chritton in *Batman* #410 (August 1987).

"You've made her a dominatrix . . ." Letter from Robin Scott Lane in *Batman* #410 (August 1987).

FN "I don't mean to make a guess . . ." Ibid.

"This is the biggest insult to any character . . ." Letter from John Craddock in *Batman* #411 (September 1987).

referred to as a "tough hooker" . . . *Legends of the Dark Knight* #1 (November 1989).

occasionally appeared in the stories that followed . . . See *Legends of the Dark Knight* #13 (December 1990), *Batman: Legends of the Dark Knight* #39 (November 1992), *Batman: Legends of the Dark Knight* #46 (June 1993).

In 1988 Alan Moore and Brian Bolland's . . . Alan Moore and Brian Bolland, *Batman: The Killing Joke* (New York: DC Comics, 1988).

FN Barbara Gordon reappeared as the . . . *Suicide Squad* #23 (April 1989).

Catwoman, sporting a purple-and-green outfit . . . *Action Comics Weekly* #611 (August 1988).

Selina gave the brooch to Holly . . . *Action Comics Weekly* #612 (August 1988).

Holly's philandering husband killed . . . *Action Comics Weekly* #613 (August 1988).

Catwoman tracked him down . . . *Action Comics Weekly* #614 (August 1988).

"In the Ruins of Innocence . . ." *Catwoman* #1 (February 1989).

"You're pissing blood . . ." Ibid.

"Don't kick the cat again, Stan . . ." *Catwoman* #2 (March 1989).

Stan, wanting to get back at Selina . . . Ibid.

This eventually led to a tense battle . . . *Catwoman* #3 (April 1989).

"I can't take it. But she can . . ." *Catwoman* #4 (May 1989).

"If enough people buy the first issue . . ." Editorial response in *Action Comics Weekly* #623 (October 1988).

Her only significant story was a two-issue . . . *Batman* #460 and #461 (March, April 1991).

"At long last, the Catwoman . . ." Letter from Neil Ahlquist in *Batman* #468 (September 1991).

**His major project in this period** . . . The first volume originally ran in *Dark Horse Presents* #51–62 (April 1991–May 1992) and was collected as Frank Miller, *Sin City: The Hard Goodbye* (Milwaukie: Dark Horse, 1992).

## Roman Holiday

All the Loeb/Sale titles have been collected and recollected several times over the years. They've been in print continually since their first release.

**the book opened with the Roman's nephew's** . . . *Batman: The Long Halloween* #1 (December 1996).

**"I don't want to help. But, I might be able . . ."** Ibid.

**"Why? Why do you help?"** . . . *Batman: The Long Halloween* #12 (November 1997).

**the story ended with Catwoman joining** . . . *Batman: The Long Halloween* #13 (December 1997).

**when the duo were seated at opposite** . . . *Batman: Dark Victory* #2 (January 2000).

**Bruce stood her up on Christmas Eve** . . . *Batman: Dark Victory* #3 (February 2000).

**and New Year's** . . . *Batman: Dark Victory* #4 (March 2000).

**"I hope you'll show a little more interest . . ."** *Batman: Dark Victory* #1 (December 1999).

**"Let's do it. Right now . . ."** *Batman: Dark Victory* #5 (April 2000).

**"I know you are my real father . . ."** *Batman: Dark Victory* #13 (December 2000).

**Selina traveled to Italy with the Riddler** . . . *Catwoman: When in Rome* #1 (November 2004).

**When she later confronted him** . . . *Catwoman: When in Rome* #4 (March 2005).

**a local gangster assured her** . . . *Catwoman: When in Rome* #6 (August 2005).

**Selina left Rome with that knowledge** . . . Ibid.

## Frank Miller Strikes Again

**He codirected a much-lauded film** . . . *Sin City*, directed by Frank Miller and Robert Rodriguez (Miramax, 2005).

**he directed *The Spirit*** . . . *The Spirit*, directed by Frank Miller (Lionsgate, 2008).

**Miller's graphic novel *300*** . . . *300*, directed by Zack Snyder (Warner Bros., 2006).

**faithful adaptations of *Batman: The Dark Knight Returns*** . . . *Batman: The Dark Knight Returns*, part 1, directed by Jay Oliva (Warner Bros., 2012);

*Batman: The Dark Knight Returns*, part 2, directed by Jay Oliva (Warner Bros., 2013).

and *Batman: Year One* . . . *Batman: Year One*, directed by Sam Liu and Lauren Montgomery (Warner Bros., 2011).

Batman's lieutenant Carrie Kelly . . . *The Dark Knight Strikes Again* #1 (December 2001).

so too was Carrie savagely beaten . . . *The Dark Knight Strikes Again* #3 (July 2002).

the first issue sold 261,000 copies . . . Data available at John Jackson Miller, "Comic Book Sales by Month," *Comichron: The Comics Chronicles*, www.comichron.com/monthlycomicssales.html.

"I'm the goddamn Batman" . . . *All Star Batman & Robin the Boy Wonder* #2 (November 2005).

"Get lost. I've heard rumors on how . . ." *All Star Batman & Robin the Boy Wonder* #8 (January 2008).

she lay collapsed in an alley . . . *All Star Batman & Robin the Boy Wonder* #10 (August 2008).

"Don't talk, baby. You're safe" . . . Ibid.

Miller announced that he was working . . . Hilary Goldstein, "WonderCon '06: Holy Terror, Batman!" *IGN*, February 12, 2006, http://ca.ign.com /articles/2006/02/12/wondercon-06-holy-terror-batman.

"[The Fixer's] got a tremble running . . ." Frank Miller, *Holy Terror* (Burbank, CA: Legendary Comics, 2011).

"Okay. So maybe I'm in love, too" . . . Ibid.

"one of the most appalling, offensive . . ." Spencer Ackerman, "Frank Miller's *Holy Terror* is Fodder for Anti-Islam Set," *Wired*, September 28, 2011, www.wired.com/2011/09/holy-terror-frank-miller/.

"a hateful, ill-considered, simplistic . . ." David Brothers, "Frank Miller's 'Holy Terror': A Propaganda Comic that Fights Faith Instead of Evil," *Comics Alliance*, September 26, 2011, http://comicsalliance.com /frank-millers-holy-terror-review/.

FN DC also released an oversized special . . . *The Dark Knight Returns: The Last Crusade* #1 (August 2016).

the first issue revealed another promotion . . . *The Dark Knight III: The Master Race* #1 (January 2016).

## 6. Hear Me Roar

a cheaply produced pair of specials . . . "The Challenge" and "The Roast," *Legends of the Superheroes* (TV), directed by Bill Carruthers and Chris Darley (Warner Bros., 1979).

producers Michael Uslan and Benjamin Melniker . . . Michael Uslan, *The Boy Who Loved Batman: A Memoir* (San Francisco: Chronicle Books, 2011), 194.

the project wasn't officially greenlit until . . . Mark Salisbury, *Burton on Burton* (London: Faber and Faber, 2006), 71.

The film began with Batman taking on . . . *Batman*, directed by Tim Burton (Warner Bros., 1989).

it broke the opening weekend box office . . . "Batman," Box Office Mojo, www.boxofficemojo.com/movies/?id=batman.htm.

Burton wasn't keen to return . . . Alan Jones, "Batman in Production," *Cinefantastique*, November 1989, 75–88.

## This Hit, That Ice Cold

*Batman Returns* is available on DVD and various streaming services, though I've learned that if you suggest watching *Batman Returns* every time you browse said streaming service, your friends and/or family will get annoyed with you. They're wrong to do so; *Batman Returns* should be watched regularly. But still, just a warning for your social relationships.

"dark and elegant, fine-boned . . ." Sam Hamm, *Batman 2*, screenplay draft, n.d., via Daily Script, www.dailyscript.com/scripts/batman-returns _unproduced.html.

"POSING for him in a little private . . ." Ibid.

he wanted to start fresh . . . Clive J. Matthews and Jim Smith, *Tim Burton* (London: Virgin, 2002), 111.

"Hamm went back to the way comic . . ." Judy Sloan, "Daniel Waters on Writing," *Film Review* (August 1995): 67–69.

Selina Kyle was Shreck's mousy assistant . . . *Batman Returns*, directed by Tim Burton (Warner Bros., 1992).

"Every major movie star from 17 . . ." Matthews and Smith, *Tim Burton*, 117.

"I thought it would be a couple of scenes . . ." Michelle Pfeiffer interviewed in "The Many Faces of Catwoman."

"I read the script and I found her . . ." Ibid.

"I didn't care, I would've done it anyway . . ." Ibid.

"She just broke all of the stereotypes . . ." Matthews and Smtih, *Tim Burton*, 118.

she spent four hours a day doing . . . Dominic Wells, "Michelle Pfeiffer: Claws & Effect," *Dominic Wells*, www.dominicwells.com/journalist/pfeiffer/.

She also trained with a professional whip . . . Ibid.

"She really did something incredible . . ." Tim Burton interviewed in "The Many Faces of Catwoman."

Pfeiffer was able to kickbox in high heels . . . Wells, "Michelle Pfeiffer."

skintight costume as an "ordeal" . . . "Michelle Pfeiffer," *Inside the Actors Studio*, season 13, episode 9 (Bravo, 2007).

it was so tight that she could only . . . Wells, "Michelle Pfeiffer."

Burton kept the set so cold . . . Ibid.

she opted to use the live bird . . . "Shadows of the Bat: The Cinematic Saga of the Dark Knight—Dark Side of the Knight," *Batman Returns: Special Edition* (DVD), directed by Constantine Nasr (Warner Bros., 2005).

*Batman Returns* broke the opening weekend . . . "Batman Returns," Box Office Mojo, www.boxofficemojo.com/movies/?id=batmanreturns.htm.

"The runaway star here is Pfeiffer . . ." Owen Gleiberman, "*Batman Returns*: EW Review," *Entertainment Weekly*, June 26, 1992, www.ew.com /article/1992/06/26/batman-returns.

"Catwoman is no bimbo in black . . ." Peter Travers, "Batman Returns," *Rolling Stone*, June 19, 1992, www.rollingstone.com/movies/reviews /batman-returns-19920619.

FN Pfeiffer's Catwoman proved so popular. . . . The IMDb "Trivia" page for *Batman Returns* reports that not only were the Catwoman posters stolen but the Plexiglas holders in bus stops were broken so often in these thefts that some cities assigned police officers to patrol the bus stops. IMDb's trivia isn't fact checked, and I was unable to find outside confirmation that such measures were taken. However, a report from a television entertainment show in Kansas City does confirm the theft of a Catwoman poster. See Entertainment Spectrum (entertainmentspctrum), "Clips from Entertainment Spectrum Batman Returns Show," YouTube, July 21, 2008, www.youtube.com/watch?v=VW3CPNSs9zE.

## Whipping the Patriarchy

Vicki Vale's role followed . . . *Batman* (1989).

"I'm afraid we haven't properly housebroken . . ." *Batman Returns* (1992).

"I don't know about you, Miss Kitty . . ." Ibid.

"I just love a big strong man . . ." Ibid.

"You make it so easy, don't you? . . ." Ibid.

"The thought of busting Batman makes . . ." Ibid.

"Couldn't you just die?" . . . Ibid.

"The world tells boys to conquer . . ." Daniel Waters, *Batman II*, screenplay draft, May 20, 1991, via Daily Script, www.dailyscript.com/scripts /batman-returns_early.html.

"He knocked me off a building . . ." *Batman Returns* (1992).

"Bruce, I would love to live with you . . ." Ibid.

### The Real Protagonist

"Penguin—Man or Myth or Something Worse?" . . . *Batman Returns* (1992).

*Batman* had ended with the Bat-Signal . . . *Batman* (1989).

Instead, a downcast Bruce Wayne . . . *Batman Returns* (1992).

The Catwoman shot was a late addition . . . "Shadows of the Bat," *Batman Returns: Special Edition* (DVD).

There were rumors that if Burton . . . David Crow, "Why Tim Burton's Batman 3 Never Happened," *Den of Geek!*, June 16, 2016, www.denofgeek.com /us/movies/batman/239632/why-tim-burtons-batman-3-never-happened.

new director Joel Schumacher . . . *Batman Forever*, directed by Joel Schumacher (Warner Bros., 1995).

the studio knew that Pfeiffer's . . . Michael Fleming, "Dish," *Variety*, June 17, 1993, http://variety.com/1993/voices/columns/dish-6-107881/.

# 7. Leaping into Animation

The Batman half of *The Batman/Superman Hour* is collected on DVD as *The Adventures of Batman: The Complete Series*, while *The New Adventures of Batman* is collected under its original title.

"He carries a hardware store . . ." "The Nine Lives of Batman," *The Batman/ Superman Hour*, season 1, episode 4 (Warner Bros., 1968).

She stole from the Penguin in one episode . . . "Bubi, Bubi, Who's Got the Ruby," *The Batman/Superman Hour*, season 1, episode 5 (Warner Bros., 1968).

refused to work with the Joker . . . "A Game of Cat and Mouse," *The Batman/ Superman Hour*, season 1, episode 10 (Warner Bros., 1968).

"Now Catwoman shall reign . . ." "Partners in Peril," *The Batman/Superman Hour*, season 1, episode 7 (Warner Bros., 1968).

cat rockets and cat robots . . . "Trouble Identity," *The New Adventures of Batman*, season 1, episode 3 (Warner Bros., 1977).

stole heating oil with a tractor beam . . . "Curses! Oiled Again!" *The New Adventures of Batman*, season 1, episode 12 (Warner Bros., 1977).

"the four vilest villains . . ." "Have an Evil Day, Part 1," *The New Adventures of Batman*, season 1, episode 14 (Warner Bros., 1977).

FN Artist Alex Toth did design a Catwoman model . . . Marc Tyler Nobleman, "Super '70s and '80s: 'Super Friends'—Darrell McNeil, Animator," *Noblemania*, July 29, 2011, http://noblemania.blogspot.ca/2011/07/super -70s-and-80s-super-friendsdarrell.html.

### Batman: The Animated Series

*Batman: The Animated Series* is collected on several DVD sets, while the *Gotham Girls* webisodes remain online today and are collected in the DVD set of the first and only season of *Birds of Prey*. Episodes will be cited by airdate and not production.

Timm returned to his desk . . . Paul Dini and Chip Kidd, *Batman Animated* (New York: Dey Street Books, 1998).

"We had a love/hate thing going on . . ." Eric Nolen-Weathington, *Modern Masters*, vol. 3, *Bruce Timm* (Raleigh, NC: TwoMorrows, 2004), 38.

"At the time," he said, "I was kind of put . . ." Nolen-Weathington, *Bruce Timm*, 39.

the studio deemed it "close enough" . . . Ibid., 40.

Her audition was just five or six lines . . . "Adrienne Barbeau," *The Bat-Podcast*, episode 5, YouTube, July 31, 2014, www.youtube.com /watch?v=F4RPjTp_nh0.

"She does not play the part sexy . . ." Dini and Kidd, *Batman Animated*.

began with Catwoman scaling . . . "The Cat and the Claw, Part 1," *Batman: The Animated Series*, season 1, episode 1, directed by Kevin Altieri (Warner Bros., 1992).

"Please understand, it's purely for . . ." Ibid.

"What this situation needs is a woman's touch" . . . "The Cat and the Claw, Part 2," *Batman: The Animated Series*, season 1, episode 8, directed by Dick Sebast (Warner Bros., 1992).

"The Catwoman of the animated series . . ." Dini and Kidd, *Batman Animated*.

"In order to play Selina Kyle . . ." "Adrienne Barbeau," *The BatPodcast*.

"Part of us, I think, as women viewers . . ." Dini and Kidd, *Batman Animated*.

the Mad Hatter had Batman trapped . . . "Perchance to Dream," *Batman: The Animated Series*, season 1, episode 26, directed by Boyd Kirkland (Warner Bros., 1992).

"If you ever don your Catwoman costume . . ." "Cat Scratch Fever," *Batman: The Animated Series*, season 1, episode 33, directed by Boyd Kirkland (Warner Bros., 1992).

Batman was less helpful in Selina's . . . "Tyger Tyger," *Batman: The Animated Series*, season 1, episode 30, directed by Frank Paur (Warner Bros., 1992).

It was only in her final appearance . . . "Almost Got 'im," *Batman: The Animated Series*, season 1, episode 35, directed by Eric Radomski (Warner Bros., 1992).

Timm began developing a potential . . . Nolen-Weathington, *Bruce Timm*, 47.

"I prowled through Gotham each evening . . ." "Catwalk," *Batman: The Animated Series*, season 4, episode 3, directed by Boyd Kirkland (Warner Bros., 1995).

"I said I'd let them take me . . ." "Batgirl Returns," *Batman: The Animated Series*, season 3, episode 8, directed by Dan Riba (Warner Bros., 1994).

She stole the British Crown Jewels . . . *The Batman Adventures* #2 (November 1992).

took out Batgirl, Harley Quinn . . . *The Batman Adventures* #12 (September 1993).

"I can't believe I'm going to hear . . ." *The Batman Adventures* #36 (October 1995).

The Kids' WB censors were far more amenable . . . Rob Allstetter, "The Dark Knight Returns," *Wizard*, no. 72 (August 1997), 50–54.

she teamed up with Nightwing . . . "You Scratch My Back," *The New Batman Adventures*, season 1, episode 5, directed by Dan Riba (Warner Bros., 1997).

Catwoman tried another double cross . . . "Cult of the Cat," *The New Batman Adventures*, season 2, episode 3, directed by Butch Lukic (Warner Bros., 1998).

"If one of them dies . . . you're next!" . . . *Batman: Gotham Adventures* #4 (September 1998).

statue that turned Batgirl into a cat . . . "Lap Bat," *Gotham Girls*, season 1, episode 2 (Warner Bros., 2000).

the gals entering the Miss Criminal . . . "Miss Un-congeniality," *Gotham Girls*, season 2, episode 2 (Warner Bros., 2001).

Catwoman hiring Harley Quinn . . . "Gotham Noir," *Gotham Girls*, season 2, episode 8 (Warner Bros., 2001).

ended with the disappearance . . . "Ms-ing in Action," *Gotham Girls*, season 3, episode 1 (Warner Bros., 2002).

The police blamed the disappearances on . . . "Gotham in Pink," *Gotham Girls*, season 3, episode 2 (Warner Bros., 2002).

leading Batgirl to team up with the villains . . . "Honor Among Thieves," *Gotham Girls*, season 3, episode 7 (Warner Bros., 2002).

Catwoman broke into Reesedale's apartment . . . "Gotham in Blue," *Gotham Girls*, season 3, episode 4 (Warner Bros., 2002).

FN Batgirl did refer to her as "he" . . . "Signal Fires," *Gotham Girls*, season 3, episode 9 (Warner Bros., 2002).

When Reesedale returned later in the season . . . Ibid.

a six-minute short that was an extra . . . "Chase Me," *Batman: Mystery of the Batwoman* (DVD), directed by Curt Veda (Warner Bros., 2003).

## Animation Duplication

*The Batman, Batman: The Brave and the Bold,* and *Beware the Batman* are all collected on DVD.

**the lowest-rated and most poorly received** . . . Jim Harvey, "Ratings for 'Beware the Batman'; July 2011 Episode Airings on Cartoon Network," *World's Finest,* August 2013, www.worldsfinestonline.com/2013/08/ratings-for -beware-the-batman-july-2013-episode-airings-on-cartoon-network/.

**which premiered on the Kids' WB** . . . "The Bat in the Belfry," *The Batman,* season 1, episode 1, directed by Seung Eun Kim (Warner Bros., 2004).

**"I'm not really a villain in this . . ."** Joe Dangelo, "New Batman Cartoon Gets Edgy Theme from U2 Guitarist," MTV News, September 10, 2004, www.mtv.com/news/1490911/new-batman-cartoon-gets-edgy-theme -from-u2-guitarist/?headlines=true.

**she was after a Japanese jade lion** . . . "The Cat and the Bat," *The Batman,* season 1, episode 4, directed by Sam Liu (Warner Bros., 2004).

**attempted robberies of Egyptian artifacts** . . . "The Cat, the Bat, and the Very Ugly," *The Batman,* season 2, episode 1, directed by Brandon Vietti (Warner Bros., 2005).

**animation cels** . . . "Ragdolls to Riches," *The Batman,* season 2, episode 9, directed by Seung Eun Kim (Warner Bros., 2005).

**and leopards** . . . "The Laughing Cats," *The Batman,* season 3, episode 7, directed by Joseph Kuhr (Warner Bros., 2005).

**FN she even stole Wonder Woman's lasso** . . . *The Batman Strikes* #3 (January 2005).

**"You've let larceny taint your loveliness . . ."** "Inside the Outsiders!" *Batman: The Brave and the Bold,* season 1, episode 24, directed by Michael Chang (Warner Bros., 2009).

**"The most dangerous game, Batman . . ."** "Shadow of the Bat!" *Batman: The Brave and the Bold,* season 3, episode 3, directed by Michael Goguen (Warner Bros., 2011).

**"While all the boys can always save the day . . ."** "The Mask of Matches Malone!" *Batman: The Brave and the Bold,* season 2, episode 24, directed by Michael Chang (Warner Bros., 2011).

**After airing eleven episodes Cartoon Network** . . . Dan Seitz, "'Beware the Batman' Might Have Been Already Cancelled," *Uproxx,* October 22, 2013, http://uproxx.com/gammasquad/beware-the-batman-might-have -already-been-canceled/.

***DC Super Hero Girls* reimagines** . . . The DC Super Hero Girls star in a variety of videos, books, and more. You can learn all about their multimedia adventures at http://play.dcsuperherogirls.com.

## 8. Glaring Fixations

after a new gang took over her neighborhood . . . The Catwoman feature ran in *Showcase '93* #1–4 (January–April 1993).

"a fortune on a custom virus . . ." *Catwoman* #1 (August 1993).

her dominatrix period took up only . . . *Catwoman* #0 (October 1994).

*Catwoman*'s annual showed Selina . . . *Catwoman Annual* #2 (July 1995).

The issue ended with the assassin shooting . . . *Catwoman* #1 (August 1993).

tracked the assassin to the . . . *Catwoman* #2 (September 1993).

saved the island's leader from . . . *Catwoman* #4 (November 1993).

discovered that Bane was behind . . . Ibid.

returning to Gotham to take revenge . . . Ibid.

### The Women Behind Catwoman

This era of *Catwoman* is not well collected in print, but the issues are available online via ComiXology.

"It's Robin Hood with a selfish twist . . ." Letter from Jeffrey DesRosiers, *Catwoman* #5 (December 1993).

"Thank you for giving a female . . ." Letter from Andrea, *Catwoman* #8 (March 1994).

"We don't need another bimbo" . . . Letter from Richard D. Stewart, *Catwoman* #5 (December 1993).

she helped an environmental group . . . The arc began in *Catwoman* #6 (January 1994).

she prevented the death of the developers . . . *Catwoman* #8 (March 1994).

breaking into a medical facility . . . *Catwoman* #10 (May 1994).

"I just want it because it's pretty . . ." *Catwoman* #22 (July 1995).

Weis put Catwoman in a world . . . *Catwoman Annual* #3 (June 1996).

"All those stories in which Batman and . . ." Editorial response, *Catwoman* #5 (December 1993).

they were pirate lovers . . . *Detective Comics Annual* #7 (1994).

paramours in a medieval fantasy . . . *Catwoman Annual* #1 (1994).

monstrous cat and bat beasts . . . *Batman Annual* #20 (1996).

"As long as I know you're suffering . . ." *Catwoman* #54 (February 1998).

Grayson moved Catwoman to Manhattan . . . *Catwoman* #66 (March 1999).

Selina Kyle blackmailed her way into . . . *Catwoman* #67 (April 1999).

soon she was running for mayor . . . *Catwoman* #68 (May 1999).

she faked her own death . . . *Catwoman* #71 (August 1999).

Maria, Selina's mother, was Latina . . . *Catwoman* #81 (June 2000).

**Frank Miller was ambiguous about Selina's** . . . Frank Miller and David Mazzucchelli, *Batman: Year One Deluxe Edition* (New York: DC Comics, 2007).

**"long, lean black woman"** . . . Frank Miller, *Batman: Year One*, screenplay draft, n.d., via Leon's Script Collection, http://leonscripts.users5.50megs.com/scripts/BATMANYEARONEscript.htm.

**Chuck Dixon had a lengthy run** . . . Starting in *Catwoman* #12 (July 1994).

**Doug Moench took over** . . . Starting in *Catwoman* #41 (January 1997).

**John Ostrander also had a brief** . . . Starting in *Catwoman* #72 (September 1999).

**women wrote only 15 percent of DC's books in 2016** . . . Tim Hanley, "Gendercrunching December 2016—the Year in Genderetrospect," *Bleeding Cool*, February 19, 2017, www.bleedingcool.com/2017/02/19/gendercrunching-december-2016/.

## The Art of Jim Balent

**assistant editors often had to go through** . . . Joseph P. Illidge, "Do not even get me started on that version of CATWOMAN. I spent time circling nipples for Production to remove. Time!" *Twitter*, October 18, 2015, https://twitter.com/JosephPIllidge/status/655911760524890112.

**tiny maid outfits** . . . *Catwoman* #22 (July 1995).

**leopard-print bikinis** . . . *Catwoman* #44 (April 1997), *Catwoman* #48 (August 1997).

**her blazer was cut almost** . . . *Catwoman* #67 (April 1999).

**a brawl in a castle in the Alps** . . . *Catwoman* #18 (February 1995).

**the cybernetic armor of Cyber-Cat** . . . *Catwoman* #42 (February 1997).

**another busty feline character named She-Cat** . . . Ibid.

**Catwoman teamed up with Vampirella** . . . *Catwoman/Vampirella: The Furies* #1 (February 1997).

**Catwoman was the hero of Gotham City** . . . *Catwoman: Guardian of Gotham* #1 (August 1999).

**FN "to write comics that women would read . . ."** Neil Gaiman quoted in Vertigo Comics, "I really wanted to write comics that women would read [. . .] and that didn't have characters that looked like they had 2 watermelons strapped to their chest," *Twitter*, November 9, 2015, https://twitter.com/vertigo_comics/status/663883517508476928.

**"Jim Balent is one of the best artists . . ."** Letter from Jay McIntyre, *Catwoman* #6 (January 1994).

**"The art is worth looking at over . . ."** Letter from Dale Mayer, *Catwoman* #13 (August 1994).

"Jim Balent is, in my opinion . . ." Letter from Jeffrey Bridge, *Catwoman* #31 (March 1996).

"I would print letters from women . . ." Editorial response, *Catwoman* #8 (March 1994).

Gorfinkel ran a column of letters written . . . *Catwoman* #12 (July 1994).

"This new series is off to a fine . . ." Letter from Shelby C. Pankratz in *Catwoman* #6 (January 1994).

"You're proving that a female super-hero . . ." Letter from Andrea, *Catwoman* #8 (March 1994).

"while Selina Kyle has been a part . . ." Letter from Mark Lucas, *Catwoman* #8 (March 1994).

"I know you're sick of hearing this . . ." Laura McLellan letter, *Catwoman* #12 (July 1994).

The chart above shows the sales . . . "Comic Book Sales by Month," *Comichron*.

### Tarot: Witch of the Black Rose

"the young voluptuous warrior witch . . ." "Broadsword Projects," *Jim Balent's BroadSword Comics*, www.jimbalentstudios.com/broadsword-projects/.

The book premiered in March 2000 . . . *Tarot: Witch of the Black Rose* #1 (March 2000).

"The style of *Catwoman* sort of . . ." Derek Royal, "Comics Alternative Interview: Jim Balent and Holly Golightly," *Comics Alternative*, November 3, 2014, http://comicsalternative.com/interviews-balent/.

Tarot had a friend named Boo Cat . . . First appeared in *Tarot: Witch of the Black Rose* #6 (January 2001).

and the 3 Little Kittens . . . First appeared in *Tarot: Witch of the Black Rose* #28 (September 2004).

FN "If all you could see of me are my breasts . . ." *Tarot: Witch of the Black Rose* #3 (July 2000).

an errant sword cut . . . *Tarot: Witch of the Black Rose* #51 (July 2008).

or a magical spell . . . *Tarot: Witch of the Black Rose* #41 (November 2006).

"a book that's little more than a supernatural . . ." Chris Sims, "'Tarot' #63 Explains What Breasts Are for to Naked Lady Werewolves," *Comics Alliance*, August 19, 2010, http://comicsalliance.com/tarot-63 -naked-werewolves/.

"I envision the books to first 'entertain' . . ." Lynn Robison, "The Nicest Man at Comic-Con—Jim Balent," *Sequential Tart*, www.sequentialtart.com /archive/sept04/jbalent.shtml.

"I am still amazed to see that it is acceptable . . ." Ibid.

"a very unhealthy way of looking at the human . . ." David Bitterbaum, "Jim Balent and Holly Golightly Interview!" YouTube, December 4, 2014, www.youtube.com/watch?v=JnGSNa1W8Ak.

"The magick of you is that you are unique . . ." *Tarot: Witch of the Black Rose* #43 (March 2007).

the fans who come to see Balent . . . Robison, "The Nicest Man."

BroadSword's official Twitter account . . . As of September 2015.

"I received a lot of positive mail from . . ." Scott Williams, "Jim Balent and Holly G Interview," *Fanboy Buzz*, December 28, 2009, www.fanboybuzz .com/2009/12/jim-balent-holly-g-interview/.

Sometimes this was done for suspense . . . For examples, see *Tarot: Witch of the Black Rose* #21 (July 2003), *Tarot: Witch of the Black Rose* #32 (May 2005), *Tarot: Witch of the Black Rose* #45 (July 2007).

Other times it was supposed to be comedic . . . For examples, see *Tarot: Witch of the Black Rose* #13 (March 2002), *Tarot: Witch of the Black Rose* #17 (November 2002).

# 9. A Novel Perspective

"kind of insulting to women readers" . . . Chris Sims, "Ed Brubaker Looks Back on Batman, Part Three: Catwoman," *Comics Alliance*, December 11, 2014, http://comicsalliance.com/ed-brubaker-looks-back-on-batman -part-three-catwoman/.

"What you should do is figure out . . ." Ibid.

that he could get a new artist . . . Ibid.

Brubaker loved his stylish, cartoonish . . . Tom Spurgeon, "An Interview with Ed Brubaker," *Comics Reporter*, September 2, 2006, www.comicsreporter.com /index.php/resources/interviews/6073/.

he couldn't resist and agreed . . . Markisan Naso, "The Darwyn Cooke Inter-view," *Comics Journal*, May 16, 2016, www.tcj.com/the-darwyn-cooke -interview-by-markisan-naso/2/.

"sexy [and] strong, not sleazy" . . . Robert Greenberger and Matthew Man-ning, *The Batman Vault: A Museum-in-a-Book with Rare Collectibles from the Batcave* (New York: Running Press, 2009).

They felt that the new take on Catwoman . . . Sims, "Ed Brubaker Looks Back."

*Catwoman* ended in July 2001 . . . *Catwoman* #94 (July 2001).

Gotham City's corrupt mayor . . . *Detective Comics* #759 (August 2001).

The mayor's goons beat Slam . . . *Detective Comics* #762 (November 2001).

When *Catwoman* #94 ended . . . "Comic Book Sales by Month," *Comichron*.
Brubaker and Cooke's new *Catwoman* . . . Ibid.

## Brubaker's Three Dozen and One

This entire era of *Catwoman* was collected in a series of graphic novels during
the original run and has recently been reprinted in a new series of collections.
Everything is also available digitally on ComiXology.

Catwoman's main sidekick . . . *Catwoman* #1 (January 2002).
FN Brubaker later explained Holly's "resurrection" . . . *Catwoman Secret
     Files and Origins* #1 (November 2002).
soon Holly was dating Karon . . . *Catwoman* #6 (June 2002).
He also clashed with Batman . . . *Catwoman* #22 (October 2003).
"I will speak for them. Because no one else will" . . . *Catwoman* #1 (January
     2002).
"I believe that deep down, you're a really . . ." Ibid.
"And if that runs out . . . well, I can . . ." *Catwoman* #4 (April 2002).
"Y'know, I'm not really sure" . . . Ibid.
witnessing the murder of an undercover cop . . . *Catwoman* #6 (June 2002).
finance a new community center . . . *Catwoman* #12 (December 2002).
her friend Sylvia from her . . . Ibid.
and her sister, Maggie, now out . . . Ibid.
it was blown up by minions of Black Mask . . . *Catwoman* #13 (January 2003).
Sylvia was revealed to be in league . . . *Catwoman* #14 (February 2003).
Maggie and Simon got kidnapped . . . Ibid.
Slam got hit by a car . . . Ibid.
Holly was assaulted . . . *Catwoman* #15 (March 2003).
Simon died from the constant . . . *Catwoman* #16 (April 2003).
Holly went into shock . . . Ibid.
"It's about surviving terrible things . . ." Arune Singh, "Look What the
     Cat Dragged In: Ed Brubaker Talks 'Catwoman,'" *Comic Book
     Resources*, January 31, 2003, www.cbr.com/look-what-the-cat-dragged
     -in-ed-brubaker-talks-catwoman/.
"one of my favorite things . . ." Sims, "Ed Brubaker Looks Back."
The story picked up six weeks later . . . *Catwoman* #17 (May 2003).
"I'm so tired of hating myself" . . . *Catwoman* #19 (July 2003).
Selina and Holly got out of Gotham . . . *Catwoman* #20 (August 2003).
Holly trained with the superhero Wildcat . . . Ibid.
Catwoman took over Sylvia's street gang . . . *Catwoman* #26 (February 2004).
"I was very conscious of wanting . . ." Sims, "Ed Brubaker Looks Back."
Holly and Karon kissed for the first time . . . *Catwoman* #5 (May 2002).

he was worried that DC would cut it . . . Sims, "Ed Brubaker Looks Back."

"It's great to see a depiction of a normal . . ." "DC's Catwoman Honored with GLAAD Award," Diamond Comics official website, accessed January 6, 2017, www.diamondcomics.com/Home/1/1/3/116?articleID=10043.

Brubaker had been laying the groundwork . . . Sims, "Ed Brubaker Looks Back."

Then Holly threw her a surprise birthday . . . *Catwoman* #37 (January 2005).

she was the chief suspect after a televangelist . . . *Gotham Central* #26 and #27 (February-March 2005).

iconic run on *Captain America* . . . *Captain America* #1 (January 2005).

FN Brubaker cameoed in the film as one . . . *Captain America: The Winter Soldier*, directed by Joe and Anthony Russo (Marvel Studios, 2014).

## Den Mother

Catwoman shot Black Mask in the head . . . *Catwoman* #52 (April 2006).

began with Selina in the hospital . . . *Catwoman* #53 (May 2006).

After killing Black Mask . . . *Catwoman* #62 (February 2007).

"The Marvel universe is founded on daddy issues" . . . Albert Ching, "Wonder-Con 2012: Carol Danvers is the New CAPTAIN MARVEL," *Newsarama*, March 18, 2012, www.newsarama.com/9237-wondercon-2012-carol-danvers-is-the-new-captain-marvel.html.

"Yes, Father. I shall become . . ." *Batman* #404 (February 1987).

have two kids, Franklin and Valeria . . . Franklin debuted in *Fantastic Four Annual* #6 (November 1968), and Valeria first appeared in *Fantastic Four* #15 (March 1999).

Clark Kent and Lois Lane briefly adopted . . . *Action Comics* #845 (January 2007).

racing across rooftops . . . *Catwoman* #55 (July 2006).

her babysitter was out cold . . . *Catwoman* #56 (August 2006).

brought in the magician Zatanna . . . *Catwoman* #58 (October 2006).

Selina had to break her out of jail . . . *Catwoman* #60 (December 2006).

stop a rampaging gorilla . . . Ibid.

asked the villain Calculator to erase . . . *Catwoman* #63 (March 2007).

break into LexCorp . . . *Catwoman* #64 (April 2007).

Blitzkrieg . . . *Catwoman* #66 (June 2007).

Hammer and Sickle . . . *Catwoman* #67 (July 2007).

vicious Amazon splinter group . . . *Catwoman* #70 (October 2007).

taking out Karon when she was babysitting . . . *Catwoman* #68 (August 2007).

Hammer got blasted out a window . . . Ibid.

She kept dreaming about other villains . . . *Catwoman* #71 (November 2007).

Bruce Wayne found her a good family . . . *Catwoman* #72 (December 2007).

she asked Zatanna to wipe Helena . . . Ibid.

*Catwoman* was way down the sales chart . . . "Comic Book Sales by Month,"
   *Comichron.*

*Catwoman* had fallen to 124th . . . Ibid.

## Identities and Events

Many of the books mentioned in this section were big event books or came
out in the past decade or so, and thus most of them remain in print today in
collected form or are recently out of print but still generally available. And
everything's on ComiXology to boot!

its final issue sold double the amount . . . "Comic Book Sales by Month,"
   *Comichron.*

stealing a briefcase full of ransom . . . *Batman* #608 (December 2002).

against Killer Croc . . . *Batman* #610 (February 2003).

Harley Quinn . . . *Batman* #613 (May 2003).

the Joker . . . *Batman* #614 (June 2003).

even Superman . . . *Batman* #612 (April 2003).

Batman revealed his secret identity . . . *Batman* #615 (July 2003).

The romance didn't work out . . . *Batman* #619 (November 2003).

Sue Dibny, was killed in *Identity Crisis* . . . *Identity Crisis* #1 (August 2004).

Jean Loring, was the book's villain . . . *Identity Crisis* #7 (February 2005).

Stephanie Brown, died in "War Games" . . . *Batman* #633 (December 2004).

Wonder Woman became a scapegoat . . . *Infinite Crisis* #1 (December 2005).

Lucy, died during the "New Krypton" event . . . *Supergirl* #59 (February 2011).

"We're going to help you. Help you . . ." *Catwoman* #50 (February 2006).

she killed Black Mask, partly as a reaction . . . *Catwoman* #52 (April 2006).

*Salvation Run* #1 premiered way down . . . "Comic Book Sales by Month,"
   *Comichron.*

sales going up for the first issue . . . Ibid.

sales for *Catwoman* were lower . . . Ibid.

Hush attacked her and cut out her heart . . . *Detective Comics* #848 (November 2008).

"because I wanted to hurt you . . ." *Detective Comics* #849 (December 2008).

and even teamed up with a few of her . . . *Detective Comics* #850 (January 2009).

kicked Catwoman off a roof . . . *Battle for the Cowl: The Underground* #1
   (June 2009).

The book began with Catwoman still reeling . . . *Gotham City Sirens* #1
   (August 2009).

Selina's sister, Maggie, returned . . . *Gotham City Sirens* #12 (July 2010).

ultimately begged Selina to kill her . . . *Gotham City Sirens* #22 (June 2011).

Talia al Ghul came after . . . *Gotham City Sirens* #19 (March 2011).

She took on a protégé, Kitrina . . . *Batman* #697 (May 2010).

When Batman told her that it wasn't safe . . . *Batman* #704 (January 2011).

"I'm my own woman. I'm doing what . . ." *Gotham City Sirens* #26 (October 2011).

## 10. Cinematic Catastrophe

"you don't win a Razzie without . . ." Razzie Channel, "Halle Berry Accepts Her RAZZIE Award," YouTube, January 13, 2011, www.youtube.com /watch?v=U-7s_yeQuDg.

### Development Hell

Dan Waters was hired to pen . . . Michael Fleming, "Another Life at WB for Catwoman and Tim Burton?" *Variety*, July 22, 1993, http://variety.com/1993 /voices/columns/another-life-at-wb-for-catwoman-and-burton-109036/.

Michelle Pfeiffer wanted to reprise . . . Ibid.

"definitely not a fun-for-the-whole . . ." Sloane, "Daniel Waters on Writing."

an amnesiac Selina Kyle . . . Daniel Waters, *Catwoman*, screenplay draft, June 16, 1995, via Sci Fi Scripts, www.scifiscripts.com/scripts/catwoman.txt.

"We stopped being lame and . . ." Ibid.

"Men realize more than ever . . ." Ibid.

Waters delivered it on the same weekend . . . Sloane, "Daniel Waters on Writing."

It also earned more at the box office . . . "Batman Forever," Box Office Mojo, www.boxofficemojo.com/movies/?id=batmanforever.htm.

"it was really his vision that made it . . ." WENN, "Pfeiffer Keeps Her Claws from Catwoman Judd," IMDB, January 28, 2002, www.imdb.com/news /ni0064187/.

There were likeness-rights issues . . . Chris Sims, "War Rocket Ajax #113: John Rogers Talks 'D&D,' Thrillbent and the Catwoman Movie," *Comics Alliance*, May 21, 2012, http://comicsalliance.com /war-rocket-ajax-113-john-rogers-talks-dandd-thrillbent-and-th/.

Ashley Judd boarded the film . . . "Film Notes: Ashley Judd Takes on 'Catwoman,'" *ABC News*, April 3, 2001, http://abcnews.go.com/Entertainment /story?id=107435&page=1#.UBRt9WGe5n8.

The lead character was Patience Price . . . Described in Jim Vejvoda, "The Stax Report: Script Review of *Catwoman*!" *IGN*, April 4, 2001, http://ca.ign.com /articles/2001/04/04/the-stax-report-script-review-of-catwoman.

"lame, derivative, and a tremendous letdown" . . . Ibid.

felt more like *Scooby-Doo* than a superhero . . . Jim Vejvoda, "Catwoman Movie Still Alive and Purring?" *IGN*, February 5, 2011, http://ca.ign.com /articles/2001/02/05/catwoman-movie-still-alive-and-purring.

he thought that they'd pulled a prank . . . Sims, "War Rocket Ajax #113."

"had no coherent attitude . . ." Ibid.

"daytime Patience uses her brain . . ." Ibid.

FN They offered the part to Nicole Kidman . . . Gary Susman, "Will Nicole Kidman Play Catwoman?" *Entertainment Weekly*, February 5, 2003, www.ew.com/article/2003/02/05/will-nicole-kidman-play-catwoman.

Their script followed the same formula . . . Melissa Ewey Johnson, *Halle Berry: A Biography* (Santa Barbara, CA: Greenwood, 2010), 77.

"female superheroes must have a female . . ." Sims, "War Rocket Ajax #113."

"tear-down-and-build-again . . ." Chris Faile, "Ed Solomon Gets Nod as 'Catwoman' Scribe," *Filmjerk*, June 20, 2003, www.filmjerk.com/news /article.php?id_new=283.

"Well, how bad could it get . . ." Sims, "War Rocket Ajax #113."

## The *Catwoman* Calamity

*Catwoman* is available on DVD and a variety of streaming services, so you can watch it there. You shouldn't; it's terrible. But you can.

"I knew we were in trouble just from . . ." Earwolf Media, "Catwoman," *How Did This Get Made?*, December 20, 2011, www.earwolf.com/episode /catwoman/.

"It all started on the day that I died" . . . *Catwoman*, directed by Pitof (Warner Bros., 2004).

"OK, then let me try the remix . . ." Ibid.

"Wanna see a pretty ridiculous photo . . ." Harry Knowles, "Wanna See a Pretty Ridiculous Photo of Halle in the CATWOMAN Outfit," *Ain't It Cool News*, September 29, 2003, www.aintitcool.com/node/16208.

"Oh no, Halle! Say it isn't so!" . . . "FIRST Picture of Halle as Catwoman Now Online!!" *Comic Book Movie*, September 29, 2003, www .comicbookmovie.com/other/first-picture-of-halle-as-catwoman-now -online-a814.

"Well, she looks like a Quebecois . . ." Sims, "War Rocket Ajax #113."

"I watched hours and hours of videotape . . ." Halle Berry interviewed in "The Many Faces of Catwoman."

"You see, sometimes I'm good . . ." *Catwoman* (2004).

came in third at the box office . . . "July 23–25, 2004—Weekend," Box Office Mojo, www.boxofficemojo.com/weekend/chart/?view=&yr =2004&wknd=30&p=.htm.

The film ultimately grossed . . . "Catwoman," Box Office Mojo, www .boxofficemojo.com/movies/?id=catwoman.htm.

"What a letdown" . . . Roger Ebert, review of *Catwoman*, RogerEbert.com, July 19, 2004, www.rogerebert.com/reviews/catwoman-2004.

"essentially an excuse to pose Berry . . ." Keith Phipps, review of *Catwoman*, *A.V. Club*, July 26, 2004, www.avclub.com/review/catwoman-4998.

"plays like a Lifetime movie . . ." David Rooney, review of *Catwoman*, *Variety*, July 22, 2004, http://variety.com/2004/film/markets-festivals /catwoman-1200532062/.

"Me-Ouch!" . . . Richard Corliss, "Me-Ouch!" *Time*, July 28, 2004, http:// content.time.com/time/arts/article/0,8599,673554,00.html.

## White Male Superhero Domination

"It's produced by people of color . . ." Wilson Morales, "*Catwoman*: An Interview with Edward L. McDonnell, *Black Film*, May 2004, www.blackfilm .com/20040521/features/edwardmcconnell.shtml.

"More films with people of color . . ." "Halle Berry," *The Oprah Winfrey Show*, May 25, 2004.

"Lone and Phillips are racially ambiguous . . ." Whaley, "Black Cat Got Your Tongue," 16.

Warner Bros.' *Suicide Squad* in 2016 . . . *Suicide Squad*, directed by David Ayers (Warner Bros., 2016).

the news that Michael B. Jordan . . . Mannie Holmes, "Michael B. Jordan on 'Fantastic Four' Casting Backlash: I'll 'Shoulder All This Hate,'" *Variety*, May 22, 2015, http://variety.com/2015/film/news/michael-b-jordan -fantastic-four-casting-backlash-shouldering-hate-1201504000/.

the North American film industry is vastly . . . Eric Deggans, "Hollywood Has a Major Diversity Problem, USC Study Finds," NPR, February 22, 2016, www.npr.org/sections/thetwo-way/2016/02/22/467665890 /hollywood-has-a-major-diversity-problem-usc-study-finds.

"Catwoman was one of the most important . . ." Eliana Dockterman, "Marvel CEO Says in Leaked Email That Female Superhero Movies Have Been a 'Disaster,'" *Time*, May 5, 2015, http://time.com/3847432 /marvel-ceo-leaked-email/.

three Spider-Mans . . . Spider-Man has been played by Tobey Maguire, Andrew Garfield, and Tom Holland.

two different versions of the Fantastic Four . . . The two cinematic sets of Fantastic Four were played by Ioan Gruffudd, Jessica Alba, Chris Evans, and Michael Chiklis and Miles Teller, Kate Mara, Michael B. Jordan, and Jamie Bell.

three Hulks . . . The three Hulks were played by Eric Bana, Ed Norton, and Mark Ruffalo.

the audience for the majority of these blockbusters . . . For example, women accounted for 44 percent of the opening weekend audience for *Guardians of the Galaxy* (Ray Subers, "Weekend Report: 'Guardians of the Galaxy' Obliterates August Record," Box Office Mojo, August 3, 2014, www.boxofficemojo.com/news/?id=3885&p=.htm), and 46 percent of *Suicide Squad*'s opening day (Pamela McClintock, "Box Office: 'Suicide Squad' Snubs Naysayers, Eyes $145–$150M Weekend," *Hollywood Reporter*, August 6, 2016, www.hollywoodreporter.com/news /box-office-suicide-squad-eyes-150-million-weekend-917819).

## 11. Sidekick Tales

*The Dark Knight*, broke the North American . . . "The Dark Knight," Box Office Mojo, www.boxofficemojo.com/movies/?id=darkknight.htm.

Disney bought the company . . . Brooks Barnes and Michael Cieply, "Disney Swoops into Action, Buying Marvel for $4 Billion," *New York Times*, August 31, 2009, www.nytimes.com/2009/09/01/business /media/01disney.html?_r=0.

### Film and Television

All the Nolan Batman films and the first two seasons of *Gotham* are available on DVD and various streaming services.

"an extraordinary character against . . ." Paul Hechinger, "'Dark Knight' Director Chris Nolan Talks About Keeping Batman Real," *BBC America*, December 2012, www.bbcamerica.com/shows//blog/2012/12 /dark-knight-director-christopher-nolan-discusses-keeping-batman-real.

"You've gotta have her, because . . ." Josh Wilding, "Christopher Nolan on Introducing Catwoman and His Involvement with MAN OF STEEL," *Comic Book Movie*, May 28, 2012, www.comicbookmovie.com/batman /christopher-nolan-on-introducing-catwoman-and-his-involvement-with -man-of-a60580.

"a bit of a con-woman, something . . ." Ibid.

Nolan auditioned several actresses . . . Tom Dichiara, "Keira Knightley, Anne Hathaway Among 6 Actresses Vying for 2 Roles in 'The Dark Knight

Rises,'" MTV News, January 12, 2011, www.mtv.com/news/2438263 /keira-knightley-anne-hathaway-the-dark-knight-rises-roles/.

**Hathaway actually thought that . . .** Chris Begley, "Anne Hathaway thought she was auditioning for Harley Quinn in 'The Dark Knight Rises,'" *Batman News*, April 13, 2012, http://batman-news.com/2012/04/13 /anne-hathaway-harley-quinn-the-dark-knight-rises/.

**working five days a week on straight . . .** Cathy Horyn, "Anne Hathaway's New World: The Interview," *Harper's Bazaar*, June 27, 2011, www.harpersbazaar.com/celebrity/latest/news/a744/anne-hathaway -interview/.

**"I always thought I had worked . . ."** Steve Weintraub, "Anne Hathaway Talks Fighting in Heels, Adapting to Nolan's Universe, Filming in IMAX and More on the Set of THE DARK KNIGHT RISES," *Collider*, May 27, 2012, http://collider.com/anne-hathaway-the-dark-knight-rises-interview/.

**"Oops. Nobody told me it was uncrackable"** . . . *The Dark Knight Rises*, directed by Christopher Nolan (Warner Bros., 2012).

**"I started out doing what I had to do . . ."** Ibid.

**"There's more to you than that"** . . . Ibid.

***The Dark Knight Rises* was a hit . . .** "The Dark Knight Rises," Box Office Mojo, www.boxofficemojo.com/movies/?id=batman3.htm.

**"the sensational secret . . ."** Anne Hornaday, "The Dark Knight Rises," *Washington Post*, July 19, 2012, www.washingtonpost.com/gog/movies /the-dark-knight-rises,1208568.html.

**"the most dynamic character . . ."** Scott Tobias, Review of *The Dark Knight Rises*, *A.V. Club*, July 18, 2012, www.avclub.com/review/the-dark-knight-rises -review-batman-82624.

**"It's Anne Hathaway's movie"** . . . David Edelstein, "Edelstein: *The Dark Knight Rises* Closes Out the Most Ambitious Superhero Movie Cycle Ever," *Vulture*, July 20, 2012, www.vulture.com/2012/07/movie-review -david-edelstein-on-the-dark-knight-rises.html#.

**"slinky, light-fingered, high-kicking . . ."** Tom Charity, "Review: 'Dark Knight Rises' Disappointingly Clunky, Bombastic," CNN, July 19, 2012, www .cnn.com/2012/07/19/showbiz/movies/dark-knight-rises-review-charity/.

**"bringing welcome humor to . . ."** Peter Travers, "The Dark Knight Rises," *Rolling Stone*, July 16, 2012, www.rollingstone.com/movies/reviews /the-dark-knight-rises-20120716.

**Katie Holmes played Bruce's . . .** *Batman Begins*, directed by Christopher Nolan (Warner Bros., 2005).

**Maggie Gyllenhaal took over . . .** *The Dark Knight*, directed by Christopher Nolan (Warner Bros., 2008).

**Selina's romantic feelings for Batman . . .** *The Dark Knight Rises* (2012).

**Bruce Wayne was a main character** . . . "Pilot," *Gotham* (TV), season 1, episode 1, directed by Danny Cannon (Warner Bros., 2014).

**relied on the character description** . . . Christina Radish, "Camren Bicondova Talks GOTHAM, the Audition Process, Becoming Part of the DC Universe, Delving into the Origins of Catwoman, and More," *Collider*, October 6, 2014, http://collider.com/camren-bicondova-gotham-interview/.

**She also put her dance training to use** . . . Ibid.

**FN Newmar is a big fan of Bicondova** . . . Hallmark Channel, "TV's Catwoman Camren Bicondova & Julie Newmar," *Home & Family*, May 11, 2016, www.hallmarkchannel.com/home-and-family/videos /tvs-catwoman-camren-bicondova-julie-newmar-home-family.

**Showrunner Bruno Heller was so impressed** . . . Michael Calia, "'Gotham' Returns: Here's What We Can Expect," *Wall Street Journal*, January 2, 2015, http://blogs.wsj.com/speakeasy/2015/01/02 /gotham-returns-heres-what-we-can-expect/.

**The show's pilot opened with Selina** . . . "Pilot."

**After she was rounded up to be sent** . . . "Selina Kyle," *Gotham* (TV), season 1, episode 2, directed by Danny Cannon (Warner Bros., 2014).

**used a pen to escape her handcuffs** . . . "The Balloonman," *Gotham* (TV), season 1, episode 3, directed by Dermott Downs (Warner Bros., 2014).

**he sent her to stay at Wayne Manor** . . . "Harvey Dent," *Gotham* (TV), season 1, episode 9, directed by Karen Gaviola (Warner Bros., 2014).

**the duo fled to the city** . . . "Lovecraft," *Gotham* (TV), season 1, episode 10, directed by Guy Ferland (Warner Bros., 2014).

**While their relationship was strained** . . . "Welcome Back, Jim Gordon," *Gotham* (TV), season 1, episode 13, directed by Wendey Stanzler (Warner Bros., 2005).

**Bruce was about to push him out** . . . "Beasts of Prey," *Gotham* (TV), season 1, episode 19, directed by Eagle Egilsson (Warner Bros., 2015).

**FN Selina also helped Bruce break into** . . . "Under the Knife," *Gotham* (TV), season 1, episode 20, directed by T. J. Scott (Warner Bros., 2015).

**"Do yourself a favor, treacle, and jog on"** . . . "Strike Force," *Gotham* (TV), season 2, episode 4, directed by T. J. Scott (Warner Bros., 2015).

**Selina thought was bad news** . . . "Mommy's Little Monster," *Gotham* (TV), season 2, episode 7, directed by Kenneth Fink (Warner Bros., 2015).

**reconnecting with her friend, Bridget** . . . "Scarification," *Gotham* (TV), season 2, episode 5, directed by Bill Eagles (Warner Bros., 2015).

**"You remind me of me, if I was . . ."** "By Fire," *Gotham* (TV), episode 6, directed by T. J. Scott (Warner Bros., 2015).

**Bridget ultimately took a dark turn** . . . Ibid.

**She broke into Silver's apartment . . .** "The Son of Gotham," *Gotham* (TV), season 2, episode 10, directed by Rob Bailey (Warner Bros., 2015).

**Selina led a team that included . . .** "Worse Than a Crime," *Gotham* (TV), season 2, episode 11, directed by Jeffrey Hunt (Warner Bros., 2015).

**letting him stay with her . . .** "This Ball of Mud and Madness," *Gotham* (TV), season 2, episode 14, directed by John Behring (Warner Bros., 2016).

**Selina stitched him up . . .** "Mad Grey Dawn," *Gotham* (TV), season 2, episode 15, directed by Nick Copus (Warner Bros., 2016).

**put up with his Robin Hood tendencies . . .** "Into the Woods," *Gotham* (TV), season 2, episode 17, directed by Oz Scott (Warner Bros., 2016).

**Selina broke into Arkham . . .** "Unleashed," *Gotham* (TV), season 2, episode 20, directed by Paul Edwards (Warner Bros., 2016).

**She also saved Bruce and Jim Gordon . . .** "Transference," *Gotham* (TV), season 2, episode 22, directed by Eagle Egilsson (Warner Bros., 2016).

## Games and Toys

**"This game should not be part . . ."** Marc Nix, "Catwoman," *IGN*, February 1, 2000, http://ca.ign.com/articles/2000/02/02/catwoman-11.

**the game had Batman fighting through . . .** *Batman: Arkham Asylum*, Rocksteady Studios, 2009.

**it sold eight million copies . . .** "Game Database," *VGChartz*, www.vgchartz.com/gamedb/?name=arkham+asylum.

**Catwoman was a playable character . . .** *Batman: Arkham City*, Rocksteady Studios, 2011.

**"The best thing about playing . . ."** Kirk Hamilton, "This is Why *Batman: Arkham City*'s Locked Catwoman Content Makes Buying the Game New the Wiser Choice," *Kotaku*, October 14, 2011, http://kotaku.com/5849771/this-is-why-batman-arkham-citys-locked-catwoman-content-makes-buying-the-game-new-the-smart-choice.

**"It's not like 90% of misogynistic . . ."** Alex Cranz, "*Batman: Arkham City* Isn't Misogynistic in Its Use of the Word Bitch," *FemPop*, October 31, 2011, www.fempop.com/2011/10/31/batman-arkham-city-isnt-misogynistic-in-its-use-of-the-word-bitch/.

**"Sorry to disappoint you, boys . . ."** *Batman: Arkham City* (2011).

**A prequel miniseries . . .** Collected as Paul Dini and Carlos D'Anda, *Batman: Arkham City* (New York: DC Comics, 2011).

**The debut issue of the follow-up . . .** *Batman: Arkham Unhinged* #1 (June 2012).

**a brief appearance in a tie-in game . . .** *Batman: Arkham Origins*, WB Games Montreal, 2013.

The game had Batman working . . . *Batman: Arkham Knight*, Rocksteady Studios, 2015.

"How should we celebrate? I know . . ." Ibid.

"'Thanks, Selina, for the daring . . .'" Ibid.

Catwoman also got her own extra . . . "Catwoman's Revenge," *Batman: Arkham Knight* DLC, Rocksteady Studios, 2015.

An animated short film . . . "Catwoman," *Batman: Year One* (DVD), directed by Lauren Montgomery (Warner Bros., 2011).

Of the thirty-two different Catwoman statues . . . This data comes from Entertainment Earth, December 2015, compiled by the author.

On DC Comics' own official online . . . This data comes from DC Collectibles' "Catwoman" page, December 2015, compiled by the author.

## 12. Perusing the New 52

they sent the Flash running . . . *Flashpoint* #5 (October 2011).

### Sexy, Sexy Times

All the comics discussed throughout this chapter came out in the last five years or so, and are well collected in a variety of graphic novels as well as readily available online via ComiXology.

"It's a very sexy title! . . ." Vaneta Rogers, "WINICK Returns to Gotham for Sexy, Violent DCnU CATWOMAN," *Newsarama*, June 11, 2011, www .newsarama.com/7787-winick-returns-to-gotham-for-sexy-violent-dcnu -catwoman.html.

"Think sexy. Think feline . . ." Ibid.

"But also think intelligent . . ." Ibid.

The cover showed Catwoman reclining . . . *Catwoman* #1 (November 2011).

"This doesn't feel like a superhero . . ." Greg McElhatton, "Catwoman #1," *Comic Book Resources*, September 21, 2011, www.cbr.com /catwoman-1/.

"Selina Kyle clearly doesn't . . ." Erik Norris, review of *Catwoman* #1, *IGN*, September 21, 2001, http://ca.ign.com/articles/2011/09/21 /catwoman-1-review.

"a bunch of gratuitous images . . ." Keith Phipps and Oliver Sava, "The New DC 52, Week 4 (*Wonder Woman*, *Batman*, *Catwoman*, and more)," *A.V. Club*, September 23, 2011, www.avclub.com/article /the-new-dc-52-week-4-iwonder-womani-ibatmani-icatw-62180.

"I hate this book from the cover down . . ." Ibid.

a beach scene in which Starfire . . . *Red Hood and the Outlaws* #1 (November 2011).

the titular character stripping . . . *Voodoo* #1 (November 2011).

FN Of the 160 creator credits . . . Tim Hanley, "Gendercrunching The DC Relaunch," *Bleeding Cool*, June 12, 2011, www.bleedingcool.com/2011 /06/12/gendercrunching-the-dc-relaunch/.

FN "Can't you show us the playful . . ." Laura Hudson, "The Big Sexy Problem with Superheroines and their 'Liberated Sexuality,'" *Comics Alliance*, September 22, 2015, http://comicsalliance.com/starfire -catwoman-sex-superheroine/.

"would very much like to see confident . . ." Ibid.

March revealed that the book's third . . . Guillem March, "CATWOMAN #03 unseen pages," *Guillem March* (blog), February 2013, 2014, http://guillemmarch.blogspot.ca/2014/02/catwoman-03-unseen-pages .html.

"I guess it all have [*sic*] to do . . ." Ibid.

she broke into a mansion via . . . *Catwoman* #8 (June 2012).

covered up a fight in her apartment . . . *Catwoman* #11 (September 2012).

March's *Catwoman* cover had her . . . "DC Comics Solicitations for September, 2012," *Comic Book Resources*, June 11, 2012, www.cbr.com /dc-comics-solicitations-for september 2012/.

most famously with the Hawkeye Initiative . . . Noelle Stevenson, "How to Fix Every Strong Female Character Pose in Superhero Comics: Replace the Character with Hawkeye Doing the Same Thing," *How Are You I'm Fine Thanks*, http://gingerhaze.tumblr.com/post/37003301441 /how-to-fix-every-strong-female-character-pose-in.

Kate Beaton of *Hark! A Vagrant* . . . The art from all of the creators mentioned here is collected in Chris Sims, "Artists Respond to DC's Back-Breaking 'Catwoman' #0 Cover," *Comics Alliance*, June 12, 2012, http://comicsalliance.com/artists-respond-dc-comics-back-breaking -catwoman-0-cover/.

When *Catwoman* #0 hit stores . . . *Catwoman* #0 (November 2012).

Artist David Finch's first issue . . . *Justice League of America* #1 (April 2013).

"My eyes are up here, sweetheart" . . . *Justice League of America* #2 (May 2013).

Catwoman was killed two issues later . . . *Justice League of America* #4 (July 2013).

soon revealed to be a fake-out . . . *Justice League of America* #5 (August 2013).

she eventually quit after the upheaval . . . *Justice League of America* #14 (July 2014).

## The Ups and Downs of Comic Book Sales

Selina's close friend Lola was . . . *Catwoman* #2 (December 2012).

from a high of 57,216 for *Catwoman* #2 . . . "Comic Book Sales by Month," *Comichron*.

to a low of 34,117 for *Catwoman* #12 . . . Ibid.

Catwoman was briefly possessed by . . . *Catwoman* #15 (February 2013).

she explored the secret cities . . . Beginning in *Catwoman* #22 (September 2013).

Catwoman was a valiant crime fighter . . . Beginning in *Catwoman* #27 (March 2014).

Catwoman returned to her roots . . . Beginning in *Catwoman* #30 (June 2014).

The first issue of Nocenti's debut . . . "Comic Book Sales by Month," *Comichron*.

by the end of the run . . . Ibid.

The chart above shows the sales figures . . . Ibid.

FN Catwoman is a side character in . . . First appeared in *DC Comics Bombshells* #5 (January 2016).


## Selina Kyle, Mob Boss

Williams and Blackman ended up quitting . . . Lucas Siegel, "WILLIAMS & BLACKMAN Quit BATWOMAN over 'Eleventh Hour' Editorial Changes," *Newsarama*, September 5, 2013, www.newsarama.com/18841 -williams-blackman-quit-batwoman-over-editorial-prevention-of -marriage.html.

"A Batman book for every fan . . ." Josie Campbell, "Doyle Promises a Batman 'for Every Fan,'" *Comic Book Resources*, December 18, 2014, www.cbr .com/doyle-promises-a-batman-for-every-fan/.

"the moral gray area she lives . . ." Vaneta Rogers, "New Writer Gives CAT-WOMAN 'Pulpy,' 'Noir' Mood . . . and a New Catwoman??" *Newsarama*, September 2, 2014, www.newsarama.com/22015-new-writer-gives -catwoman-pulpy-noir-mood-and-a-new-catwoman.html.

Selina was the daughter of Rex . . . *Batman Eternal* #23 (November 2014).

Rex told her that the only way for peace . . . Ibid.

after seeing her young friend Jade . . . *Batman Eternal* #28 (December 2014).

"the most Vertigo-esque" . . . Mark Doyle, "I say with pride that CAT-WOMAN is the most 'Vertigo-esque' book we've developed over the last few months. I hope people check it out," *Twitter*, October 22, 2014, https://twitter.com/markedoyle/status/524953587303337985.

The bright colors were gone . . . *Catwoman* #35 (December 2014).

"lots of shimmering cities . . ." Cameron Hatheway, "Talking to Garry Brown about The Massive and Catwoman at Long Beach Comic Expo," *Bleeding Cool*, March 3, 2015, www.bleedingcool.com/2015/03/03 /talking-garry-brown-massive-catwoman-long-beach-comic-expo/.

selling caches of guns . . . *Catwoman* #35 (December 2014).

slyly sabotaging a shipment of heroin . . . *Catwoman* #36 (January 2015).

she had him killed . . . *Catwoman* #37 (February 2015).

Valentine quoted a letter from Queen Elizabeth . . . *Catwoman* #35 (December 2014).

Queen Elizabeth was a favorite . . . In *Catwoman* #35, #38, #43.

As was Lucrezia Borgia . . . In *Catwoman* #36, #39, #41.

Caterina Sforza . . . In *Catwoman* #45.

Cleopatra . . . In *Catwoman* #40.

Eleanor of Aquitane . . . In *Catwoman* #44.

Empress Pulcheria . . . In *Catwoman* #42.

FN Chinese poet Li Bai's . . . In *Catwoman* #37.

Antonia became her second in command . . . *Catwoman* #36 (January 2015).

Eiko Hasigawa . . . First appeared in *Catwoman* #35 (December 2014).

took up the mantle of Catwoman . . . *Catwoman* #36 (January 2015).

"I can't help you after this . . ." *Catwoman* #39 (April 2015).

"wasn't a revelation so much as a confirmation" . . . Alison Flood, "Catwoman Revealed as Bisexual in New DC Comic," *Guardian*, February 27, 2015, www.theguardian.com/books/2015/feb/27 /catwoman-revealed-bisexual-new-dc-comic.

*Vanity Fair* . . . Julie Miller, "Catwoman Writer Confirms Selina Kyle Is Bisexual," *Vanity Fair*, February 26, 2015, www.vanityfair.com /hollywood/2015/02/selina-kyle-catwoman-bisexual.

CNN . . . Henry Hanks, "Catwoman Comes Out as Bisexual," CNN, February 27, 2015, www.cnn.com/2015/02/26/entertainment/catwoman -bisexual-feat/.

the BBC . . . "Catwoman 'Comes Out as Bisexual,'" *BBC News*, February 27, 2015, www.bbc.com/news/entertainment-arts-31663989.

FN "Boy oh boy. Normalizing perversion . . ." Comment from Resonantg, in Kipp Jones, "Latest Comic Confirms DC's Catwoman Is Bisexual," *Breitbart*, February 26, 2015, www.breitbart.com/big-hollywood/2015/02/26 /latest-comic-confirms-dcs-catwoman-is-bisexual/.

FN "Leftys have to defile everything" . . . Comment from headache, in Jones, "Latest Comic Confirms."

"Is it accurate to say that Angela is the first . . ." Axel Alonso, "Dragging 'Angela' to Hell, Entering X-Men's 'Extraordinary' Era,"

*Comic Book Resources*, October 30, 2015, www.cbr.com/dragging
-angela-to-hel-entering-x-mens-extraordinary-era/.

**Alonso definitively stated that he . . .** Axel Alonso, "Course-Correcting Diversity Probelms, Bendis' Iron Man Expansion," *Comic Book Resources*, July 31, 2015, www.cbr.com/course-correcting-diversity-problems-bendis
-iron-man-expansion/.

**DC launched a new series starring Midnighter . . .** *Midnighter* #1 (August 2015).

**longtime pals Harley Quinn and Poison Ivy . . .** Donna Dickens, "Creators Confirm Harley Quinn And Poison Ivy Are Definitely Hooking Up," *Hitfix*, June 16, 2015, www.hitfix.com/harpy/creators-confirm
-harley-quinn-and-poison-ivy-are-definitely-hooking-up.

**The Calabreses had to partner with the Penguin . . .** *Catwoman* #40 (May 2015).

**He ultimately turned on the Hasigawas . . .** *Catwoman* #44 (November 2015).

**She threw a party for the families . . .** *Catwoman* #46 (January 2016).

**The run started out with sales . . .** "Comic Book Sales by Month," *Comichron*.

**and ended at 21,661 . . .** Ibid.

**a fine, conventional caper . . .** *Catwoman* #47 (February 2016).

*Catwoman* **#47 sold only . . .** "Comic Book Sales by Month," *Comichron*.

**FN Catwoman recently resurfaced . . .** *Batman* #9 (December 2016).

## Conclusion

**Catwoman tauntingly counted down . . .** *Batman Returns* (1992).

**"Not bad, as ninth lives go" . . .** *Catwoman* #35 (December 2014).

**"Well, what's the matter? . . ."** *Batman* #1 (Spring 1940).

# Bibliography

ABC News. "Film Notes: Ashley Judd Takes on 'Catwoman.'" *ABC News*, April 3, 2001. http://abcnews.go.com/Entertainment/story?id=107435&page=1#.UBRt9WGe5n8.

Ackerman, Spencer. "Frank Miller's *Holy Terror* Is Fodder for Anti-Islam Set." *Wired*, September 28, 2011. www.wired.com/2011/09/holy-terror-frank-miller/.

*The Adventures of Batman: The Complete Series*. DVD. Warner Bros., 2014.

Allstetter, Rob. "The Dark Knight Returns." *Wizard* 72 (August 1997): 50–54.

Alonso, Axel. "Course-Correcting Diversity Problems, Bendis' Iron Man Expansion." *Comic Book Resources*, July 31, 2015. www.cbr.com/course-correcting-diversity-problems-bendis-iron-man-expansion/.

———. "Dragging 'Angela' to Hell, Entering X-Men's 'Extraordinary' Era." *Comic Book Resources*, October 30, 2015. www.cbr.com/dragging-angela-to-hel-entering-x-mens-extraordinary-era/.

Amash, Jim. "Building 'Batman'—and Other True Legends of the Golden Age." *Alter Ego* 39 (August 2004): 11–12.

Bails, Jerry. "If the Truth Be Known, or 'A Finger in Every Plot!'" *CAPA-alpha* 12 (September 1965).

Barnes, Brooks, and Michael Cieply, "Disney Swoops into Action, Buying Marvel for $4 Billion." *New York Times*, August 31, 2009. www.nytimes.com/2009/09/01/business/media/01disney.html?_r=0.

*Batman*. Directed by Tim Burton. Warner Bros., 1989.

*Batman: Arkham Asylum*. Rocksteady Studios, 2009.

*Batman: Arkham City*. Rocksteady Studios, 2011.

*Batman: Arkham Knight*. Rocksteady Studios, 2015.

*Batman: Arkham Origins*. WB Games Montréal, 2013.

*Batman Begins*. Directed by Christopher Nolan. Warner Bros., 2005.

*Batman Forever*. Directed by Joel Schumacher. Warner Bros., 1995.

*Batman: Return of the Caped Crusaders*. DVD. Directed by Rick Morales. Warner Bros., 2016.

*Batman Returns*. Directed by Tim Burton. Warner Bros., 1992.

*Batman: The Animated Series*. Vols. 1–4. DVD. Warner Bros., 2004–2005.

*Batman: The Brave and the Bold*. Seasons 1–3. DVD. Warner Bros., 2012–2014.

*The Batman: The Complete Series*. DVD. Warner Bros., 2008.

*Batman: The Complete Television Series*. DVD. Warner Bros., 2014.

*Batman: The Dark Knight Returns*. Part 1. DVD. Directed by Jay Oliva. Warner Bros., 2012.

*Batman: The Dark Knight Returns*. Part 2. DVD. Directed by Jay Oliva. Warner Bros., 2013.

*Batman: The Movie*. Directed by Leslie H. Martinson. Warner Bros., 1966.

*Batman: Year One*. DVD. Directed by Sam Liu and Lauren Montgomery. Warner Bros., 2011.

*The BatPodcast*. "Adrienne Barbeau." Episode 5. YouTube, July 31, 2014. www.youtube.com/watch?v=F4RPjTp_nh0.

Beaty, Bart. *Fredric Wertham and the Critique of Mass Culture*. Jackson: University Press of Mississippi, 2005.

Bedard, Tony, and Peter Calloway. *Gotham City Sirens*, vol. 2. New York: DC Comics, 2015.

Begley, Chris. "Anne Hathaway Thought She Was Auditioning for Harley Quinn in 'The Dark Knight Rises.'" *Batman News*, April 13, 2012. http://batman-news.com/2012/04/13/anne-hathaway-harley-quinn-the-dark-knight-rises/.

*Beware the Batman*. Vols. 1–2. DVD. Warner Bros., 2014.

Billinghurst, Jane. *Temptress: From the Original Bad Girls to Women on Top*. New York: Douglas & McIntyre, 2012.

Bitterbaum, David. "Jim Balent and Holly Golightly Interview!" YouTube, December 4, 2014. www.youtube.com/watch?v=JnGSNa1W8Ak.

Booker, M. Keith. *Comics Through Time: A History of Icons, Idols, and Ideas*. Vol. 2, *1960–1980*. Santa Barbara, CA: Greenwood, 2014.

Boucher, Geoff. "'Dark Knight Rises' Star Anne Hathaway: 'Gotham City Is Full of Grace.'" Hero Complex, *Los Angeles Times*, December 29, 2011. http://herocomplex.latimes.com/movies/dark-knight-rises-star-anne-hathaway-gotham-city-is-full-of-grace/.

Bronfen, Elisabeth. "Femme Fatale—Negotiations of Tragic Desire." In *Rethinking Tragedy*, edited by Rita Felski. Baltimore: Johns Hopkins University Press, 2008.

Brothers, David. "Frank Miller's 'Holy Terror': A Propaganda Comic That Fights Faith Instead of Evil [Review]." *Comics Alliance*, September 26, 2011. http://comicsalliance.com/frank-millers-holy-terror-review/.

Brownstein, Charles. *Eisner/Miller*. Milwaukee: Dark Horse, 2005.

Brubaker, Ed, and Darwyn Cooke. *Trail of the Catwoman*. Vol. 1 of *Catwoman*. New York: DC Comics, 2012.

Brubaker, Ed, and Paul Gulacy. *Under Pressure*. Vol. 3 of *Catwoman*. New York: DC Comics, 2014.

Brubaker, Ed, and Cameron Stewart. *No Easy Way Out*. Vol. 2 of *Catwoman*. New York: DC Comics, 2013.

Calia, Michael. "'Gotham' Returns: Here's What We Can Expect." *Wall Street Journal*, January 2, 2015. http://blogs.wsj.com/speakeasy/2015/01/02/gotham-returns-heres-what-we-can-expect/.

Campbell, Josie. "Doyle Promises a Batman 'for Every Fan.'" *Comic Book Resources*, December 18, 2014. www.cbr.com/doyle-promises-a-batman-for-every-fan/.

Canby, Vincent. "The Screen: 'Mackenna's Gold' in Apache Country." *New York Times*, June 19, 1969. www.nytimes.com/movie/review?res=9A0CE4DE1639EF3BBC4152DFB0668382679EDE.

"Catwoman." *Batman: Year One*. DVD. Directed by Lauren Montgomery. Warner Bros., 2011.

*Catwoman*. Directed by Pitof. Warner Bros., 2004.

Charity, Tom. "Review: 'Dark Knight Rises' Disappointingly Clunky, Bombastic." CNN, July 19, 2012. www.cnn.com/2012/07/19/showbiz/movies/dark-knight-rises-review-charity/.

"Chase Me." *Batman: Mystery of the Batwoman*. DVD. Directed by Curt Veda. Warner Bros., 2003.

Ching, Albert. "WonderCon 2012: Carol Danvers Is the New CAPTAIN MARVEL," *Newsarama*, March 18, 2012. www.newsarama.com/9237-wondercon-2012-carol-danvers-is-the-new-captain-marvel.html.

*Comic Book Movie*. "FIRST Picture of Halle as Catwoman Now Online!!" September 29, 2003. www.comicbookmovie.com/other/first-picture-of-halle-as-catwoman-now-online-a814.

Corliss, Richard. "Me-Ouch!" *Time*, July 28, 2004. http://content.time.com/time/arts/article/0,8599,673554,00.html.

Couch, Aaron. "William Shatner to Voice Two-Face in 'Batman: Return of the Caped Crusaders' Sequel." *Hollywood Reporter*, October 6, 2016. www.hollywoodreporter.com/heat-vision/william-shatner-voice-two-face-936010

Cranz, Alex. "*Batman: Arkham City* Isn't Misogynistic in Its Use of the Word Bitch." *FemPop*, October 31, 2011. www.fempop.com/2011/10/31 /batman-arkham-city-isnt-misogynistic-in-its-use-of-the-word-bitch/.

Cronin, Brian. "TV Legends Revealed: Catwoman's Invention Provided Cheeky Assist?" *Comic Book Resources*, June 26, 2013. www.cbr.com/tv -legends-revealed-catwomans-invention-provided-cheeky-assist/.

Crow, David. "Why Tim Burton's Batman 3 Never Happened." *Den of Geek!* June 16, 2016. www.denofgeek.com/us/movies/batman/239632/why-tim -burtons-batman-3-never-happened.

Dangelo, Joe. "New Batman Cartoon Gets Edgy Theme from U2 Guitarist." MTV News, September 10, 2004. www.mtv.com/news/1490911/new-batman -cartoon-gets-edgy-theme-from-u2-guitarist/?headlines=true.

Daniels, Les. *Batman: The Complete History.* San Francisco: Chronicle Books, 1999.

———. *Wonder Woman: The Complete History.* San Francisco: Chronicle Books, 2000.

*The Dark Knight.* Directed by Christopher Nolan. Warner Bros., 2008.

*The Dark Knight Rises.* Directed by Christopher Nolan. Warner Bros., 2012.

Deggans, Eric. "Hollywood Has a Major Diversity Problem, USC Study Finds." NPR, February 22, 2016. www.npr.org/sections/thetwo-way /2016/02/22/467665890/hollywood-has-a-major-diversity-problem-usc -study-finds.

Diamond Comics. "DC's Catwoman Honored with GLAAD Award." Official website, accessed January 6, 2017. www.diamondcomics.com/Home /1/1/3/116?articleID=10043.

Dichiara, Tom. "Keira Knightley, Anne Hathaway Among 6 Actresses Vying for 2 Roles in 'The Dark Knight Rises.'" MTV News, January 12, 2011. www.mtv.com/news/2438263/keira-knightley-anne-hathaway -the-dark-knight-rises-roles/.

Dickens, Donna. "Creators Confirm Harley Quinn And Poison Ivy Are Definitely Hooking Up." *Hitfix*, June 16, 2015. www.hitfix.com/harpy /creators-confirm-harley-quinn-and-poison-ivy-are-definitely-hooking-up.

Dini, Paul, and Carlos D'Anda. *Batman: Arkham City.* New York: DC Comics, 2011.

Dini, Paul, and Chip Kidd. *Batman Animated.* New York: Dey Street Books, 1998.

Dini, Paul, and Guillem March. *Gotham City Sirens*, vol. 1. New York: DC Comics, 2014.

Dini, Paul, and Dustin Nguyen. *Batman: Heart of Hush.* New York: DC Comics, 2010.

Doane, Mary Ann. *Femmes Fatales: Feminism, Film Theory, Psychoanalysis.* New York: Routledge, 1991.

Dockterman, Eliana. "Marvel CEO Says in Leaked Email That Female Superhero Movies Have Been a 'Disaster.'" *Time*, May 5, 2015. http://time .com/3847432/marvel-ceo-leaked-email/.

Earwolf Media. "Catwoman." *How Did This Get Made?*, December 20, 2011. www.earwolf.com/episode/catwoman/.

Ebert, Roger. Review of *Catwoman.* RogerEbert.com, July 19, 2004, www .rogerebert.com/reviews/catwoman-2004.

Edelstein, David. "Edelstein: *The Dark Knight Rises* Closes Out the Most Ambitious Superhero Movie Cycle Ever." *Vulture*, July 20, 2012. www .vulture.com/2012/07/movie-review-david-edelstein-on-the-dark-knight -rises.html#.

Eisner, Joel. "The Batscholar on Batman: The Movie." *To the Batpoles* (blog), October 4, 2011, http://tothebatpoles.blogspot.ca/2011/10/batscholar -on-batman-movie.html.

————. *The Official Batman Batbook: The Revised Edition.* Bloomington: AuthorHouse, 2008.

Entertainment Spectrum (entertainmentspctrum). "Clips from Entertainment Spectrum Batman Returns Show." Youtube, July 21, 2008. www .youtube.com/watch?v=VW3CPNSs9zE.

Eury, Michael, and Michael Kronenberg. *The Batcave Companion.* Raleigh, NC: TwoMorrows, 2009.

Faile, Chris. "Ed Solomon Gets Nod as 'Catwoman' Scribe." *Filmjerk*, June 20, 2003. www.filmjerk.com/news/article.php?id_new=283.

Find a Grave. "Bob Kane." August 12, 2000. www.findagrave.com/cgi-bin /fg.cgi?page=gr&GRid=11708.

Finger, Bill, et al. *Catwoman: A Celebration of 75 Years.* New York: DC Comics, 2015.

Finger, Bill, Edmond Hamilton, Leo Dorfman, Gardner Fox, Frank Robbins, Dough Moench, Devin Grayson, Ty Templeton, and Ed Brubaker. *Catwoman: Nine Lives of a Feline Fatale.* New York: DC Comics, 2004.

Finger, Bill, and Bob Kane. *The Batman Chronicles.* Vols. 1–9. New York: DC Comics, 2005–2010.

Fleming, Michael. "Another life at WB for Catwoman and Tim Burton?" *Variety*, July 22, 1993. http://variety.com/1993/voices/columns/another -life-at-wb-for-catwoman-and-burton-109036/.

Fleming, Michael. "Dish," *Variety*, June 17, 1993. http://variety.com/1993 /voices/columns/dish-6-107881/.

Flood, Alison. "Catwoman Revealed as Bisexual in New DC Comic." *Guardian*, February 27, 2015. www.theguardian.com/books/2015/feb/27/catwoman-revealed-bisexual-new-dc-comic.

Flora, Carlin. "Eartha Kitt: She Growls, She Purrs." *Psychology Today*, September 1, 2006. www.psychologytoday.com/articles/200609/eartha-kitt-she-growls-she-purrs.

Fox, Gardner, et al. *Showcase Presents: Batman*. Vols. 1–6. New York: DC Comics, 2006–2016.

Gaines, William S. "Testimony of William S. Gaines, Publisher, Entertaining Comics Group, New York, N.Y." April 21, 1954. www.thecomicbooks.com/gaines.html.

Garcia, Bob. "Batman: Catwoman." *Cinefantastique* 26/27, no. 6/1 (February 1994).

Glieberman, Owen. "*Batman Returns*: EW Review." *Entertainment Weekly*, June 26, 1992. www.ew.com/article/1992/06/26/batman-returns.

Goldstein, Hilary. "WonderCon '06: Holy Terror, Batman!" *IGN*, February 12, 2006. http://ca.ign.com/articles/2006/02/12/wondercon-06-holy-terror-batman.

*Gotham*. Seasons 1–2. DVD. Warner Bros., 2015–2016.

Greenberger, Robert, and Matthew Manning. *The Batman Vault: A Museum-in-a-Book with Rare Collectibles from the Batcave*. New York: Running Press, 2009.

Groth, Gary. "Jerry Robinson: Been There, Done That." *Comics Journal*, February 5, 2011. www.tcj.com/jerry-robinson-been-there-done-that/2/.

Hajdu, David. *The Ten-Cent Plague: The Great Comic Book Scare and How It Changed America*. New York: Farrar, Straus and Giroux, 2008.

Hallmark Channel. "TV's Catwoman Camren Bicondova & Julie Newmar." *Home & Family*, May 11, 2016. www.hallmarkchannel.com/home-and-family/videos/tvs-catwoman-camren-bicondova-julie-newmar-home-family.

Hamilton, Kirk. "This is Why *Batman: Arkham City*'s Locked Catwoman Content Makes Buying the Game New the Wiser Choice." *Kotaku*, October 14, 2011. http://kotaku.com/5849771/this-is-why-batman-arkham-citys-locked-catwoman-content-makes-buying-the-game-new-the-smart-choice.

Hamm, Sam. *Batman 2*. Screenplay draft, n.d. Via Daily Script. www.dailyscript.com/scripts/batman-returns_unproduced.html.

Hanks, Henry. "Catwoman Comes Out as Bisexual." CNN, February 27, 2015. www.cnn.com/2015/02/26/entertainment/catwoman-bisexual-feat/.

Hanley, Tim. "Gendercrunching December 2016—the Year in Genderetrospect." *Bleeding Cool*, February 19, 2017. www.bleedingcool.com/2017/02/19/gendercrunching-december-2016/.

———. "Gendercrunching the DC Relaunch." *Bleeding Cool*, June 12, 2011. www.bleedingcool.com/2011/06/12/gendercrunching-the-dc-relaunch/.

———. *Wonder Woman Unbound: The Curious History of the World's Most Famous Heroine.* Chicago: Chicago Review Press, 2014.

Harvey, Jim. "Ratings for 'Beware the Batman'; July 2011 Episode Airings on Cartoon Network." *World's Finest*, August 2013. www.worldsfinestonline.com/2013/08/ratings-for-beware-the-batman-july-2013-episode-airings-on-cartoon-network/.

Hatheway, Cameron. "Talking to Garry Brown About *The Massive* and *Catwoman* at Long Beach Comic Expo." *Bleeding Cool*, March 3, 2015. www.bleedingcool.com/2015/03/03/talking-garry-brown-massive-catwoman-long-beach-comic-expo/.

Hechinger, Paul. "'Dark Knight' Director Chris Nolan Talks About Keeping Batman Real." *BBC America*, December 2012. www.bbcamerica.com/shows//blog/2012/12/dark-knight-director-christopher-nolan-discusses-keeping-batman-real.

Holmes, Mannie. "Michael B. Jordan on 'Fantastic Four' Casting Backlash: I'll 'Shoulder All This Hate.'" *Variety*, May 22, 2015. http://variety.com/2015/film/news/michael-b-jordan-fantastic-four-casting-backlash-shouldering-hate-1201504000/.

Hornaday, Anne. "The Dark Knight Rises." *Washington Post*, July 19, 2012. www.washingtonpost.com/gog/movies/the-dark-knight-rises,1208568.html.

Horyn, Cathy. "Anne Hathaway's New World: The Interview." *Harper's Bazaar*, June 27, 2011. www.harpersbazaar.com/celebrity/latest/news/a744/anne-hathaway-interview/.

Hudson, Laura. "The Big Sexy Problem with Superheroines and Their 'Liberated Sexuality.'" *Comics Alliance*, September 22, 2015. http://comicsalliance.com/starfire-catwoman-sex-superheroine/.

*Inside the Actors Studio.* "Michelle Pfeiffer." Season 13, episode 9. Bravo, 2007.

Johns, Geoff, and David Finch. *Justice League of America.* Vol. 1, *World's Most Dangerous.* New York: DC Comics, 2014.

Johnson, Melissa Ewey. *Halle Berry: A Biography.* Santa Barbara, CA: Greenwood, 2010.

Jones, Alan. "Batman in Production." *Cinefantastique*, November 1989, 75–88.

Jones, Kipp. "Latest Comic Confirms DC's Catwoman Is Bisexual." *Breitbart*, February 26, 2015. www.breitbart.com/big-hollywood/2015/02/26 /latest-comic-confirms-dcs-catwoman-is-bisexual/.

Kane, Bob. "An Open Letter to All 'Batmanians' Everywhere." *Batmania Annual* #1 (April 1967).

Kane, Bob, and Thomas Andrae. *Batman & Me.* Forestville, CA: Eclipse Books, 1989.

Kaplan, Arie. *From Krakow to Krypton: Jews and Comic Books.* Philadelphia: Jewish Publication Society, 2008.

Knowles, Harry. "Wanna See a Pretty Ridiculous Photo of Halle in the CATWOMAN Outfit." *Ain't It Cool News*, September 29, 2003. www .aintitcool.com/node/16208.

Leth, Kate. "Zip Up!" *Kate or Die*, March 20, 2013. http://kateordiecomics .com/archive/xyz/.

Levitz, Paul, and Joe Staton. *Huntress: Dark Knight Daughter.* New York: DC Comics, 2006.

Loeb, Jeph, and Jim Lee. *Batman: Hush.* New York: DC Comics, 2009.

Loeb, Jeph, and Tim Sale. *Batman: Dark Victory.* New York: DC Comics, 2002.

———. *Batman: The Long Halloween.* New York: DC Comics, 1998.

———. *Catwoman: When in Rome.* New York: DC Comics, 2007.

Mainon, Dominique, and James Ursini. *Femme Fatale: Cinema's Most Unforgettable Lethal Ladies.* New York: Limelight Editions, 2009.

"The Many Faces of Catwoman." *Catwoman.* DVD. Directed by Jeffrey Lerner. Warner Bros., 2005.

March, Guillem. "CATWOMAN #03 Unseen Pages." *Guillem March* (blog), February 23, 2014. http://guillemmarch.blogspot.ca/2014/02/catwoman -03-unseen-pages.html.

Mars, Scotty. "Interview with Catwoman Julie Newmar." YouTube, May 3, 2013. www.youtube.com/watch?v=96i9u-ynA4A.

Matthews, Clive J., and Jim Smith, *Tim Burton.* London: Virgin, 2002.

McClintock, Pamela. "Box Office: 'Suicide Squad' Snubs Naysayers, Eyes $145–$150M Weekend." *Hollywood Reporter*, August 6, 2016. www .hollywoodreporter.com/news/box-office-suicide-squad-eyes-150 -million-weekend-917819

McElhatton, Greg. "Catwoman #1." *Comic Book Resources*, September 21, 2011. www.cbr.com/catwoman-1/.

Miller, Frank. *Batman: Year One.* Screenplay draft, n.d. Via Leon's Script Collection. http://leonscripts.users5.50megs.com/scripts/BATMAN YEARONEscript.htm.

———. *Holy Terror.* Burbank, CA: Legendary Comics, 2011.

————. *Sin City: The Hard Goodbye*. Milwaukie: Dark Horse, 1992.

Miller, Frank, and Klaus Janson. *Daredevil by Frank Miller and Klaus Janson*. Vols. 1–3. New York: Marvel Comics, 2008–2009.

Miller, Frank, and Jim Lee. *All Star Batman and Robin, the Boy Wonder*. New York: DC Comics, 2009.

Miller, Frank, and David Mazzucchelli. *Batman: Year One Deluxe Edition*. New York: DC Comics, 2007.

————. *Daredevil: Born Again*. New York: DC Comics, 2010.

Miller, Frank, and Lynn Varley. *Batman: The Dark Knight Returns*. New York: DC Comics, 1997.

————. *Batman: The Dark Knight Strikes Again*. New York: DC Comics, 2004.

————. *Elektra Lives Again*. New York: Marvel, 1990.

Miller, John Jackson. "Comic Book Sales by Month." *Comichron: The Comics Chronicles*. www.comichron.com/monthlycomicssales.html.

Miller, Julie. "Catwoman Writer Confirms Selina Kyle Is Bisexual." *Vanity Fair*, February 26, 2015. www.vanityfair.com/hollywood/2015/02/selina-kyle-catwoman-bisexual.

Moore, Alan, and Brian Bolland. *Batman: The Killing Joke*. New York: DC Comics, 1988.

Morales, Wilson. "*Catwoman*: An Interview with Edward L. McDonnell." *Black Film*, May 2004. www.blackfilm.com/20040521/features/edward mcconnell.shtml.

Naso, Markisan. "The Darwyn Cooke Interview." *Comics Journal*, May 16, 2016. www.tcj.com/the-darwyn-cooke-interview-by-markisan-naso/2/.

*The New Adventures of Batman*. DVD. Warner Bros., 2007.

Newell, Mindy, and J. J. Birch. *Catwoman: Her Sister's Keeper*. New York: DC Comics, 1991.

Nix, Marc. "Catwoman." *IGN*, February 1, 2000. http://ca.ign.com/articles/2000/02/02/catwoman-11.

Nobleman, Marc Tyler. *Bill the Boy Wonder: The Secret Co-creator of Batman*. Watertown, MA: Charlesbridge, 2012.

————. "Interview with Co-author of Bob Kane's Autobiography." *Noblemania* (blog), March 30, 2014. http://noblemania.blogspot.ca/2014/03/interview-with-co-author-of-bob-kanes.html.

————. "Super '70s and '80s: 'Super Friends'—Darrell McNeil, Animator." *Noblemania* (blog), July 29, 2011. http://noblemania.blogspot.ca/2011/07/super-70s-and-80s-super-friendsdarrell.html.

Nocenti, Ann, and Patrick Oliffe. *Catwoman*. Vol. 5, *Race of Thieves*. New York: DC Comics, 2014.

Nocenti, Ann, and Rafa Sandoval. *Catwoman.* Vol. 3, *Death of the Family.* New York: DC Comics, 2013.

Nocenti, Ann, and Rafa Sandoval. *Catwoman.* Vol. 4, *Gotham Underground.* New York: DC Comics, 2014.

Nolen-Weathington, Eric. *Modern Master.* Vol. 3, *Bruce Timm.* Raleigh, NC: TwoMorrows, 2004.

Norris, Erik. Review of *Catwoman* #1. *IGN,* September 21, 2001. http:// ca.ign.com/articles/2011/09/21/catwoman-1-review.

Nyberg, Amy Kiste. *Seal of Approval: The History of the Comics Code.* Jackson: University Press of Mississippi, 1998.

Obenzinger, Eric. "Ruth Steel Interview (Age 96)—May 22, 2011." YouTube, May 27, 2011. www.youtube.com/watch?v=0HfIuUKpTPU.

Pfeifer, Will, and David Lopez. *Catwoman.* Vol. 5, *Backward Masking.* New York: DC Comics, 2016.

Pfeifer, Will, and Pete Woods. *Catwoman.* Vol. 4, *The One You Love.* New York: DC Comics, 2015.

Pfeifer, Will, and various. *Catwoman.* Vol. 6, *Final Jeopardy.* New York: DC Comics, 2017.

Phipps, Keith. Review of *Catwoman.* *A.V. Club,* July 26, 2004. www.avclub .com/review/catwoman-4998.

Phipps, Keith, and Oliver Sava. "The New DC 52, Week 4 (*Wonder Woman, Batman, Catwoman,* and more)." *A.V. Club,* September 23, 2011. www.avclub.com/article/the-new-dc-52-week-4-iwonder-womani -ibatmani-icatw-62180.

Place, Janey. "Women in Film Noir." *Women in Film Noir.* Ed. E. Ann Kaplan. London: BFI Pub., 1998.

Polo, Susana. "The Writer Who Made Me Love Comics Taught Me to Hate Them." *Polygon,* March 1, 2016. www.polygon.com/2016/3/1/11139828 /the-dark-knight-returns.

Porter, Alan J. "The Dubious Origins of the Batman." In *Batman Unauthorized: Vigilantes, Jokers, and Heroes in Gotham City,* edited by Dennis O'Neil and Leah Wilson. Dallas: BenBella Books, 2008.

Quattro, Ken. "Woolfolk on Weisinger." *Comics Detective* (blog), April 16, 2012. http://thecomicsdetective.blogspot.com/2012/04/woolfolk-on-weisinger .html.

Radish, Christina. "Camren Bicondova Talks GOTHAM, the Audition Process, Becoming Part of the DC Universe, Delving into the Origins of Catwoman, and More." *Collider,* October 6, 2014. http://collider.com /camren-bicondova-gotham-interview/.

Razzie Channel. "Halle Berry Accepts Her RAZZIE Award." YouTube, January 13, 2011. www.youtube.com/watch?v=U-7s_yeQuDg.

Reed, Robby. "The Haunting of Robert Kane, Part 3!" *Dial B for Blog.* www
.dialbforblog.com/archives/391/.

Robison, Lynn. "The Nicest Man at Comic-Con—Jim Balent." *Sequential
Tart.* www.sequentialtart.com/archive/sept04/jbalent.shtml.

Rogers, John. "Writing: Arbitration Letters." *Kung Fu Monkey* (blog), March
15, 2007. http://kfmonkey.blogspot.ca/2007/03/writing-arbitration
-letters.html.

Rogers, Vaneta. "New Writer Gives CATWOMAN 'Pulpy,' 'Noir' Mood
. . . and a New Catwoman??" *Newsarama*, September 2, 2014. www
.newsarama.com/22015-new-writer-gives-catwoman-pulpy-noir-mood
-and-a-new-catwoman.html.

———. "WINICK Returns to Gotham for Sexy, Violent DCnU CAT-
WOMAN." *Newsarama*, June 11, 2011. www.newsarama.com/7787
-winick-returns-to-gotham-for-sexy-violent-dcnu-catwoman.html.

Rooney, David. "Review: 'Catwoman.'" *Variety*, July 22, 2004. http://variety
.com/2004/film/markets-festivals/catwoman-1200532062/.

Royal, Derek. "Comics Alternative Interview: Jim Balent and Holly Golightly."
*Comics Alternative*, November 3, 2014. http://comicsalternative.com
/interviews-balent/.

Salisbury, Mark. *Burton on Burton.* London: Faber and Faber, 2006.

San Diego County News Channel (sdcnewschannel). "Interview with
Lee Meriwether." YouTube, July 28, 2011. www.youtube.com
/watch?v=p4lijTeld3Q.

Schiff, Jack, and Gene Reed. "Reminiscences of a Comic Book Editor." *The
Comic Book Price Guide.* Ed. Robert M. Overstreet. Vol. 13. 1982. 64–70.

Schumer, Arlen. "The Bat-Man Cover Story." *Alter Ego* 2, no. 5 (Summer 1999).

Schwartz, Julius, and Brian M. Thomsen. *Man of Two Worlds.* New York:
HarperCollins, 2000.

Seitz, Dan. "'Beware The Batman' Might Have Been Already Cancelled."
*Uproxx*, October 22, 2013. http://uproxx.com/gammasquad/beware
-the-batman-might-have-already-been-canceled/.

"Shadows of the Bat: The Cinematic Saga of the Dark Knight—Dark Side of
the Knight." *Batman Returns: Special Edition.* DVD. Directed by Constantine Nasr. Warner Bros., 2005.

Siegel, Lucas. "WILLIAMS & BLACKMAN Quit BATWOMAN over 'Eleventh Hour' Editorial Changes." *Newsarama*, September 5, 2013. www
.newsarama.com/18841-williams-blackman-quit-batwoman-over
-editorial-prevention-of-marriage.html.

Sims, Chris. "Artists Respond to DC's Back-Breaking 'Catwoman' #0
Cover." *Comics Alliance*, June 12, 2012. http://comicsalliance.com
/artists-respond-dc-comics-back-breaking-catwoman-0-cover/.

———. "Ed Brubaker Looks Back on Batman, Part Three: Catwoman." *Comics Alliance*, December 11, 2014. http://comicsalliance.com /ed-brubaker-looks-back-on-batman-part-three-catwoman/.

———. "'Tarot' #63 Explains What Breasts Are for to Naked Lady Werewolves." *Comics Alliance*, August 19, 2010. http://comicsalliance.com /tarot-63-naked-werewolves/.

———. "War Rocket Ajax #113: John Rogers Talks 'D&D,' Thrillbent and the Catwoman Movie." *Comics Alliance*, May 21, 2012. http://comicsalliance .com/war-rocket-ajax-113-john-rogers-talks-dandd-thrillbent-and-th/.

*Sin City*. Directed by Frank Miller and Robert Rodriguez. Miramax, 2005.

Singh, Arune. "Look What the Cat Dragged In: Ed Brubaker Talks 'Catwoman.'" *Comic Book Resources*, January 31, 2003. www.cbr.com /look-what-the-cat-dragged-in-ed-brubaker-talks-catwoman/.

Sloan, Judy. "Daniel Waters on Writing." *Film Review*, August 1995. 67–69.

Smith, Ronald L. *Sweethearts of '60s TV*. New York: St. Martin's Press, 1989.

Sneddon, Laura. "Catwoman: The Hyper-Sexualisation of a Sexual Woman." *comicbookGRRRL* (blog), June 12, 2011. www.comicbookgrrl.com /2011/06/12/catwoman-the-hyper-sexualisation-of-a-sexual-woman/.

Snyder, Scott, and James Tynion IV. *Batman Eternal*. Vol. 1. New York: DC Comics, 2014.

———. *Batman Eternal*. Vol. 2. New York: DC Comics, 2015.

*The Spirit*. Directed by Frank Miller. Lionsgate, 2008.

Spurgeon, Tom. "An Interview with Ed Brubaker." *Comics Reporter*, September 2, 2006. www.comicsreporter.com/index.php/resources/interviews /6073/.

Steranko, Jim. *The Steranko History of Comics*. Vol. 1. Reading, PA: Supergraphics, 1970.

Subers, Ray. "Weekend Report: 'Guardians of the Galaxy' Obliterates August Record." Box Office Mojo, August 3, 2014. www.boxofficemojo.com /news/?id=3885&p=.htm.

*Suicide Squad*. Directed by David Ayer. Warner Bros., 2016.

Susman, Gary. "Will Nicole Kidman Play Catwoman?" *Entertainment Weekly*, February 5, 2003. www.ew.com/article/2003/02/05/will-nicole -kidman-play-catwoman.

Taraborrelli, Randy J. *The Secret Life of Marilyn Monroe*. New York: Grand Central Publishing, 2009.

*300*. Directed by Zack Snyder. Warner Bros., 2006.

Tieri, Frank, and Inaki Miranda. *Catwoman*. Vol. 8, *Run Like Hell*. New York: DC Comics, 2016.

Tilley, Carol L. "Seducing the Innocent: Fredric Wertham and the Falsifications That Helped Condemn Comics." *Information & Culture*. Vol. 47. No. 4. 2012. 383–413.

*Time.* "Horror on the Newsstands." September 27, 1954. www.time.com/time
/magazine/article/0.9171,820350,00.html.

Tobias, Scott. Review of *The Dark Knight Rises.* *A.V. Club,* July 18, 2012.
www.avclub.com/review/the-dark-knight-rises-review-batman-82624.

Travers, Peter. Review of *Batman Returns. Rolling Stone,* June 19, 1992.
www.rollingstone.com/movies/reviews/batman-returns-19920619.

———. Review of *The Dark Knight Rises. Rolling Stone,* July 16, 2012. www
.rollingstone.com/movies/reviews/the-dark-knight-rises-20120716.

Uslan, Michael. *The Boy Who Loved Batman: A Memoir.* San Francisco:
Chronicle Books, 2011.

———. Introduction to *Catwoman: Nine Lives of a Feline Fatale,* by Bill Finger et al. New York: DC Comics, 2014.

Valentine, Genevieve, and Garry Brown. *Catwoman.* Vol. 6, *Keeper of the
Castle.* New York: DC Comics, 2015.

Valentine, Genevieve, and David Messina. *Catwoman.* Vol. 7, *Inheritance.*
New York: DC Comics, 2016.

Vaz, Mark Cotta. *Tales of the Dark Knight: Batman's First Fifty Years, 1939–
1989.* New York: Ballantine, 1989.

Vejvoda, Jim. "Catwoman Movie Still Alive and Purring?" *IGN,* February 5,
2011. http://ca.ign.com/articles/2001/02/05/catwoman-movie-still-alive
-and-purring.

———. "The Stax Report: Script Review of *Catwoman!*" *IGN,* April 4, 2001.
http://ca.ign.com/articles/2001/04/04/the-stax-report-script-review-of
-catwoman.

Ward, Burt. *Boy Wonder: My Life in Tights.* Los Angeles: Logical Figments,
1995.

Waters, Daniel. *Batman II.* Screenplay draft, May 20, 1991. Via Daily Script.
www.dailyscript.com/scripts/batman-returns_early.html.

———. *Catwoman.* Screenplay draft, June 16, 1995. Via Sci Fi Scripts. www
.scifiscripts.com/scripts/catwoman.txt.

Weintraub, Steve. "Anne Hathaway Talks Fighting in Heels, Adapting
to Nolan's Universe, Filming in IMAX and More on the Set of THE
DARK KNIGHT RISES." *Collider,* May 27, 2012. http://collider.com
/anne-hathaway-the-dark-knight-rises-interview/.

Weldon, Glen. *The Caped Crusade: Batman and the Rise of Nerd Culture.*
New York: Simon & Schuster, 2016.

Wells, Dominic. "Michelle Pfeiffer: Claws & Effect." *Dominic Wells.* www
.dominicwells.com/journalist/pfeiffer/.

WENN. "Pfeiffer Keeps Her Claws from Catwoman Judd." IMDb, January
28, 2002. www.imdb.com/news/ni0064187/.

Wertham, Fredric. *Seduction of the Innocent.* New York: Rinehart & Company, 1954.

————. "Testimony of Dr. Fredric Wertham, Psychiatrist, Director, Lafargue Clinic, New York, N.Y." April 21, 1954. www.thecomicbooks.com /wertham.html.

West, Adam, with Jeff Rovin. *Back to the Batcave.* New York: Berkley Books, 1994.

Whaley, Deborah Elizabeth. "Black Cat Got Your Tongue? Catwoman, Blackness, and the Alchemy of Postracialism." *Journal of Graphic Novels and Comics* 2, no. 1 (June 2011): 3–23.

————. *Black Women in Sequence: Re-inking Comics, Graphic Novels, and Anime.* Seattle: University of Washington Press, 2016.

Wilding, Josh. "Christopher Nolan on Introducing Catwoman and His Involvement with MAN OF STEEL." *Comic Book Movie*, May 28, 2012. www.comicbookmovie.com/batman/christopher-nolan-on-introducing -catwoman-and-his-involvement-with-man-of-a60580.

Williams, John L. *America's Mistress: The Life and Times of Eartha Kitt.* London: Quercus, 2014.

Williams, Scott. "Jim Balent and Holly G Interview." *Fanboy Buzz*, December 28, 2009. www.fanboybuzz.com/2009/12/jim-balent-holly-g-interview/.

Winick, Judd, and Guillem March. *Catwoman.* Vol. 1, *The Game.* New York: DC Comics, 2012.

————. *Catwoman.* Vol. 2, *Dollhouse.* New York: DC Comics, 2013.

Wright, Bradford. *Comic Book Nation: The Transformation of Youth Culture in America.* Baltimore: Johns Hopkins University Press, 2001.

Zimmerman, Dwight. "Interview with Fred Finger." In *Alter Ego: The Comic Book Artist Collection.* Raleigh: TwoMorrows, 2001.

# Index

# *About the Author*

Tim Hanley is a comic book historian and the author of *Wonder Woman Unbound: The Curious History of the World's Most Famous Heroine* and *Investigating Lois Lane: The Turbulent History of the Daily Planet's Ace Reporter*. He also contributed to *Wonder Woman Psychology: Lassoing the Truth*, and his work has appeared in the *Atlantic*, the *Los Angeles Review of Books*, and the *Comics Journal*. His column on female creator statistics in the superhero comic book industry, "Gendercrunching," runs monthly at *Bleeding Cool*, and he writes regularly about gender and comics at his blog, *Straitened Circumstances* (https://thanley.wordpress.com/). He lives in Halifax, Nova Scotia, between his massive stacks of comic books. You can find him on Twitter at @timhanley01.